TOAD Handbook

Bert Scalzo
Dan Hotka

DEVELOPER'S
LIBRARY

Sams Publishing, 800 East 96th Street, Indianapolis, Indiana 46240

TOAD Handbook

International Standard Book Number: 0-672-32486-5

Library of Congress Catalog Card Number: 2002111195

Printed in the United States of America

First Printing: February 2003

05   04   5   4   3   2

Trademarks

Warning and Disclaimer

Associate Publisher
Michael Stephens

Acquisitions Editor
Todd Green

Development Editor
Songlin Qiu

Managing Editor
Charlotte Clapp

Project Editor
Andy Beaster

Copy Editor
Margaret Berson

Indexer
Sharon Shock

Proofreader
Jody Larsen

Technical Editors
Jim McDaniel
Darren Lynch
Patrick McGrath

Team Coordinator
Lynne Williams

Interior Designer
Gary Adair

Cover Designer
Alan Clements

Page Layout
Michelle Mitchell

Contents at a Glance

Table of Contents

4   TOAD Procedure Editor   77

About the Authors

Bert Scalzo is a product architect for Quest Software and a member of the TOAD development team. He designed many of the features in the TOAD DBA module.

Mr. Scalzo has worked as an Oracle DBA with versions 4 through 9i. He has worked for both Oracle Education and Consulting. Mr. Scalzo holds several Oracle Masters, a BS, MS, and PhD in Computer Science, an MBA, and several insurance industry designations. His key areas of DBA interest are Linux and data warehousing (he designed 7-Eleven Corporation's multi-terabyte, star-schema data warehouse). Mr. Scalzo has also written articles for Oracle's Technology Network, Oracle Informant, PC Week, Linux Journal, Oracle Magazine, and www.linux.com. He also has written *Oracle DBA Guide to Data Warehousing and Star Schemas*. Mr. Scalzo can be reached at bscalzo@attbi.com or Bert.Scalzo@Quest.com.

Dan Hotka has over 24 years in the computer industry and over 19 years experience with Oracle products. He is an internationally recognized Oracle expert with Oracle experience dating back to the Oracle V4.0 days. He has authored the books *Oracle9i Development By Example* and *Oracle8i from Scratch* published by Que and has coauthored the popular books *Oracle Unleashed*, *Oracle8 Server Unleashed*, and *Oracle Development Unleashed* published by SAMS and *Special Edition using Oracle8/8i* published by Que. He is frequently published in Oracle trade journals, and regularly speaks at Oracle conferences and user groups around the world. Visit his Web site at www.DanHotka.com. Dan can be reached at dhotka@earthlink.net.

Dedication

from Bert Scalzo
To my best friend in the whole world,
Ziggy—my miniature Schnauzer.

Acknowledgments

from **Bert Scalzo**

I'd like to thank Jim McDaniel and his entire TOAD development team for permitting me to work with them. Jim's love for his product is contagious. You can't help but become a rabid fanatic because it's such fun to work with these guys. Ideas go from whiteboard to design spec to code to QA in a matter of days or weeks. There are no lengthy design docs and long, drawn-out design meetings—just ideas translated into product as quickly as is humanly possible. That's how Jim and the team work. It's such fun that many times we work right through evenings and weekends (even NFL Sundays) because we get so excited by the whole TOAD development process. I've never before seen anything like this.

I'd also like to thank the TOAD user community. As Jim says, the users own and direct TOAD. It's not a bunch of "ivory tower" architects building their solution, but rather a grass-roots movement that has evolved into the premier PL/SQL development and DBA tool. From the Yahoo TOAD bulletin boards to the TOAD User Group meetings held across the country, it's been great fun working with the TOAD users. Their opinions and enthusiasm have helped to make the product what it is.

Finally I'd like to thank Dan Hotka for helping out with this book. Dan not only wrote a lot of the book, but also and more importantly opened the door for this book idea with the publisher. If it had not been for Dan, this book might have never gotten to first base.

from **Dan Hotka**

I have now been writing about Oracle-related topics for over seven years. What started out as something to help utilize my time while on United Airlines has turned into a rather substantial second job. I again want to thank those who have not only contributed to my work in this book but have made a positive difference in my career and life.

A special thanks goes out to my wife of 24 years, Gail Hackett, and my family. Her patience, love, and understanding have allowed me to take on opportunities such as writing and the travel that comes with my work. The family suffers the most with my line of work. I want to thank Elizabeth (Libby), Emily, and Thomas, my children, for giving me the foundation that continues to fuel my success.

A big "thank you very much!" goes to Bert Scalzo for inviting me along on this book.

I want to make sure to thank the people who help make my writing a success. Tim Gorman has to be the most Oracle-knowledgeable person I know. His advice and wisdom have definitely enhanced most every Oracle project I have undertaken. Other technical advice has been gleaned from (not in any particular order): Bradley Brown, Gary Dodge, Daniel Fink, Dave Oldroyd, Guy Harrison, Rich Niemiec, Swamy Kanathur, Robert Nightengale, Marlene Theriault, Paul Masterson, Jonathan Lewis, and D. Scott Wheeler. Thank you for your technical assistance on this project and through the years.

I want to thank those managers who have helped mold my career into the success that I continue to enjoy today: Karl Lenk (Sperry-Rand, Inc.), Gary Dodge (Oracle Corp.), and Deb Jenson (Platinum Technology, Inc. and Quest Software, Inc.).

Thanks to those editors who trusted me through the years to produce quality manuscript: Todd Green, Michelle Newcomb, Angela Koslowski, Heidi Frost, Farion Grove, and Rosemarie Graham, as well as their staffs.

Thank you to all the people listed below, who have made a positive difference in my life and career: Tom Villhauer, Adrian Tate, Alice Meyer, Bert Scalzo, Bert Spencer, Bob Emley, Bob Kenward, Bradley Brown, Brian Hengen, Bill and Debbie Wallace, Bonnie Vermillion, Buff Emslie, Cam White, Carol Thompson, Carolyn Smith, Cathy (CW) Fountain, Cathy (CL) Langhurst, Chauncey Kupferschmidt, Cheryl McCarthy, Chet and Kathy Gniadek, Cindy Swartz, Colette Simpson, Colin Blignault, Conny Vandeweyer, Craig Mullins, Cristina Nunes, Dan Wulfman, Dave Brainard, David Darnell, David Letsch, David Metcalf, David Pearson, David Wagner, Dawn Simmons, Deb Goodnow, Debra M. Smith, Dee Pollock, Derek Ashmore, Don Bishop, Donald Hotka, Don Kerker, Don Schroeder, Dorothy Campbell, Doug Evers, Doug Garn, Doug Tracy, Dwight Miller, Ed Grinbukh, Elsie Bishop, Floyd Sturgeon, Francesca Castiglione, Gaja Vaidyanatha, Garrett Cook, Gayln Underwood, Geri McGinnis, Gloria Brenneman, Greg Goodnow, Greg Slaymaker, Greg Spence, Haydn Pinnell, Heath Race, Heidi Yocki, Huub Commandeur, Jacqueline Fry, Jane Hambright, Janet Jones, Janice Ford, Jason Dean, Jay Johnson, Jeff Sheppard, Jerry Fox, Jerry Greenlee, Jerry Matza, Jerry Meyers, Jerry Wegner, Jim Cox, Jim "Toadman" McDaniel, Jim and Mary Sanders, Joe Gniadek, Joe Smith, John Beresniewicz, John Koszarek, John Theis, Jon Styre, Julian Good, Julie Ferry,

Julie Nelson, Karen Wicker, Karin Jung, Kat Yarbrough, Kate Freeman, Kathie Danielson, Kathleen Morehouse, Kathy Metcalf, Kelsey Thompson, Ken Jacobs, Kevin McGinnis, Kevin Schell, Larry and Joan Birk, Larry Kleinmeyer, Laurie Nelson, Leyria Walters, Linda Calibro, Linda Litton, Linda McMahon, Lisa Ciccarelli, Lora Grossenbacker, Lora Powers, Lu Johnson, Lynette Kleinmeyer, Mariam Giesler, Marjorie Olsen, Marita Welch, Mark and Ann Sierzant, Mark Harry, Martin N. Greenfield, Martin Rapetti, Marv Troutman, Mary Bricker, Mary Kenyon, Mary Villhauer, Melvin Morehouse, Michel Clerin, Michelle Campbell, Michelle Pregler, Mike Cannon, Mike Carroll, Mike Coffman, Mike Curtis, Mike Fisher, Mike Hotz, Mike Metcalf, Mike Nelson, Mike Sanchez, Mike Swing, Nancy Taslitz, Nicole Tokarski, Niel Bauman, Ofelia Albrecht, Paul Sanderson, Pat McMahon, Patricia Hemphill, Patrick and Misty Gniadek, Patrick McGrath, Penny Loupakos, Rachel Carmichael, Ramon Graham, Ramsina Lazari, Randy Spiese, Richard Neimiec, Richard Scholtz, Rick Born, Rick Magnuson, Rita Liddel, Robert Hotz, Robert Nightingale, Robert Thompson, Robyn Cincinnati, Rowland Schweigl, Ron Danielson, Ron Hahn, Ron Innis, Ron Mattia, Ron Miles, Ron Smith, Ross Walters, Rudy Neimiec, Russ Greene, Sandra Kay, Sarah Hackett, Scott Bickel, Scott Kane, Sean Kennedy, Sean McGrath, Sharon Reynolds, Sheri Ballard, Shona Freese, Simon Pearce, Simone Abawat, Steve Albrecht, Steve Black, Steve Blair, Steve Healy, Steve Jaschen, Steve Renneer, Susan Ferguson, Svet Bricker, TA Meyer, Tam Nguyen, Ted Cohen, Tom Bickel, Tom Parkinson, Tony Foley, Troy Amyett, Valda-Jean Robison, Vinny Smith, Walt Bricker, Wass Pogerelov, and Wayne Smith.

And finally, thank you very much to my parents, Philip and Dorothy Hotka; my in-laws, Dean and Marian Hackett; my siblings, Mike Hotka and Janice Hotka; and to my grandmothers, Mamie and Gladys, who will always have a special place in my heart.

We Want to Hear from You!

As the reader of this book, you are our most important critic and commentator. We value your opinion and want to know what we're doing right, what we could do better, what areas you'd like to see us publish in, and any other words of wisdom you're willing to pass our way.

As an associate publisher for Sams Publishing, I welcome your comments. You can email or write me directly to let me know what you did or didn't like about this book—as well as what we can do to make our books better.

Please note that I cannot help you with technical problems related to the *topic* of this book. We do have a User Services group, however, where I will forward specific technical questions related to the book.

When you write, please be sure to include this book's title and author as well as your name, email address, and phone number. I will carefully review your comments and share them with the author and editors who worked on the book.

Email: feedback@samspublishing.com
Mail: Michael Stephens, Associate Publisher
          Sams Publishing
          800 East 96th Street
          Indianapolis, IN 46240 USA

For more information about this book or another Sams title, visit our Web site at www.samspublishing.com. Type the ISBN (excluding hyphens) or the title of a book in the Search field to find the page you're looking for.

Foreword (by the Toadman)

I've been working on TOAD now for more than six years. Or has it been seven? I no longer really remember. But the very same incentives that motivated me to create TOAD are still the driving factors behind the continued development of TOAD: a constant desire to create a better development tool for Oracle developers; one that provides a simple GUI interface over all the daily tasks that a developer might encounter.

I have to back up and amend that last statement to include DBAs because the introduction of the DBA module now pushes the number one tool for Oracle developers into the DBA arena. TOAD has truly become the ubiquitous Oracle utility.

TOAD has been popular and remains popular for many reasons, the majority of which I attribute to a very passionate core group of users who drive the product and never allow us to slow down. They maintain the pace and accept nothing less than total encapsulation of their tasks within their favorite tool. And we—the TOAD team— obligingly comply. The TOAD users—the Toadies—are our inspiration, our motivation, and ultimately, the source of our rewards. One of my favorite user remarks was a simple "bodacious tool, dude." Such direct feedback from our users keeps our programming fires fueled.

One of the greatest benefits of the growth of TOAD has been the opportunity to work with Oracle experts whose feedback helps make TOAD a more valuable product for the users, including experts such as Bert Scalzo and Dan Hotka with whom I've had the pleasure of working these past few years. Dan has been a long time supporter of TOAD and Bert has been the architect for many of the DBA features in TOAD today. I take a great deal of pride in knowing that these two have come together in collaboration to publish this resource for TOAD users.

In closing, I'd like to thank Dan and Bert for this effort. I had been asked in the past to write a TOAD guide but just could not find the free time. I'd also like to thank y'all for your continued support and feedback. I hope Mr. Toad's Wild Ride continues for years to come.

Jim McDaniel, Toadman

Introduction

This is the first complete book on the market that covers the ever-popular Oracle development tool, TOAD (Tool for Oracle Application Developers). This book covers all features of TOAD, including new features of version 7.4 and the Quest DBA module for TOAD. An updated book is planned for each new release of TOAD. This book covers TOAD features, tips, tricks, and techniques, and does not focus on any particular version of Oracle RDBMS, unless otherwise noted.

The focus of this book is for all users of TOAD. It is the only complete reference book available for TOAD to date. This book is perfect for those who are new to Oracle and TOAD, the power user, and the more sophisticated/experienced users of TOAD. TOAD has so many features and benefits that it was difficult to include all of them in this book. Each chapter focuses on a particular topic, covering it in depth with illustrations, tips, and techniques from the Oracle experts Bert Scalzo and Dan Hotka.

This book is ideal for the following readers:

- The power user wanting easy access to data, help with SQL, and help with occasional coding assignments

- Anyone who wants to increase his or her productivity using the Oracle RDBMS

- IT professionals already familiar with TOAD but needing help with additional features

- Developers who want to do a specific task but cannot remember how

- Any TOAD user, as a tool for learning additional features

This book is intended to be a complete, single source of information, usage, tips, and techniques for the TOAD tool. The book focuses on the following topics:

- TOAD installation and setup

- Developing PL/SQL, SQL, and SQL scripts in an easy and intuitive environment

- Tuning SQL and debugging PL/SQL

- Modeling any user's schema

- Routine and advanced DBA tasks

- Exporting of data into various formats

- Using additional features such as FTP, TKProf, and adding your own favorite editors and programs

Approach of This Book

Note that this book's approach is very task-oriented and extremely visual. Each chapter covers logically related tasks that a TOAD user might perform, with ample figures to both elaborate and demonstrate key features for that task. For example, the section showing how to use TOAD's Create New Database wizard walks the user through screen snapshots of each phase, with highlights of those issues that are critical to achieve the greatest success in using that feature. Although this format makes for more figures than other books, we feel that the information is presented in the absolute best format for achieving the greatest success in leveraging TOAD's many features.

How This Book Is Organized

This book doesn't make assumptions about prior TOAD or Oracle development background and therefore all the tips and techniques are presented. The main focus of this book is to illustrate using TOAD and to be a handy reference for anyone using the TOAD tool. This book is liberally illustrated with working examples of all the topics. The chapters are organized as follows:

Chapter 1, "Setting Up TOAD for Successful Use," discusses the various installation options for most any computing environment. This chapter begins with basic operational issues, such as TOAD's database connectivity requirements, Oracle-based security, and required schema objects. The chapter then delves into more advanced TOAD security settings, including various read-only mode options available. It concludes with Windows scripts for saving and restoring your various TOAD settings.

Chapter 2, "Using TOAD's Schema Browser," covers the main TOAD interface for exploring your databases' structure and content (that is, metadata and data). This chapter also introduces you to the various keystrokes available in this browser. This chapter also includes how to model your schema to visualize or print the various object relationships. This chapter covers all the browser's advanced display options and capabilities, as well as various key startup and control options. This chapter also includes how to filter the schemas, objects, and their data. In addition, this chapter introduces the use of the Favorites tab for a customized browser experience.

Chapter 3, "TOAD SQL Editor," covers all the features available for building and maintaining SQL code and SQL scripts. This chapter covers all of the shortcuts and hotkeys available in depth and in a convenient reference grid. This chapter includes how to build SQL with code templates and advanced topics like "scripts that write scripts."

Chapter 4, "TOAD Procedure Editor," covers all the features available for building and maintaining PL/SQL, procedures, functions, and triggers. This chapter will also illustrate just how easy it is to see the various object relationships. This chapter also covers using the powerful PL/SQL symbolic debugger! This chapter covers all of the shortcuts and hotkeys available in depth and in a convenient reference grid.

The book then turns its focus to database administration.

Chapter 5, "Using TOAD for Routine DBA Tasks," covers the routine DBA tasks such as instance status, monitoring of key database elements and user sessions, checking and correcting fragmentation, and the easy creation and maintenance of database objects. Anyone who has to do database administration (possibly even the power user) will find this chapter useful.

Chapter 6, "Using TOAD for Non-Routine DBA Tasks," covers the rest of the database administration story. This chapter illustrates how TOAD can do even complex DBA tasks such as creating new databases, estimating object sizes, creating schema scripts, additional monitoring, and even the management of INIT.ORA parameters, rollback segments, and redo logs.

The remainder of the book covers various TOAD topics not previously discussed.

Chapter 7, "Generating Database Reports via TOAD," covers the various reports that come with TOAD, including HTML reports, and covers how to generate additional reports.

Chapter 8, "Exporting Table Data," illustrates how easy it is to get data out of Oracle into a variety of customized formats using TOAD. This chapter also discusses how TOAD easily works with existing Oracle features such as Export and Import.

Chapter 9, "Using Other Powerful TOAD Tools," covers the remaining features of TOAD. These features include browsing master-detail data; building SQL visually using the SQL Modeler; creating "poor man's" mini-ERDs via the Schema Browser hook to the SQL modeler; registering external programs for quick launch from within TOAD; visually comparing text files for differences; running network utilities such as FTP, telnet, and rexec; maintaining tnsnames files; running TKPROF; making subsets of data; and managing libraries of scripts via TOAD's script manager.

Chapter 10, "Knowing the TOAD World and Its Add-ons," covers the various TOAD prepackaged options currently available (that is, freeware, standard, professional, expert) as separately purchasable options, plus additional features or interfacing products available from Quest Software, Inc. Tools covered include Knowledge Xperts for PL/SQL and Oracle Administration, SQLab Xpert (SQL tuning), Benchmark Factory (stress testing), and QDesigner (data modeling).

Conventions Used in This Book

This book uses certain conventions to help make the book more readable and helpful:

- SQL code listings, SQL statements, and screen messages appear in a special monospace font.

- Placeholders (words that are substitutes for what you actually type) appear in monospace italic.

- Terms being introduced or defined appear in *italics*.

- Menu selections are separated with a comma. For example, "Select File, Open" means that you pull down the File menu and choose the Open option.

- Sometimes a line of SQL code is too long to fit on a single line of this book. When this happens, the line is broken and continued on the next line, preceded by a ➡ character.

In addition, this book uses special sidebars that are set apart from the rest of the text. These sidebars include Notes, Tips, Cautions.

Source Code and Updates

For updates to this book, and to download the source code and examples presented in this book, visit http://www.samspublishing.com. From the home page, type this book's ISBN (0672324865) into the search window, and click on "Search" to access information about the book and a direct link to the source code.

We hope you enjoy using this book as much as we have enjoyed writing it.

Bert Scalzo and Dan Hotka

1

Setting Up TOAD for Successful Use

Congratulations! You've just bought TOAD and are now getting ready to deploy it in your organization. When TOAD is correctly configured, you will find it to be the single most productive integrated development environment (IDE) for SQL and PL/SQL on the market. With a quarter million registered users and possibly double that using the freeware, TOAD has been almost universally accepted as the "de facto" standard for doing Oracle application development and administration. But even the world's greatest tool requires a little attention to detail for both setup and configuration in order to achieve the greatest success. So by spending just a few minutes wisely up front, you can make all your TOAD users (both DBAs and developers) more productive.

Meeting TOAD's Database Connectivity Needs

TOAD must be able to communicate with your Oracle database. That means TOAD must be able to both connect and then work with your database whether it's local (on PC) or remote (on server). This requires that the Oracle network client libraries exist on your PC for TOAD to call. Of course, Oracle in its infinite wisdom has renamed the client software and libraries as shown in Table 1.1.

TABLE 1.1   Oracle Connectivity

Version	Terminology	Client Library
Oracle 7	SQL*Net	ORA7x.DLL
Oracle 8	Net8	ORACLIENT8.DLL
Oracle 8i	Net8	ORACLIENT8.DLL
Oracle 9i	Oracle Net	ORACLIENT9.DLL
Oracle 9iR2	Oracle Net	ORACLIENT9.DLL

Furthermore, you must also verify that your PC's environment variable for PATH includes the directory where those network client libraries are installed (that is, the Oracle installation directory). Of course, this too has changed over the Oracle versions and can also be modified by the person doing the install. Here are some examples of locations where they might be found:

- `C:\ORAWIN\BIN`
- `C:\ORAWIN95\BIN`
- `C:\ORANT\BIN`
- `C:\ORACLE\BIN`
- `C:\ORACLE\ORA92\BIN`

Failure to install and reference these client libraries will prevent TOAD from functioning. However, you must also keep in mind your version of the client libraries versus the database you are talking to. Having client libraries from an older version of Oracle but talking to newer versions of Oracle is a recipe for disaster. You may encounter Oracle OCI API error messages from within TOAD. This might occur as TOAD attempts to call an OCI function for some new features or capability of the newer database version that the older network client library does not support.

For example, using an 8i client with a 9i database and attempting to work with columns whose data type is XMLTYPE will yield the cryptic message: `OCI-21500: internal error code, arguments: [kocgpn129], [2], [], [], [], [], [], []`. This is not a TOAD bug or lack of TOAD support for new features, but a simple user error of trying to use old or incompatible network client libraries with newer versions of the database. The best advice is to always use the latest and greatest network client, as it is always backward-compatible with prior database versions.

Understanding TOAD's Oracle-Based Security

Probably the most frequently asked question by DBAs new to TOAD is: "Will TOAD permit my developers to do things that they should not?" The simple answer is definitely not, because TOAD cannot override or supersede Oracle's security. TOAD users have only whatever roles, system privileges, or object grants that exist for them within the database. Thus they can do no more in TOAD than they could in SQL*Plus (they just can do it more easily and faster). To reiterate, TOAD only permits users to do whatever the DBA has granted them—there are no loopholes or exceptions.

But this does require the DBAs managing the Oracle schemas (that is, users) to have a very firm grasp on all the privileges they are actually handing out. For example, far too many DBAs still grant the predefined roles CONNECT, RESOURCE, and DBA to their users—even though Oracle states that these roles are there merely for backward compatibility and that you should create and grant your own customized roles. Unfortunately, many people seem to have missed this fact and still overuse the predefined roles. But some DBAs do not fully realize which system privileges the predefined roles grant. So granting a schema CONNECT means that the user can create clusters, database links, sequences, synonyms, tables, and views via TOAD, because those are the privileges that CONNECT possesses. So know your predefined roles well if you're going to use them. However, the recommendation is to create your own custom roles and grant those to your DBAs and developers, as in the following example. (Of course, you could create these roles by using TOAD's GUI for managing roles from the Schema Browser as shown in Figure 1.1.)

```
-- Role: Junior Developer
-- Trusted to do some things
CREATE ROLE DEVELOPER_JR NOT IDENTIFIED;
--
-- Obviously required priv's
GRANT CREATE SESSION TO DEVELOPER_JR;
GRANT ALTER SESSION TO DEVELOPER_JR;
GRANT ALTER USER TO DEVELOPER_JR;
--
-- Junior Developer Priv's
GRANT CREATE PROCEDURE TO DEVELOPER_JR;
GRANT CREATE SEQUENCE TO DEVELOPER_JR;
GRANT CREATE SYNONYM TO DEVELOPER_JR;
GRANT CREATE TRIGGER TO DEVELOPER_JR;
GRANT CREATE TYPE TO DEVELOPER_JR;
GRANT CREATE VIEW TO DEVELOPER_JR;


-- Role: Senior Developer
-- Trusted to do most things
CREATE ROLE DEVELOPER_SR NOT IDENTIFIED;
--
```

```
-- Inherit All Junior Priv's
GRANT DEVELOPER_JR TO DEVELOPER_SR;
--
-- Senior Developer Priv's
GRANT CREATE DATABASE LINK TO DEVELOPER_SR;
GRANT CREATE DIMENSION TO DEVELOPER_SR;
GRANT CREATE INDEXTYPE TO DEVELOPER_JR;
GRANT CREATE LIBRARY TO DEVELOPER_SR;
GRANT CREATE MATERIALIZED VIEW TO DEVELOPER_SR;
GRANT CREATE OPERATOR TO DEVELOPER_JR;
GRANT CREATE TABLE TO DEVELOPER_SR;
```

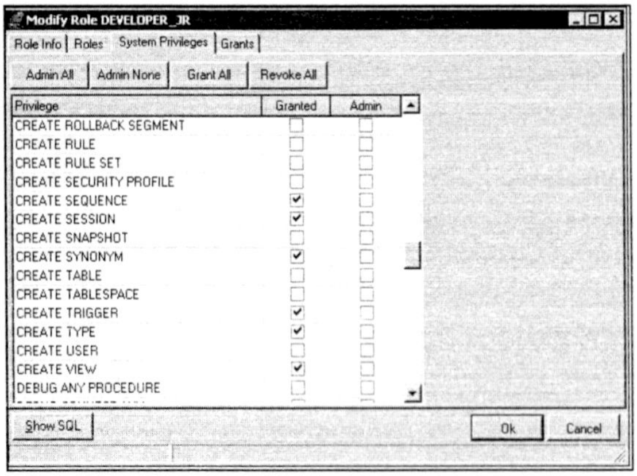

Another area of possible security oversight is to forget the PUBLIC schema and its granted roles, system privileges, or object grants. For example, granting SELECT ANY TABLE to PUBLIC (which is generally not advisable) means that TOAD users can see the entire database's table data. So manage PUBLIC wisely. But do note that TOAD uses the data dictionary views for ALL_xxx and DBA_xxx that have been granted to PUBLIC. And don't worry about the DBA_xxx views; again, TOAD only allows users to see

FIGURE 1.1   TOAD role management screen.

those based upon Oracle security. Thus a user must have SELECT ANY TABLE, SELECT ANY DICTIONARY, or SELECT_CATALOG_ROLE (depending on Oracle version and O7_DICTIONARY_ACCESSIBILITY setting) in order for TOAD to reference the DBA_xxx views. Remember that as you create roles for users who will be using TOAD's DBA module. For those users, one of the following security scenarios should be adopted:

- O7_DICTIONARY_ACCESSIBILITY = true

- O7_DICTIONARY_ACCESSIBILITY = true, SELECT ANY DICTIONARY granted, SELECT ANY TABLE not granted (second best recommendation)

- O7_DICTIONARY_ACCESSIBILITY = true, SELECT ANY DICTIONARY granted, SELECT ANY TABLE granted

- O7_DICTIONARY_ACCESSIBILITY = true, SELECT ANY DICTIONARY not granted, SELECT ANY TABLE not granted, SELECT_CATALOG_ROLE granted (best recommendation)

Creating the All-Important TOAD Schema

Strictly speaking, you do not have to create any database server-side objects in order to use TOAD. You can simply install TOAD on your PC and go on your merry way. But there are screens where a developer will require access to an Oracle explain plan table. For example, the SQL Editor window has a tab for displaying the explain plan for the current SQL statement. Thus TOAD will need access to a plan table in order to process and then display the resulting explain plan. You have three options here.

First, sometimes DBAs prefer to create a DBA schema-owned, general-purpose and shared explain plan table using Oracle's scripts. So the steps to implement might look something like this:

- Connect as SYSTEM (or other DBA account).

- Run Oracle's RDBMS/ADMIN/UTLXPLAN.SQL.

- GRANT ALL ON SYSTEM.PLAN_TABLE TO PUBLIC

- CREATE PUBLIC SYNONYM PLAN_TABLE FOR SYSTEM.PLAN_TABLE

TOAD can work with such a setup. You should merely set the TOAD options for the Explain Plan Table Name field under the Oracle category to PLAN_TABLE (meaning the public synonym for the general-purpose table set up by the DBA). The TOAD Options screen is launched from the main menu at View, Options and is shown in Figure 1.2.

There are two caveats with this method. First, you must make sure the DBA schema-owned explain plan table is current for the Oracle version being used. It's really quite easy to forget to update this table with major Oracle upgrades. This can cause TOAD to encounter problems with missing columns (that is, a call to Oracle will try to populate newer columns that don't exist in the old plan table structure). And second, TOAD will not be able to save and recall plans if you use this method because TOAD requires its own plan table to support such operations. You must instead use one of the two remaining methods.

Second (and recommended), you can also create a special TOAD schema to own a general-purpose and shared explain plan table using TOAD's TOADPREP.SQL script (found in the TEMPS subdirectory of the TOAD install directory). TOADPREP.SQL first creates the TOAD schema, and then creates its required explain plan objects. To accomplish this implementation, the steps are as follows:

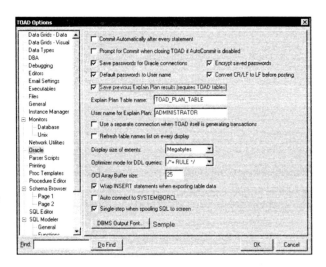

FIGURE 1.2   TOAD Options: Oracle explain plans.

1. Edit TOAD's TEMPS/TOADPREP.SQL.

2. Connect as SYSTEM (or other DBA account).

3. Run TOAD's TEMPS/TOADPREP.SQL.

TOAD will now be able to support the save and recall of explain plans, as long as you remember to check Save Previous Explain Plan Results in the TOAD Options screen under the Oracle category, as shown in Figure 1.2.

The TOADPREP.SQL script has changed significantly with version 7.4. Although the script has always created both the TOAD schema and all its explain-plan required objects, it has been updated such that you only need to modify the first three DEFINE statements in the script in order to control the script's behavior. It used to be that you had to review the entire SQL script for possible changes. So the new TOAD-PREP.SQL script shown in Listing 1.1 is much easer to work with.

LISTING 1.1   TOADPREP.SQL Script

```
REM  This script will create TOAD objects in their own
REM  schema. If you DO NOT want to create a unique system
REM  schema for TOAD objects, load the file NOTOAD.SQL
REM
REM  Otherwise, start a new Oracle connection as SYSTEM ( or
REM  any other user with privileges to create a new USER)
REM  and, while connected as that user,  execute the following
```

LISTING 1.1   Continued

```
REM  by clicking the third toolbar button in a SQL Edit OR
REM  by selecting the menu option "SQL_Window/Execute as Script"
REM
REM  Ver  Date         Description
REM  ===  =========    =====================================
REM  1.1  10/06/1999   1. Added STORAGE clauses to the table
REM                       create commands so that not too much
REM                       disk space will be allocated.
REM                       2. Removed obsolete TOAD_TEMP and
REM                       TOAD_DEP_TEMP.
REM  1.2  11/17/1999   1. Changed index on TOAD_PLAN_TABLE from
REM                       unique to non-unique.
REM  1.3  05/23/2001   1. Added partition-related columns and
REM                       DISTRIBUTION to TOAD_PLAN_TABLE
REM  1.4  01/18/2001   1. Added OBJECTNAME function
REM  1.5  03/29/2002   Added EXECUTE ANY PROCEDURE
REM  1.6  03/31/2002   Reworked entire script so user custimizations
REM                       can be made via DEFINE variables in one place

REM --------- Make all changes right here --------------------
REM --------- Do not change the name of the TOAD user --------

DEFINE UPW_TOAD=TOAD
DEFINE DEF_TSPACE=USER_DATA
DEFINE TMP_TSPACE=TEMPORARY

REM ----------------- Create the TOAD User -----------------

DROP USER TOAD CASCADE;

CREATE USER TOAD
  IDENTIFIED BY &UPW_TOAD
  DEFAULT TABLESPACE &DEF_TSPACE
  TEMPORARY TABLESPACE &TMP_TSPACE
  QUOTA UNLIMITED ON &DEF_TSPACE
  QUOTA 0K ON SYSTEM;

GRANT CONNECT TO TOAD;
GRANT RESOURCE TO TOAD;
GRANT CREATE PUBLIC SYNONYM TO TOAD;
```

LISTING 1.1 Continued

```
--The following grant is only necessary if you intend to install the TOAD
--Profiler objects into the TOAD schema
GRANT EXECUTE ANY PROCEDURE TO TOAD;

REM ---------------- Drop public synonyms --------------------

DROP PUBLIC SYNONYM TOAD_PLAN_SQL;
DROP PUBLIC SYNONYM TOAD_PLAN_TABLE;
DROP PUBLIC SYNONYM TOAD_SEQ;

REM ---------------- Connect as TOAD -----------------------

CONNECT TOAD/&UPW_TOAD;

REM ---------------- Create the Explain Plan objects

DROP TABLE TOAD.TOAD_PLAN_SQL;
DROP TABLE TOAD.TOAD_PLAN_TABLE;
DROP SEQUENCE TOAD.TOAD_SEQ;

CREATE TABLE TOAD.TOAD_PLAN_SQL (
USERNAME     VARCHAR2(30),
STATEMENT_ID VARCHAR2(32),
TIMESTAMP    DATE,
STATEMENT    VARCHAR2(2000) )
STORAGE (INITIAL 40K NEXT 24K);

CREATE UNIQUE INDEX TOAD.TPSQL_IDX ON
TOAD.TOAD_PLAN_SQL ( STATEMENT_ID );

CREATE TABLE TOAD.TOAD_PLAN_TABLE (
STATEMENT_ID     VARCHAR2(32),
TIMESTAMP        DATE,
REMARKS          VARCHAR2(80),
OPERATION        VARCHAR2(30),
OPTIONS          VARCHAR2(30),
OBJECT_NODE      VARCHAR2(128),
OBJECT_OWNER     VARCHAR2(30),
OBJECT_NAME      VARCHAR2(30),
OBJECT_INSTANCE  NUMBER,
OBJECT_TYPE      VARCHAR2(30),
```

LISTING 1.1   Continued

```
SEARCH_COLUMNS  NUMBER,
ID              NUMBER,
COST            NUMBER,
PARENT_ID       NUMBER,
POSITION        NUMBER,
CARDINALITY     NUMBER,
OPTIMIZER       VARCHAR2(255),
BYTES           NUMBER,
OTHER_TAG       VARCHAR2(255),
PARTITION_ID    NUMBER,
PARTITION_START VARCHAR2(255),
PARTITION_STOP  VARCHAR2(255),
DISTRIBUTION    VARCHAR2(30),
OTHER           LONG)
STORAGE(INITIAL 80K NEXT 36K) ;

CREATE INDEX TOAD.TPTBL_IDX ON
TOAD.TOAD_PLAN_TABLE ( STATEMENT_ID );

CREATE SEQUENCE TOAD.TOAD_SEQ START WITH 1 CACHE 20;

CREATE PUBLIC SYNONYM TOAD_PLAN_SQL FOR TOAD.TOAD_PLAN_SQL;
CREATE PUBLIC SYNONYM TOAD_PLAN_TABLE FOR TOAD.TOAD_PLAN_TABLE;
CREATE PUBLIC SYNONYM TOAD_SEQ FOR TOAD.TOAD_SEQ;

GRANT SELECT, INSERT, UPDATE, DELETE ON TOAD.TOAD_PLAN_SQL TO PUBLIC;
GRANT SELECT, INSERT, UPDATE, DELETE ON TOAD.TOAD_PLAN_TABLE TO PUBLIC;
GRANT SELECT, ALTER ON TOAD.TOAD_SEQ TO PUBLIC;

REM -------- Create the ObjectName function for use in Kill/Trace ----------

DROP FUNCTION TOAD.MYOBJECTNAME;

CREATE OR REPLACE function TOAD.ObjectName(in_object_id in number) return
varchar
is
  return_string varchar2(100);
begin
  select OWNER||'.'||OBJECT_NAME
    into return_string
    from all_objects
```

LISTING 1.1   Continued

```
    where object_id = in_object_id;
  return return_string;
end ObjectName;
/
GRANT EXECUTE ON TOAD.OBJECTNAME TO PUBLIC;
```

Third and finally, you can also create a private TOAD explain plan table and all its required objects per TOAD user via the NOTOAD.SQL script (also found in the TEMPS subdirectory of the TOAD install directory). To accomplish this implementation, the steps are as follows:

1. Connect as each and every TOAD user.

2. Run TOAD's TEMPS/NOTOAD.SQL.

This method is supported for backward compatibility, but it's very hard to imagine a case where you would want to choose this implementation option. This method would require every TOAD user to have CREATE TABLE privilege, CREATE SEQUENCE privilege, and some tablespace quota on at least one tablespace. Plus it would result in numerous additional database objects as a whole (that is, two tables, two indexes, and one sequence created per TOAD user). But the option does exist for those who want to use it. The only advantage to this approach is that, like the prior method, it too supports the save and recall of explain plans. Because this method is not recommended, the NOTOAD.SQL script is not shown.

Activating TOAD's "Read-Only" Mode

Most people don't realize that TOAD comes with two modes of operation entirely under their control. TOAD can operate in either read/write or read-only mode, simply controlled by the license files in the TOAD install directory. When the TOAD.LIC file is a copy of the FULLTOAD.LIC file (default), TOAD operates in read/write mode. And when the TOAD.LIC file is a copy of the READONLY.LIC file, TOAD operates in read-only mode. Note that read-only refers to the fact that users cannot save or commit anything to the database. However, read-only users are still permitted to create, modify, and save other files on the local PC. They cannot do anything but read database data.

Note that this was the original method by which TOAD supported a read-only mode of operation. Beginning in version 7.3, TOAD's entirely new advanced security offering (see the following section) offers a much cleaner and simpler method for making TOAD read-only.

Using TOAD's New Advanced Security

Beginning with version 7.3, TOAD offers an entirely new and completely customizable security mechanism. With it, you can very easily define what features or functions should work in TOAD by either database user or role. For example, you can take the DEVELOPER_JR database role from the prior section and further control what a junior developer can do within TOAD as shown in Figure 1.3. This screen is callable from the main menu at Tools, Toad Security. However, to use this screen, you must first have a TOAD schema (like the one created by TOADPREP.SQL) and then run the TOADSECURITY.SQL script (found in the TEMPS subdirectory of the TOAD install directory and shown in Listing 1.2).

LISTING 1.2   TOADSECURITY.SQL Script

```
/*
    This is the script for setting up TOAD Features Security.
    This file should be run after the TOAD user has been created
    through toadprep.sql.  Load this script into the SQL Editor
    and press "Run as script."  You will be prompted for TOAD's
    password on your database.  Then you will be prompted for the name
    of the user (should be a DBA) who will serve as the TOAD
    Security administrator.  Bear in mind that users with the
    DBA role are not bound by TOAD Security.
*/
/*
Date        Description
..........  .........................................
03/05/2002  Recreated script for 7.3's rewrite of TOAD Security
*/


CONNECT TOAD

CREATE TABLE TOAD_RESTRICTIONS (
  USER_NAME  VARCHAR2(32)  NOT NULL,
  FEATURE    VARCHAR2(20)  NOT NULL,
  CONSTRAINT TOAD_RES_PK
  PRIMARY KEY ( FEATURE, USER_NAME ) );

REM  grant all to the toad tables WITH grant option to any users
REM  who will be using the TOAD Features Security Window to administer
REM  TOAD security features.
REM
GRANT ALL ON TOAD_RESTRICTIONS TO &SOME_DBA_USER WITH GRANT OPTION;
```

Examine Figure 1.3 in more detail. The left side shows a list of all the available functions, also considered enabled. These fall into two categories: menu and non-menu. Menu refers to actual menu items within TOAD, whereas non-menu means functions that might be accessible from multiple places within TOAD. The right side then shows just those functions you want to remove or disable for that user or role. Thus in Figure 1.3, the DEVELOPER_JR has had the following removed:

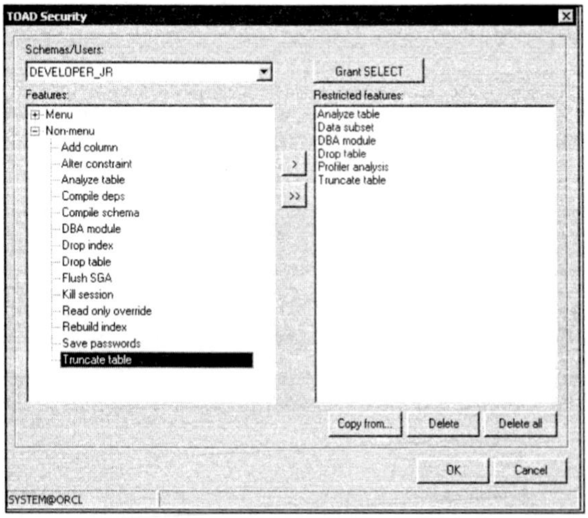

FIGURE 1.3   TOAD Security screen.

- Menu: Data subset (cannot run data subset wizard)

- Menu: Profiler analysis (cannot run TOAD profiler)

- Non-Menu: Analyze table (cannot analyze tables)

- Non-Menu: DBA module (cannot access DBA features)

- Non-Menu: Drop table (cannot drop tables)

- Non-Menu: Truncate table (cannot truncate tables)

Note that the left side offers a Non-Menu choice of "Read only override." This is the new and preferable way to activate TOAD in read-only mode (see the preceding section). This is by far the easiest and most reliable method for defining your read-only TOAD users.

Enabling TOAD's PL/SQL Profiler Support

TOAD has a very capable PL/SQL profiler for detailed analysis of code execution behavior. But many people seem to have problems initially getting this feature to work. At first, the menu item and toolbar icon may not appear as enabled. That's because there are some TOAD schema objects that must be created. People next encounter issues on the profiler screen, because unknown to them there are Oracle profiler packages that must be created by the DBA in the SYS account (and which Oracle does not create by default). But in reality the steps to set up TOAD's profiler are quite easy:

1. Connect as SYS.

2. Run Oracle's `RDBMS/ADMIN/PROFLOAD.SQL`.

3. Connect as TOAD.

4. Run TOAD's `TEMPS/TOADPROFILER.SQL`.

If you don't create and use a TOAD schema, it would still be possible to enable TOAD profiler support in one of two ways:

- Run TOAD's `TEMPS/TOADPROFILER.SQL` as SYSTEM or other DBA account, because it creates public synonyms and grants object privileges to public.

- Run TOAD's `TEMPS/TOADPROFILER.SQL` as each and every TOAD user (just remember to comment out the public grants and synonyms portions near the bottom of the script).

Saving and Restoring All Your TOAD Settings

If there's one thing TOAD has, it's lots and lots of options. So as you use TOAD over time, you will naturally set many of these options so as to customize TOAD to the way you like to work. But what happens when you go to work on a different PC (for example, if you work on your neighbor's PC while yours is being serviced)? You lose all your settings because they are stored on the local PC hard drive in both the TOAD install directory and the TEMPS subdirectory. It would take some time if you lost those settings and had to visit every screen where they are defined throughout the tool and reset them. So what's needed is a TOAD settings backup and restoration utility, which is provided in the following examples.

The following Windows command processor batch script will back up all your most important TOAD settings. You simply modify the script's first four SET statements for your particular environment and save the script to a file called TOAD_SAVE.BAT. Then you can merely type TOAD_SAVE in a command window, or better yet, place an icon on your desktop so that you can save all your settings quickly and easily with a single click.

```
@echo off

set save_dir1=c:\temp\TOAD
set save_dir2=%save_dir1%\temps

set toad_dir1=c:\program files\quest software\toad
set toad_dir2=%toad_dir1%\temps
```

```
echo.
echo *** Saving TOAD Settings ***
echo.
echo Target:
echo save_dir1 = %save_dir1%
echo save_dir2 = %save_dir2%
echo.
echo Source:
echo toad_dir1 = %toad_dir1%
echo toad_dir2 = %toad_dir2%

if not exist "%save_dir1%" mkdir "%save_dir1%"
if not exist "%save_dir2%" mkdir "%save_dir2%"
del /Q %save_dir%\*.*
del /Q %save_dir%\*.*

echo.
echo Copying Files:
for %%i in ("%toad_dir1%"\*.ini,
            "%toad_dir1%"\*.dat,
            "%toad_dir1%"\*.sdf,
            "%toad_dir1%"\*.jdf,
            "%toad_dir1%"\*.flt,
            "%toad_dir1%"\*.tni,
            "%toad_dir1%"\*.tbl,
            "%toad_dir1%"\*.tmd,
            "%toad_dir1%"\*.lst) do copy /Y "%%i" "%save_dir1%\"

for %%i in ("%toad_dir2%"\*.ini,
            "%toad_dir2%"\*.dat,
            "%toad_dir2%"\*.sdf,
            "%toad_dir2%"\*.jdf,
            "%toad_dir2%"\*.flt,
            "%toad_dir2%"\*.tni,
            "%toad_dir2%"\*.tbl,
            "%toad_dir2%"\*.tmd,
            "%toad_dir2%"\*.lst) do copy /Y "%%i" "%save_dir2%\"
```

Similarly, the following Windows command processor batch script will restore all of your most important TOAD settings. You modify the script's first four SET statements for your particular environment and save the script to a file called TOAD_RESTORE.BAT. Then you can just type TOAD_RESTORE in a command window, or better yet, place an icon on your desktop so that you can restore all your settings with a single click.

```
@echo off

set save_dir1=c:\temp\TOAD
set save_dir2=%save_dir1%\temps

set toad_dir1=c:\program files\quest software\toad
set toad_dir2=%toad_dir1%\temps

echo.
echo *** Restoring TOAD Settings ***
echo.
echo Source:
echo save_dir1 = %save_dir1%
echo save_dir2 = %save_dir2%
echo.
echo Target:
echo toad_dir1 = %toad_dir1%
echo toad_dir2 = %toad_dir2%

echo.
echo Copying Files:
for %%i in ("%save_dir1%"\*.ini,
            "%save_dir1%"\*.dat,
            "%save_dir1%"\*.sdf,
            "%save_dir1%"\*.jdf,
            "%save_dir1%"\*.flt,
            "%save_dir1%"\*.tni,
            "%save_dir1%"\*.tbl,
            "%save_dir1%"\*.tmd,
            "%save_dir1%"\*.lst) do copy /Y "%%i" "%toad_dir1%\"

for %%i in ("%save_dir2%"\*.ini,
            "%save_dir2%"\*.dat,
            "%save_dir2%"\*.sdf,
            "%save_dir2%"\*.jdf,
            "%save_dir2%"\*.flt,
            "%save_dir2%"\*.tni,
            "%save_dir2%"\*.tbl,
            "%save_dir2%"\*.tmd,
            "%save_dir2%"\*.lst) do copy /Y "%%i" "%toad_dir2%\"
```

Summary

This chapter covered basic TOAD setup and configuration steps necessary to successfully utilize the product. Although a few of these topics are quite basic and remedial for some users, other topics are much less obvious—although they can have a profound effect on how you use TOAD. People experiencing problems using TOAD often learn the hard way that they've simply failed to run some of the configuration scripts provided and discussed in this chapter.

The next chapter introduces TOAD's Schema Browser, an Explorer-like interface for navigating and managing all of your database objects.

2

Using TOAD's Schema Browser

Whether you're a DBA or a developer, TOAD's Schema Browser is a powerful and functional interface for exploring all your database objects. Not only does the Schema Browser enable you to quickly and easily navigate the complex structures within the database, but it also enables you to both manage and control all those structures (where your granted Oracle privileges permit). This screen is so extremely useful that when you're not coding or debugging, you'll most likely be exploring your database with the TOAD Schema Browser. It is accessible from the main toolbar and from the main menu at Database, Schema Browser.

Although many of today's Windows tools utilize tree views for their explorer GUI design, TOAD has pioneered and adopted a tabbed GUI design. The problem with tree views is that you end up scrolling too much when lots of information must be displayed. For example, opening a tree-view node for a user's tables might well display dozens of nodes and cause the tree view to scroll numerous other items of interest out of the main viewing area. By contrast, with the tabbed approach, less scrolling is generally required. Returning to the prior example, choosing a user's tables from the Tables tab does not cause your other main object categories (that is, tabs) to scroll off anywhere. Although it may initially take some getting used to, TOAD's tabbed GUI design is infinitely more productive in terms of wasted scrolling efforts. And time is money.

Finally, you might think you can skip this chapter because the Schema Browser is just another explorer and people use those every day. But the TOAD Schema Browser has so many features and capabilities you might never find that skipping this one chapter could make your overall TOAD usage much less productive. In fact, during the TOAD User Groups when "Tips and Tricks" are discussed, this one area alone seems to generate the most comments like "I did not know TOAD could do that." So please read on to learn how to fully utilize TOAD's Schema Browser and all its advanced capabilities.

Making Schema Browser Your Startup Screen

Many people find the Schema Browser so useful that they want TOAD to bring it up as their initial screen when TOAD either launches or creates a new database connection. The concept is that often you must navigate to something of interest and then perform work on it. Thus using the Schema Browser to locate and then operate on that object is often the most productive method for working within TOAD. To accomplish this, you simply check the box for Browser under the group Startup Windows per Connection under the StartUp category in the TOAD Options screen, as shown in Figure 2.1. The TOAD Options screen is accessible from the main menu at View, Options. Now TOAD will open a Schema Browser when you first launch it and for each new database connection.

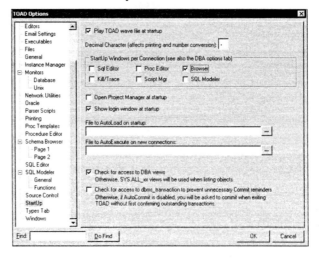

Figure 2.1   The TOAD Schema Browser option for auto-startup.

Choosing Among Schema Browser Display Styles

TOAD's novel tabbed approach can at times appear cluttered, as shown in Figure 2.2. The left-hand side (LHS) of the screen has all the tabs spanning across multiple lines, thus consuming nearly a third of the vertical real estate within which to display each tab's relevant contextual information. What if you had two dozen tables? The bottom half of the LHS would become scrollable and you would not be able to see some of the tables (unless you scrolled). For some people, this is not the optimal way to work. So TOAD offers options for how the Schema Browser display should appear.

For people who like the tabbed approach but do not want the tabs to span multiple lines and therefore chew up valuable display real estate, TOAD can also display the tabs as horizontally scrollable. To accomplish this, you simply uncheck the box for Use Multi-Line Tabs on the Left Side on Page 2 of the Schema Browser category of the TOAD Options screen as shown in Figure 2.3. The TOAD Options screen is accessible from the main menu at View, Options.

Figure 2.2 The TOAD Schema Browser: multiline tabs.

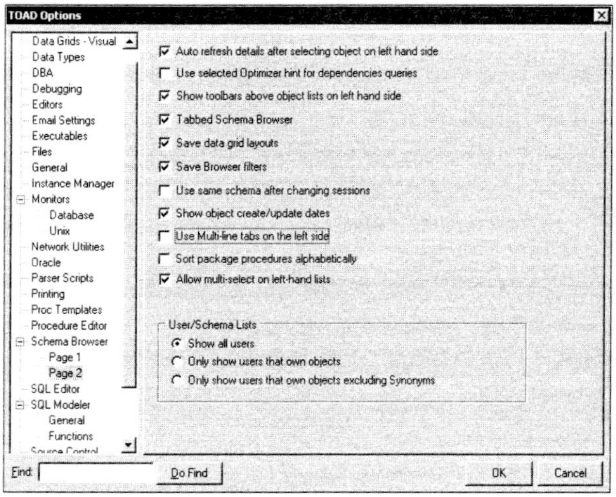

Figure 2.3 TOAD options for single-line Schema Browser.

Now the Schema Browser tabs will appear as shown in Figure 2.4. Compare Figures 2.2 and 2.4 and you'll see how this option does not consume as much real estate for the tabs and thus has more room for displaying contextual information. Of course now you must scroll left and right in order to access all of TOAD's many tabs.

Of course, some people just don't like the tabbed approach and prefer something more traditional. Thus TOAD offers a drop-down list display style for the Schema Browser as well. To choose this style of interface, you simply uncheck the box for Tabbed Schema Browser on Page 2 of the Schema Browser category of the TOAD Options screen as shown in Figure 2.5. The TOAD Options screen can be accessed from the main menu at View, Options.

Figure 2.4   TOAD Schema Browser, showing single-line tabs.

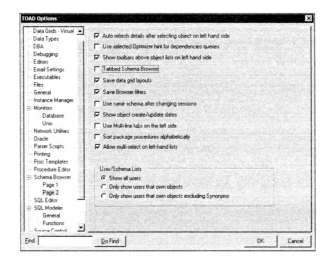

Figure 2.5   TOAD options for drop-down list style Schema Browser.

Now the Schema Browser will appear as shown in Figure 2.6 (note that the drop down lists completely replace the need for any tabs at all). Compare Figures 2.2, 2.4, and 2.6. The drop-down list style does not consume as much real estate either, but offers a simple and intuitive interface for those people who dislike the tabbed approach.

Enabling or Disabling Schema Browser Tabs

Most people do not work with every conceivable Oracle object type, but rather a select subset that fits their needs and job description. For example, a PL/SQL developer may not care to see tabs for table-spaces, rollback segments, profiles, policies, and other more DBA-relevant information. So you can simply right-click to open a context menu on any tab or a tab's toolbar and select which tabs to enable or disable for display on the Schema Browser as shown in Figure 2.7. Then you will have a Schema Browser whose displayed tabs fit your needs. This might be quite useful for people who want the tabs to span lines, but cannot accept having all the tabs being displayed and thus losing so much real estate for displaying each tab's contextual information.

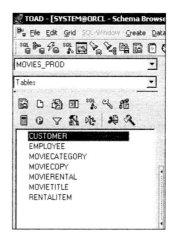
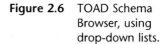

Figure 2.6   TOAD Schema Browser, using drop-down lists.

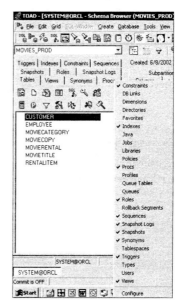

Figure 2.7   Selecting displayed tabs.

Configuring Schema Browser Tabs

Regardless of whether you choose to disable certain tabs or not as shown in Figure 2.7, you might not like the tab order or their labels. For example, you might prefer that "Snapshots" and "Snapshot Logs" be instead labeled as "MV/Snaps" and "MV/Snap Logs", respectively. Plus, you might want them to be located right next to each other (that is, not have "Roles" shown between them as shown in Figure 2.7). To accomplish this task, you simply right-click on any tab or a tab's toolbar and select the Configure choice from the context menu as shown in Figure 2.7. This will launch the Configure Browser Tabs window shown in Figure 2.8, where you control both the label and order for all the tabs.

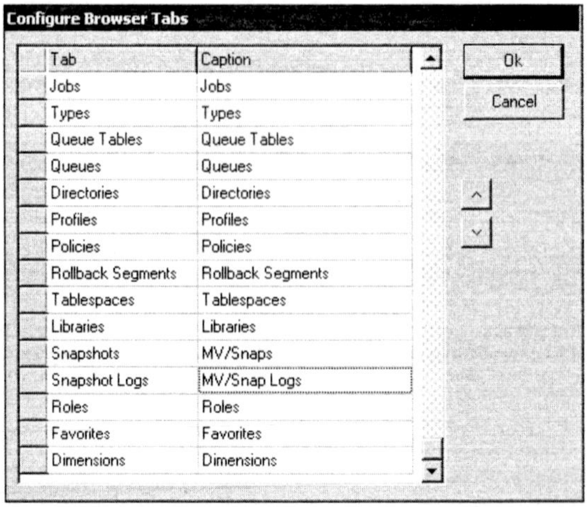

Figure 2.8   Configuring tabs in TOAD Schema Browser.

After you complete your selections and click OK to leave this screen, the Schema Browser will appear with the newly desired customizations as shown in Figure 2.9. Thus you now have the tabs labeled and ordered exactly as you wanted. These settings are permanent (i.e. remembered across TOAD across sessions), so you'll only need to make such changes once.

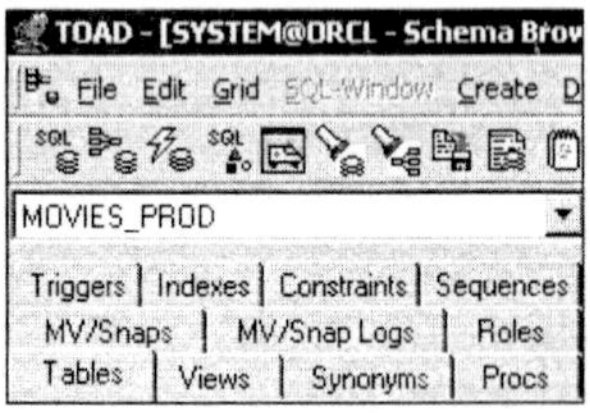

Figure 2.9   Customized tabs for MV/Snaps and MV/Snap Logs.

Filtering Schema Browser Schemas

It's not unusual for a typical database to have lots of schemas. In fact, many of today's database applications routinely create a schema per application user. These user schemas often possess no database objects, but instead access the central application tables by using grants and synonyms. When you're working within TOAD's Schema Browser, these user schemas are really of limited value. Thus you would like to see them filtered out of the drop-down list in the Schema Browser for the schema to focus upon (because they have no objects and will never really display anything). As with everywhere else in TOAD, there is an option to control this and it's simple to do.

Figure 2.10 shows the TOAD Schema Browser drop-down list for all the available schemas within the database, of which 16 are shown. But some of these schemas contain no objects, so there is really little or no value in being able to select them (i.e. their schema browser tabs would show no objects under them if displayed).

To eliminate such schemas from the drop-down list, you simply check the Only Show Users That Own Objects option under the group User/Schema Lists on Page 2 of the Schema Browser category of the TOAD Options screen as shown in Figure 2.11. You can access the TOAD Options screen from the main menu at View, Options.

Figure 2.10 TOAD Schema Browser, showing all available schemas.

Now those empty schemas will be eliminated as shown in Figure 2.12 (the choices for BERT and DBSNMP are no longer displayed). This not only keeps the drop-down list for available schemas within the database short, but also offers for selection only those schemas that would have something to display within the Schema Browser. Note that the option for Only Show Users That Own Objects Excluding Synonyms in Figure 2.11 might be the best possible choice. Because

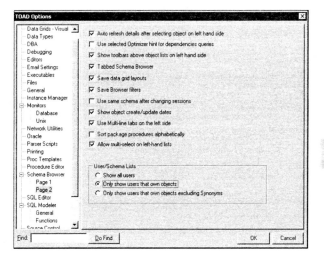
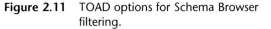

Figure 2.11 TOAD options for Schema Browser filtering.

it's not uncommon for database applications that create a schema per user to access tables via private and public synonyms, these users would display very little in the Schema Browser.

Of course, just filtering by users who own objects may not be selective enough. What if your Oracle database contains many subject areas or applications? You might need to work on just a select few, and the others may be of little or no value to you. TOAD permits you to customize the list of users available by using the Configure User Lists screen as shown in Figure 2.13. You can access this screen from the main menu at View, Oracle Users List. You simply check and uncheck those schemas of interest and then click the OK button.

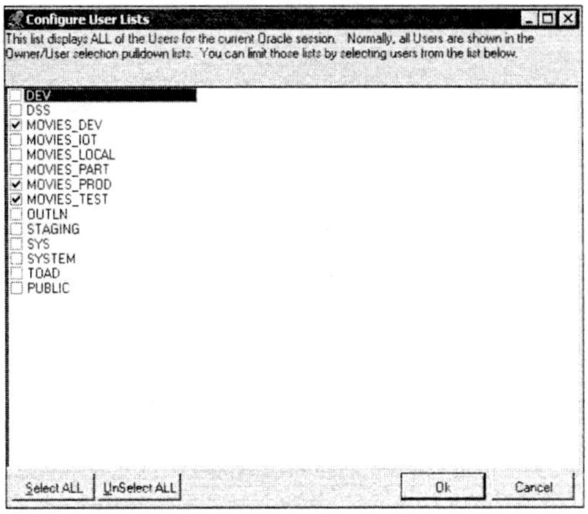

Figure 2.12 Displaying only schemas with objects.

Figure 2.13   TOAD Configure User Lists screen.

Now the Schema Browser's Schema drop-down list will display only those selected schemas as shown in Figure 2.14. This is probably the most effective way to filter the Schema Browser since most database application developers tend to work on objects owned by just a few select schemas at a time. Just remember that you've set these filters or you may mistakenly think that TOAD is not propely showing you everything within your database.

Figure 2.14 Displaying only selected schemas.

Filtering Schema Browser Objects

It's not unusual for a typical database schema to have lots of objects. For example, Enterprise Resource Planning (ERP) applications such as SAP, Peoplesoft, Siebel, and Oracle Apps can have thousands of tables. As such, they often follow some naming convention to ease the object name overload. So the general ledger table names may be prefixed with "GL_", the accounts receivable with "AR_", the accounts payable with "AP_", and so on. But as the DBA, you or the developer might not be interested in always seeing all possible choices, but instead merely a user-defined subset based on the naming standard. TOAD provides filters for most of the Schema Browser tabs for accomplishing exactly this task.

In Figure 2.15, the Schema Browser Tables tab shows nine tables, two of which are meaningless as indicated by their name (that is, name begins with the letters JUNK). To eliminate these tables, you simply click the Filter icon (the gray funnel) on that tab's toolbar, which launches the Browser Filters screen shown in Figure 2.15 (this screen will look different for the various database object types because different filter criteria options apply). For the example, you merely specify a table name that is "Not Like" and "%JUNK%".

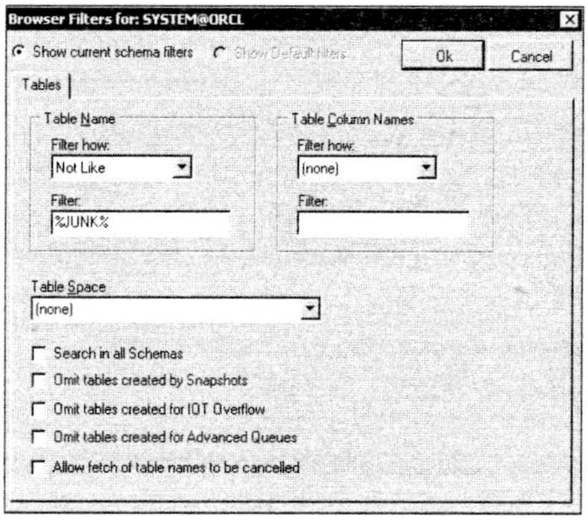

Figure 2.15 Basic name filtering.

After you apply your filter settings and click the OK button, two things will happen as shown in Figure 2.16. First, those filter settings will be applied to the information displayed for the tab. In this example, the JUNK tables were eliminated. Second, that tab's Filter toolbar icon will change in color to red, which indicates that the filter is now active. It will, of course, change back to gray if you clear the filter.

Yet another common filtering task that a DBA or developer may need is to see just those objects that contain some additional level of filtration criteria (that is, filtering beyond just that based on their name). For example, a DBA might need to work with only those tables that contain columns whose name includes the letters NAME. To specify only these tables, you again simply click the Filter icon on that tab's toolbar, which launches the Browser Filters screen shown in Figure 2.17 (this screen will look different for the various data-base object types because different filter criteria options apply). For this example, you additionally specify column names "Includes" and "%NAME%".

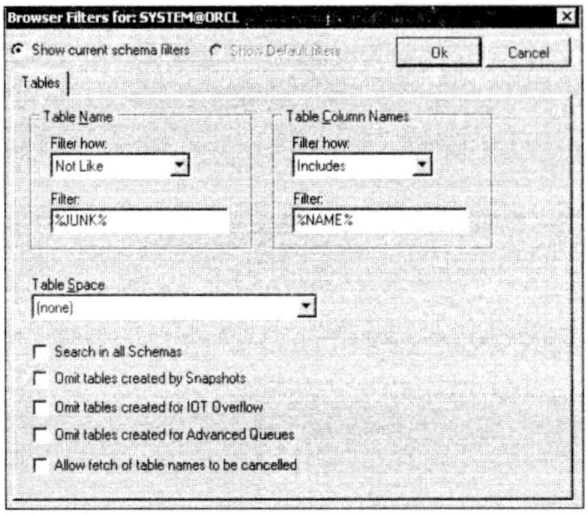

Figure 2.16   Displaying only filtered names.

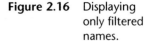

Figure 2.17   Advanced filtering options.

After you apply your filter settings and click the OK button, two things will happen as shown in Figure 2.18. First, those additional filter settings will be applied. In this example, only tables that contain columns with the names that contain NAME are displayed. And second, again that tab's Filter toolbar icon will change in color to red (that is, active).

Filtering and Sorting Schema Browser Data

With cheap disk space, today's databases are big. Likewise, many tables and views are also quite large. Thus great care should be taken when navigating the Schema Browser, for some of the left-hand-side (LHS) tabs (that is, tables, views, and snapshots) have a right-hand-side (RHS) tab for displaying the data as shown in Figure 2.19.

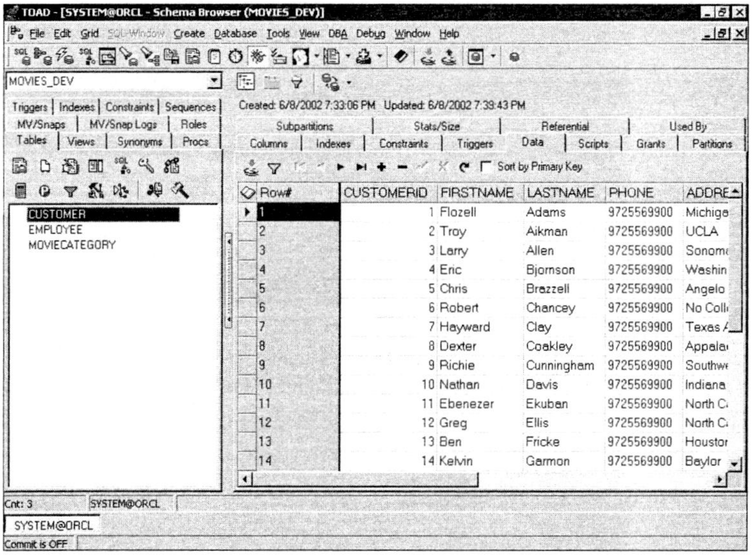

Figure 2.18 Results of applying all filters.

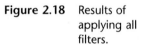

Figure 2.19 Viewing data.

And while these data grids fetch rows 25 at a time, there are user navigation scenarios that can cause problems (e.g. pressing last record button or scrolling the grid to its end). So if you select a million-row table on the LHS, choose its data tab on the RHS, and then scroll the grid to its end, TOAD will have to fetch and display a million rows. That will take some time and also chew up a lot of your PC's memory. And it's quite likely that you don't need all that data, maybe just the first 100 rows or so.

To avoid such costly queries, TOAD offers a Filter/Sort toolbar icon (that is, gray funnel) for the data tab on the RHS. Clicking the Filter/Sort icon opens the Table Sort window as shown in Figure 2.20. Using the Filter tab, you can easily select the restriction criteria upon which to filter the data, which is added to the WHERE clause used to retrieve this data from the database.

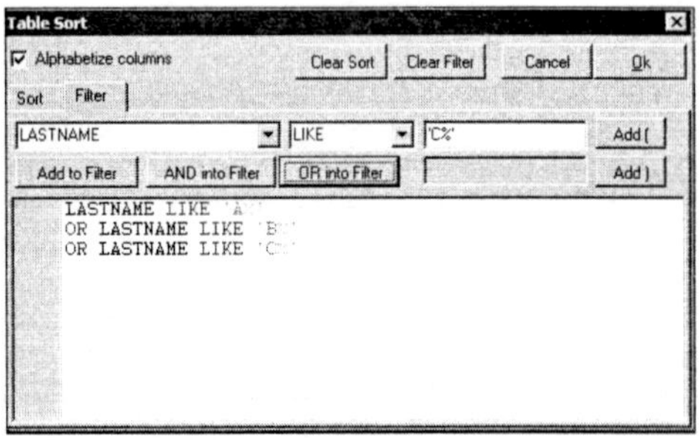

Figure 2.20   Filtering data.

Clicking the OK button (with only filtering criteria specified) will cause two things to happen as shown in Figure 2.21. First, those filter settings will be applied to the information displayed for the data grid. In this example, only those rows where the LASTNAME begins with A, B, or C are retrieved. Second, that tab's Filter toolbar icon will change in color to red, which indicates that the filter is now active. It will, of course, change back to gray if you clear the filter.

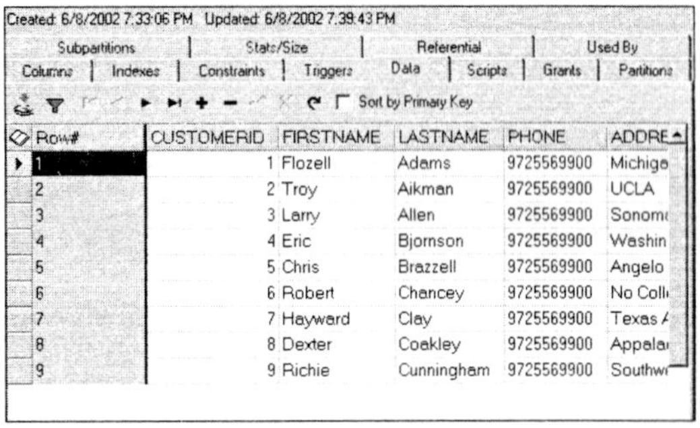

Figure 2.21   Displaying filtered data.

Of course, you can also specify to sort the data using the Sort tab as shown in Figure 2.22. This results in an ORDER BY clause being added to the SQL command to retrieve the data from the database. So you are in fact asking the Oracle database server to sort the resylt set data before returning it to the TOAD client (as opposed to having the client having to sort the possibly huge result sets).

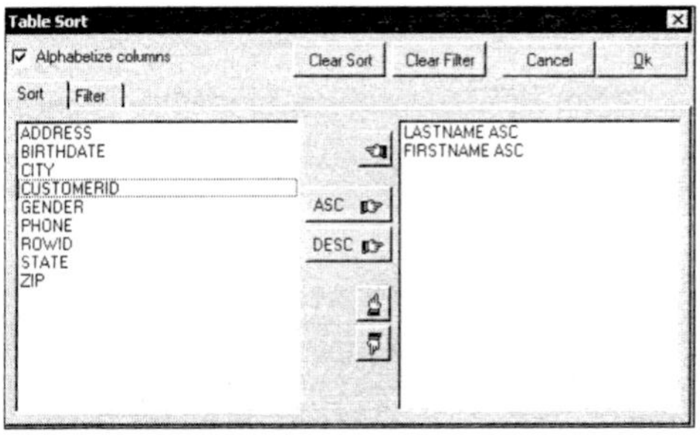

Figure 2.22   Sorting data.

Clicking the OK button (with sort criteria specified) will cause two things to happen as shown in Figure 2.23. First, those sort settings will be applied to the information displayed for the Data tab's grid. In this example, rows are sorted ascending first by LASTNAME and then by FIRSTNAME. And second, that tab's Filter toolbar icon will display a blue triangle over the funnel. If the funnel is red, both a filter and sort are being applied. If the funnel is gray, just the sort is being done. Clearing the sort will of course remove the blue triangle.

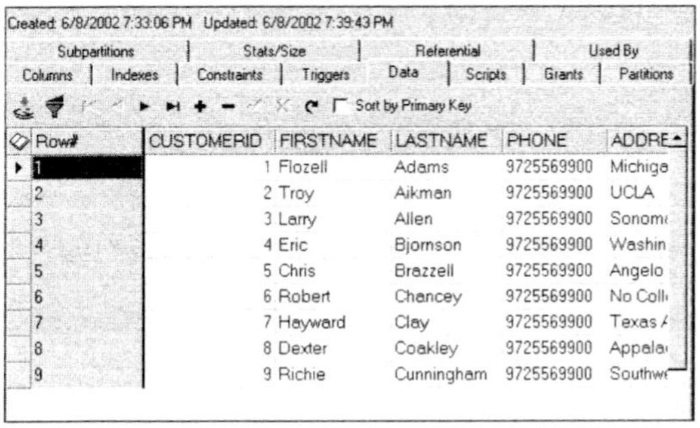

Figure 2.23   Displaying sorted data.

Using Favorites as a Custom Schema Browser

Often in TOAD, you need to work with the same group or groups of objects. For example, you might only need to routinely work with the production tables for CUSTOMER and EMPLOYEE, their indexes and views. So you would like to have a customized Schema Browser for just those objects. TOAD offers the Favorites tab so that you can easily and quickly work in this manner. It can be a huge productivity enhancer. But far too often people don't seem to know about this feature's existence, and thus are working harder than they really need to. You merely need to set it up, define your favorites, and then begin using it as your customized schema browser.

Setting Up for Successful Favorites Usage

Before attempting to use favorites, you must spend a moment to set up some basic prerequisites for success-ful favorites usage. The first thing you need to do is to enable the Schema Browser Favorites tab as shown in Figure 2.24. Of course this same logic allpies to all the other Schema Browser tabs as well, meaning that you cannot use or otherwise reference tabs which are not actively being displayed.

But that's only the beginning. Because you really want to use the Favorites tab as a customized Schema Browser, you also probably want that tab to be your primary focus (that is, when you open a Schema Browser, it starts on that tab). To accomplish this, you must select the Configure option shown in Figure 2.24 in order to open the Configure Browser Tabs window shown in Figure 2.25.

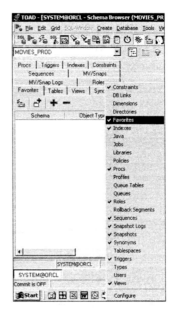

Figure 2.24   Enabling favorites.

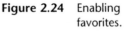

Figure 2.25   TOAD Schema Browser—favorites first.

Here you should select the Favorites Tab entry and repeatedly click the "^" button in order to move it to the top of the list, thus making the Favorites tab the initial tab of focus for the Schema Browser. Finally, you must then visit the Favorites tab and create some new favorites folders using the Add New Folder to the Favorites button (that is, the folder with a plus sign) as shown in Figure 2.26. For this scenario, the Production Work folder will be the destination.

Selecting Your Favorites Tab Entries

With the basic prerequisites for successful favorites usage in place, you must now define what constitutes your favorites. This is done simply by creating named favorites folders that contain all those items selected from the Schema Browser and then added as entries to that folder. Those items can be from the same or different schemas. However, all the items must be from the same connection. That is, you cannot pick items from different schema browsers and thus different connections to be placed within the same favorites folder. Note that the new Projects window added to TOAD in version 7.4 addresses this limitation (however, this radically new feature is still in a state of flux at this time and therefore not covered by this edition of the book).

Figure 2.26 Adding favorites folders.

Returning to our example, you now need to add the EMPLOYEE and CUSTOMER related tables, views, and indexes to your Production Work favorites folder. So you need to visit the respective tabs, select the items you want to add as favorites, and then specify which folder to add them to. Making use of the Schema Browser's multi-select for context menu options, you can quickly and easily accomplish this task.

For example, to add the CUSTOMER and EMPLOYEE tables to your favorites, you would multi-select them as shown in Figure 2.27 and specify

Figure 2.27 Adding favorite tables.

to add them to the Production Work favorites folder as shown in Figure 2.28. You would then simply repeat this process for each tab that contained objects you wanted to select for addition to your favorites folder. After you've created and populated your favorites folder in this manner, you now have a completely customized Schema Browser from which to work (as discussed in the next section).

Using Favorites as Your Schema Browser

With the prerequisites for favorites usage—your Favorites folder and its item selections—in place, you are now ready to start using the Favorites tab as your customized Schema Browser as shown in Figure 2.29.

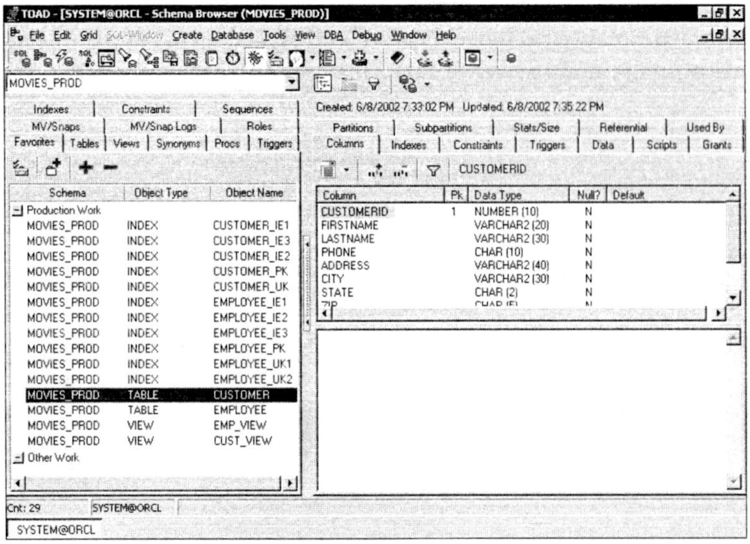

Figure 2.28   Selecting a favorite folder.

Figure 2.29   Using favorites.

Note how it displays the schema, object type, and object name. This clearly shows that you can select from various schemas and tabs in order to populate this list. Plus, note how the object type drives the right-hand-side (RHS) detailed display. Thus when you select a table, the RHS side looks the same as if you were on the Tables tab, and so on for each object type. Plus, the object type likewise controls the context menu options displayed for an entry as shown in Figure 2.30. So again, it's as if you were on the tab of interest and seeing the menu options normally available. For small to mid-sized groupings of objects, this is definitely the most efficient method of working within TOAD. However, as the list of items in your Favorites folder grows, you do reach a point where just using the Schema Browser with filters becomes a viable option. Of course, that threshold will be different for different people.

Figure 2.30 The favorites context menu.

Setting Some Advanced Schema Browser Options

TOAD's Schema Browser is a highly complex bit of code with numerous capabilities and nearly endless options. Although some of these options have already been examined within this chapter, there are still many more. In fact, there are so many options (and growing) that the TOAD Options category for the Schema Browser now has two complete pages. Unfortunately the options on each page do not seem to be based on any logical grouping, but rather just an overflow of what could fit on one page. So you'll need to visit both pages to be certain you've chosen all of the right option settings.

The first page, Page 1 as shown in Figure 2.31, offers over a dozen options for controlling general Schema Browser behavior.

- Enable DROP-ALL Buttons—Adds button to each tab for dropping all objects under that tab and is good for the current session only. This option is not as useful now that the Schema Browser supports multi-select.

- Limit Data Grids to N Number of Rows— Causes TOAD to populate the table, view, and snapshot data tab grids N rows at a time. TOAD prompts between iterations on whether to continue or not. Useful when examining very large tables and not using data filters.

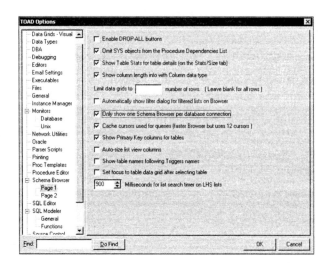

Figure 2.31   TOAD Options—Schema Browser Page 1.

- Only Show One Schema Browser per Database Connection—Because Schema Browser is a Windows resource–intensive interface by nature, limits TOAD to one Schema Browser per connection in order to save on PC resources.

- Cache Cursors Used for Queries—Speeds up the browser performance at the expense of saving 12 cursors. The DBA should have adequate INIT.ORA parameter settings based on the number of concurrent TOAD users so that this does not become an issue.

- Set Focus to Table Grid Data After Selecting Table—Some users like to examine sample data as the first step in looking at their tables. This speeds up the process by sending them there first. Recommend using either data filters or the option for Limit Data Grids to N Number of Rows when this feature is turned on. Otherwise, you may find yourself waiting when million-row tables are selected!

The second page, Page 2 as shown in Figure 2.32, also offers over a dozen options for controlling general Schema Browser behavior.

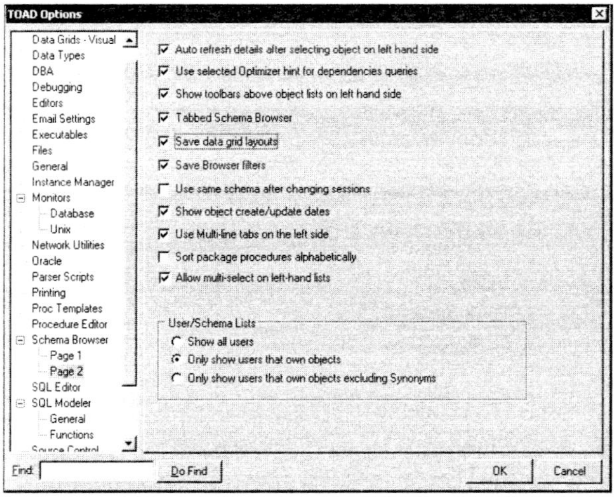

- Auto Refresh Details After Selecting Object on Left Hand Side— Causes TOAD to automatically refresh the RHS when a selection is made on the LHS. Recommend that you turn this on.

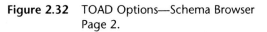

Figure 2.32 TOAD Options—Schema Browser Page 2.

- Use Selected Optimizer Hint for Dependency Queries—Forces TOAD to use the hint "Optimizer mode for DDL queries" that was specified in Options, Oracle. Recommend that you set this to "/*+ RULE */" for best results (in general).

- Save Data Grid Layouts—Causes TOAD to save the grid layouts regarding column order, fixed columns, and exclusions.

- Save Browser Filters—Causes TOAD to save both the browser object and data filters to a file named SCHEMA.FLT in the TOAD TEMPS directory.

- Allow Multi-Select on Left-Hand Lists—Allows you to use multi-select with context menu options. This option is new for TOAD version 7.4. Recommend that you turn it on.

Summary

This chapter covered TOAD's Schema Browser and its many options. Even though many people are now accustomed to using such explorer-like interfaces, TOAD's Schema Browser offers many more capabilities than meets the eye. Informed users will increase both efficiency and productivity in using the Schema Browser by choosing proper settings for options, filters, and sorts.

The next chapter introduces TOAD's industry-leading SQL Editor for writing, tuning, and executing SQL code.

3

TOAD SQL Editor

The SQL Editor is the original development area of
TOAD. This window enables you to type, save, run, and
tune SQL statements. In addition, you will learn how to
use TOAD to create and execute SQL scripts, save the
output, and examine the explain plan. This chapter will
discuss and illustrate every option available in the SQL
Editor.

Overview

TOAD provides a number of features that make SQL development easy:

- Keyboard shortcuts

- Table and column select lists

- SQL templates

- Options for creating and executing SQL scripts

- Options for reviewing, editing, and saving result-set
  data

- Compatibility with SQL*Plus

The Editor window is the basis of the entire TOAD tool,
giving you the ability to create and edit SQL: both individual SQL statements (possibly to be inserted into applications) and scripts that contain multiple SQL statements.
Figure 3.1 shows the basic SQL Editor window.

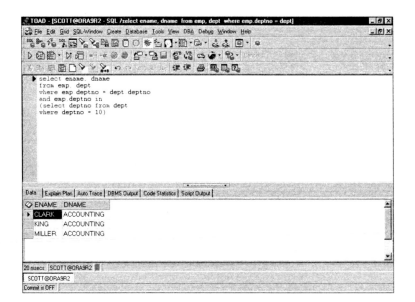

FIGURE 3.1   TOAD SQL Editor window.

This illustration shows the default SQL Editor. Notice the various buttons at the top that perform about any function (including executing the current SQL, saving the current SQL, and so on). There are three rows of buttons, or three TOAD toolbars. Hover the mouse over a button and a balloon will appear with a description of its use.

A *shortcut* is a keystroke or keystrokes that perform a certain function. F1, for example, brings up the TOAD help facility. There is a button on the toolbar for about every shortcut. The savvy TOAD user makes extensive use of the shortcuts.

  F1 brings up the TOAD help facility.

Figure 3.2 illustrates the toolbars.

FIGURE 3.2   TOAD SQL Editor window toolbars.

The first toolbar provides easy access to the main TOAD browsers and editors as well as the save functions. Some additional TOAD features also appear on this toolbar. The first toolbar (left to right) contains the following icons:

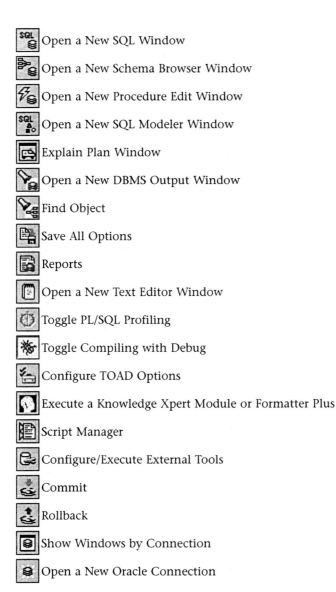

Open a New SQL Window

Open a New Schema Browser Window

Open a New Procedure Edit Window

Open a New SQL Modeler Window

Explain Plan Window

Open a New DBMS Output Window

Find Object

Save All Options

Reports

Open a New Text Editor Window

Toggle PL/SQL Profiling

Toggle Compiling with Debug

Configure TOAD Options

Execute a Knowledge Xpert Module or Formatter Plus

Script Manager

Configure/Execute External Tools

Commit

Rollback

Show Windows by Connection

Open a New Oracle Connection

The second toolbar focuses on execution. This toolbar enables you to execute code and scripts, and allows code to be loaded into the environment by a number of methods. The second (middle) toolbar contains the following icons:

Execute Statement

Execute Current Statement

Execute as a Script

Recall a Previous Statement

Recall a Personal Statement

Insert a Row

Delete Current Row

Post Data Changes

Revert Data Changes

Load a File into the Editor

Save Editor to File

Save Edits to File

Create a Code Statement

Strip All Non-SQL Syntax

Run Explain Plan for Current Statement

Tune the Current Statement using SQLab Xpert tuner

Change Session for this Window

Cancel

The third and final toolbar contains shortcuts for the standard Windows actions like cut and paste, clear, and so on. This toolbar also enables you to get information on specific objects as well. The third toolbar contains the following icons:

Cut

Copy

Paste

Select All

Clear All

Find Text

Find Next

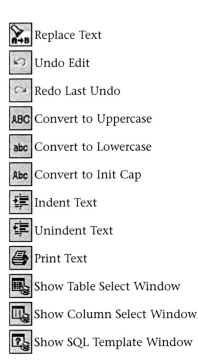

Replace Text

Undo Edit

Redo Last Undo

Convert to Uppercase

Convert to Lowercase

Convert to Init Cap

Indent Text

Unindent Text

Print Text

Show Table Select Window

Show Column Select Window

Show SQL Template Window

The first shortcut is F2. This toggles the bottom output window, or a better description might be: toggles the SQL Editor window to full screen. Shift+F2 toggles the grid output (on the bottom) to full screen. Figure 3.3 shows the SQL Editor with the output toggled off, or the full-screen grid. This is helpful when working on longer SQL statements or SQL scripts. You can easily toggle on the output tabs when you want to see the output.

 F2 toggles on/off the full-screen editor.

Shift+F2 toggles on/off the full-screen data grid.

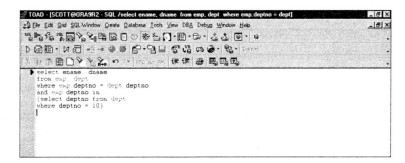

FIGURE 3.3   TOAD SQL Editor window, full-screen grid.

The lower section, or data grid, contains the result-set data from the query, the explain plan used to retrieve the data, code statistics, Auto Trace output, DBMS output, and Script output. Each of these will be covered in this chapter.

Notice that the SQL syntax appears (along with any other Oracle reserved words) in blue where the supplied columns, table names, and other variable syntax appear in black. Comments appear in green, and so on. These color patterns are controlled by the Editor Options. You can access these options by clicking Edit, Editor Options from the menu bar or by right-clicking and selecting Editing Options. Notice that TOAD lists the keyboard shortcuts whenever possible.

Figure 3.4 illustrates the Highlighting options in the SQL window. You can see that you have complete control over the editor environment (such as autoreplacement of words, general layout and text wrapping in the edit window, key assignments, and code templates).

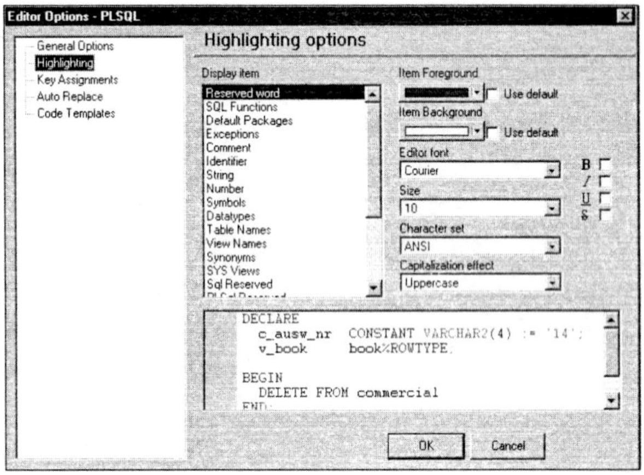

TOAD has three editors: the SQL Editor, the Procedure Editor (covered in Chapter 4), and a text editor of your choice. The editor environment applies its options to both TOAD editors. Additional editors can easily be added to TOAD. Choose View, Options from the menu bar, and then select Editors (or use the Configure TOAD Options button) to add your editor of choice. Figure 3.5 illustrates how to add the Notepad editor, for example. Be sure to use the variable %s to pass this editor the SQL that you are currently working on. If your current session has not been saved, you will be prompted to save it. Also, upon exiting your external editor, you will be prompted to reload your work from the saved file. Make sure the option Reload Files When Activating TOAD is checked on in the Procedure Editor section of the TOAD Options screen. You then use this external editor by choosing Edit, Load in External Editor from the menu bar or by using the shortcut Ctrl+F12. Figure 3.6 shows some work in the Notepad editor.

FIGURE 3.4   TOAD SQL Editor Options.

 Ctrl+F12 accesses a previously defined external editor.

TOAD supports threads, which allows SQL statements to be canceled while they are running. If you want this behavior, make sure you check the box Process Statements in Threads in the SQL Editor part of the TOAD Options screen. The Cancel button (far right button on the middle SQL Editor toolbar) will become available during the execution of a SQL statement being run in this fashion. In this same area, you can also increase or decrease the SQL statements TOAD will automatically track. These SQL statements are stored in the file SQLS.DAT in your TOAD home directory. You have control over default behavior such as whether you are prompted to save the current SQL (Prompt to Save Contents), code format options, showing execution time, and so on.

There are several ways to get SQL into the SQL Editor. You can simply type in a new SQL statement. You can use the

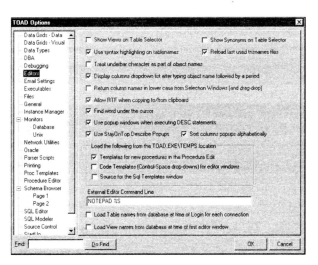

FIGURE 3.5 Defining external editors in TOAD.

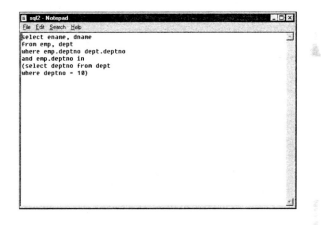

FIGURE 3.6 Using Notepad as editor in TOAD.

SQL Statement Recall button (fourth button on the middle SQL Editor toolbar) and select a SQL statement from the stored TOAD SQL history (see Figure 3.7). Pressing Alt+Up arrow and Alt+Down arrow also walks you thru the SQL statement history. You can also choose File, Open from the menu bar (or Ctrl+O), and cut and paste SQL code into the Editor from other applications. The Load option is also useful for loading in SQL from files from the pop-up menu that appears when you right-click.

Alt+Up arrow gets the previous SQL statement from the TOAD history.

Alt+Down arrow gets the next SQL statement from the TOAD history.

TOAD will also easily format your SQL into an easy-to-read format. Figure 3.8 shows how to access the formatter by right-clicking and selecting Formatting Tools, Format Code from the context menu. Figure 3.9 shows how TOAD formats the SQL.

This overview covered some of the basic concepts and features of the SQL Editor. The remainder of this chapter will cover specific topics in the SQL Editor.

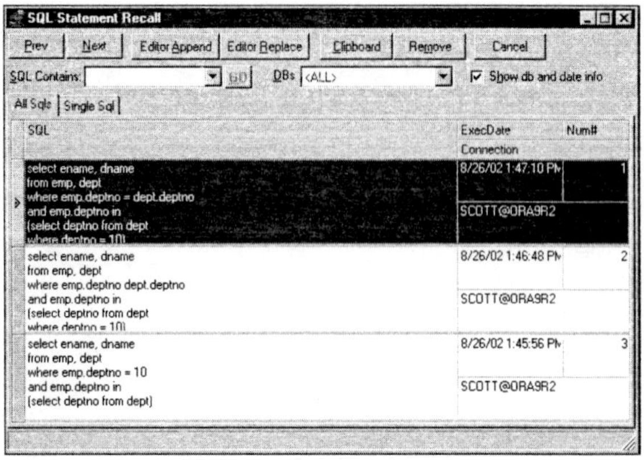

FIGURE 3.7   Selecting SQL from TOAD history.

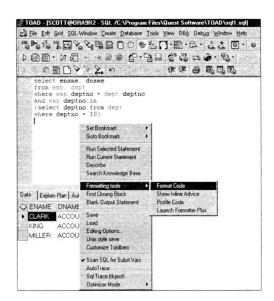

FIGURE 3.8   Accessing SQL Formatter.

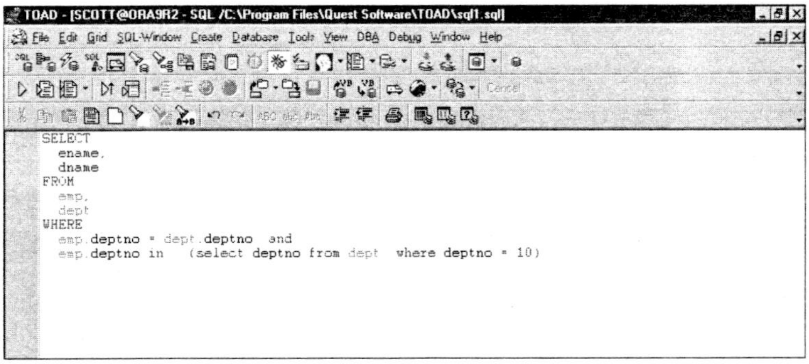

FIGURE 3.9   TOAD formatted SQL.

Predefined Shortcuts

Keyboard shortcuts are one of the features that make TOAD so powerful and easy to use. TOAD comes with a host of predefined shortcuts. These shortcuts save keystrokes and mouse actions and perform a variety of tasks such as issuing a describe on the current highlighted object, or find (find next, find previous, and so on). The shortcuts differ slightly between the SQL Editor and the PL/SQL Editor (covered in Chapter 4). This section focuses on the shortcuts for the SQL Editor only.

Table 3.1 shows all the shortcuts in keystroke order and Table 3.2 shows all the shortcuts in description order. The third column refers you to the figure in this chapter where the shortcut is illustrated.

TABLE 3.1   SQL Editor Shortcuts by Keystroke

Shortcut	Description	Illustration
F1	Windows Help File	
F2	Toggle Output Window	Figure 3.2
Shift+F2	Toggle Data Grid Window	
F3	Find Next Occurrence	
Shift+F3	Find Previous Occurrence	
F4	Describe Table, View, Procedure, Function	Figure 3.26
F5	Execute SQL as a script	Figure 3.34
F6	Toggle between SQL Editor and Results Panel	Figure 3.1
F7	Clear All Text	
F8	Recall Previous SQL Statement	
F9	Execute Statement	Figure 3.33
Ctrl+F9	Set Code Execution Parameters	Figure 3.33
Shift+F9	Execute Current SQL statement at Cursor	
F10 or right-click	Pop-up Menu	Figures 3.4, 3.10

TABLE 3.1   Continued

Shortcut	Description	Illustration
Ctrl+F12	External Editor, Pass Contents	Figures 3.5, 3.6
Ctrl+A	Select All Text	
Ctrl+C	Copy	
Ctrl+E	Execute Explain Plan on the Current Statement	Figure 3.41
Ctrl+F	Find Text	
Ctrl+G	Goto Line	
Ctrl+L	Convert Text to Lowercase	
Ctrl+M	Make Code Statement	
Ctrl+N	Recall Named SQL Statement	
Ctrl+O	Open a Text File	
Ctrl+P	Strip Code Statement	
Ctrl+R	Find and Replace	
Ctrl+S	Save File	
Shift+Ctrl+S	Save File As	Figure 3.18
Ctrl+T	Columns Drop-down	
Shift+Ctrl+R	Alias Replacement	
Shift+Ctrl+T	Columns Drop-Down no alias	Figure 3.19
Ctrl+Spacebar	Code Templates	Figure 3.30
Ctrl+U	Converts Text to Uppercase	
Ctrl+V	Paste	
Ctrl+X	Cut	
Ctrl+Z	Undo Last Change	
Ctrl+.	Display Pop-up List of Matching Table Names	Figure 3.16
Shift+Ctrl+Z	Redo Last Undo	
Alt+Up Arrow	Display Previous Statement	Figure 3.7
Alt+Down Arrow	Display Next Statement (After Alt+Up Arrow)	Figure 3.7
Ctrl+Home	In the data grid: goes to the top of the record set	
Ctrl+End	In the data grid: goes to the end of the record set	
Ctrl+Tab	Cycles through the Collection of MDI Child Windows	

The competent TOAD user makes use of Shift+F9 to execute SQL statements one at a time out of a script, and F8 to recall the previous SQL statement. The TOAD user also makes use of cut and paste to move code between TOAD windows.

Shift+F9 executes single SQL statements.

F8 recalls the previous SQL statement.

TABLE 3.2   SQL Editor Shortcuts by Description

Description	Shortcut	Illustration
Alias Replacement	Shift+Ctrl+R	
Clear All Text	F7	
Code Templates	Ctrl+Spacebar	Figure 3.30
Columns Drop-down	Ctrl+T	Figure 3.18
Columns Drop-down no alias	Shift+Ctrl+T	Figure 3.19
Convert Text to Lowercase	Ctrl+L	
Convert Text to Uppercase	Ctrl+U	
Copy	Ctrl+C	
Cut	Ctrl+X	
Cycles through the Collection of MDI Child Windows	Ctrl+Tab	
Describe Table, View, Procedure, Function, or Package	F4	
Display Next Statement (After Alt+Up Arrow)	Alt+Down Arrow	Figure 3.7
Display Previous Statement	Alt+Up Arrow	Figure 3.7
Display Pop-up List of Matching Table Names	Ctrl+.	Figure 3.16
Execute Current SQL Statement at Cursor	Shift+F9	
Execute SQL as a Script	F5	Figure 3.35
Execute Explain Plan on the Current SQL Statement	Ctrl+E	Figure 3.41
Execute SQL Statement	F9	Figure 3.34
External Editor, Pass Contents	Ctrl+F12	Figure 3.5
Find and Replace	Ctrl+R	
Find Next Occurrence	F3	
Find Previous Occurrence	Shift+F3	
Find Text	Ctrl+F	
Goto Line	Ctrl+G	
In the data grid: goes to the end of the record set	Ctrl+End	
In the data grid: goes to the top of the record set	Ctrl+Home	
Make Code Statement	Ctrl+M	
Open a Text File	Ctrl+O	
Paste	Ctrl+V	
Pop-up Menu	F10 or RT-Mouse	Figures 3.4, 3.10
Recall Named SQL	Ctrl+N	
Recall Previous SQL Statement	F8	
Redo Last Undo	Shift+Ctrl+Z	
Save File	Ctrl+S	
Save File As	Shift+Ctrl+S	
Select All Text	Ctrl+A	
Strip Code Statement	Ctrl+P	
Toggle between SQL Editor and Results Panel	F6	Figure 3.1
Toggle Full Screen Editor	F2	Figure 3.2
Undo Last Change	Ctrl+Z	
Verify Statement Without Execution (Parse)	Ctrl+F9	
Windows Help File	F1	

User-Defined Shortcuts

TOAD is completely configurable. You can easily add your own shortcuts to TOAD. It is easy to change the shortcut keystrokes for existing shortcuts, and it is just as easy to add your own shortcuts.

Access the Editor Options menu with a right-click or by pressing the F10 key and selecting Editing Options.

To change an existing keystroke assignment, select Key Assignments, locate the particular assignment to change, and click on the Edit Sequence button as illustrated in Figure 3.10.

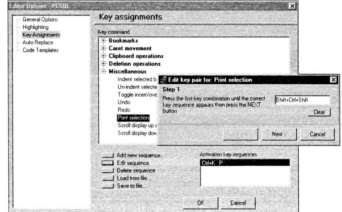

To add additional keystroke assignments, select Key Assignments, locate the particular assignment to change, and click on the Add New Sequence button. Type the sequence desired to perform the key assignment task. In Figure 3.11, notice that Shift+Ctrl+D was added by pressing and holding down the Control key while pressing Shift and d.

FIGURE 3.10   Changing shortcut keystroke assignments in TOAD.

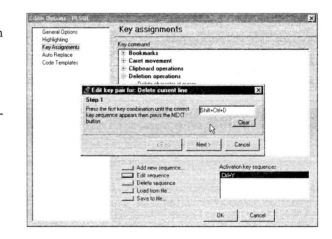

FIGURE 3.11   Adding shortcut keystroke assignments in TOAD.

Using Variables

TOAD supports all kinds of SQL, from all kinds of applications. If you were to bring in SQL, for example, from a SQL*Forms application, it will contain bind variables. Bind variables are used to supply SQL with data at execution time. This allows applications to use the same SQL statement to select and manipulate different data, depending on the data supplied to the bind variables.

> Using the same SQL statement makes efficient use of the Oracle RDBMS SQL pool as the SQL will not be reparsed when using bind variables. The text of the SQL remains the same, so Oracle will reuse the same execution plan, making for a better-performing database environment.

When TOAD encounters bind variables, it will prompt you for their value as in Figure 3.12. This illustration shows two bind variables. The Scan SQL button will check for any missing bind variables, which is particularly useful if you are adding and changing bind variables in this interface.

Substitution variables work the same way as bind variables. Do remember that substitution variables are resolved into SQL text at parse time, but bind variables won't change the actual SQL text (this

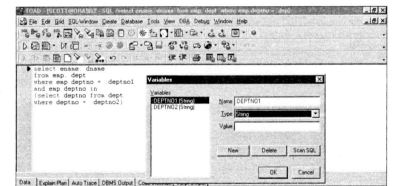

FIGURE 3.12 Resolving SQL bind variables.

greatly enables SQL reuse in the Oracle SQL pool). TOAD will prompt for the data for each substitution variable as shown in Figure 3.13.

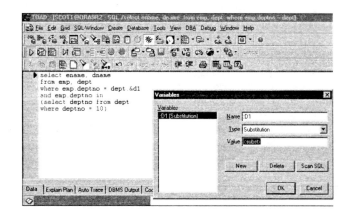

FIGURE 3.13   Resolving SQL substitution variables.

Table and Column Name Select Lists

TOAD makes it easy to find and work with tables and columns. Figure 3.14 illustrates using the Show Table Select Window button (mouse cursor is pointing to this button). This brings up the Table Name Select window, with a list of available tables for this particular user. If the user has privileges to other schemas, the drop-down list in this window can be changed to the schema owner and those objects will then appear in the select list. Double-clicking on the selected object adds the selected table to the SQL Editor as illustrated in Figure 3.14.

Similarly, columns can be added to the SQL Editor by using the Show Column Select Window button. Figure 3.15 illustrates using the Column Name Select window to add the three columns EMPNO, ENAME, and JOB to the SQL being built in the SQL Editor.

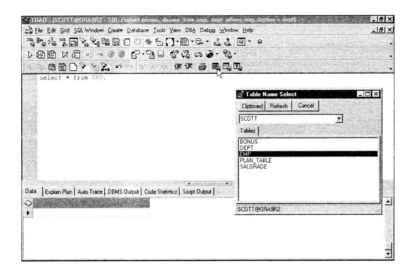

FIGURE 3.14   Table Name Select list.

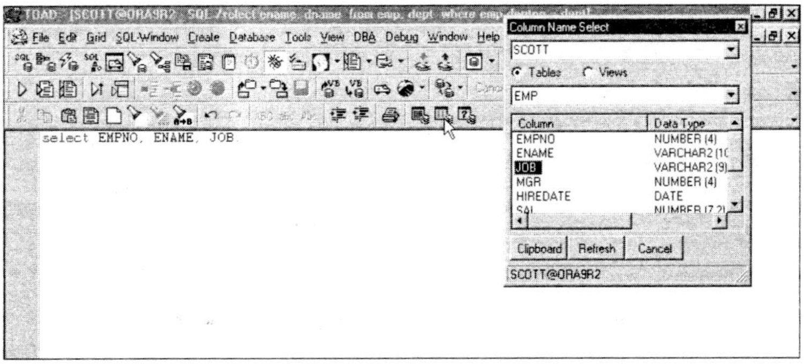

FIGURE 3.15   Column Name Select list.

> TOAD will automatically give a column select list if you type or select a valid schema table name followed by a '.'. Wait a second and the column select list will appear as illustrated in Figure 3.16!

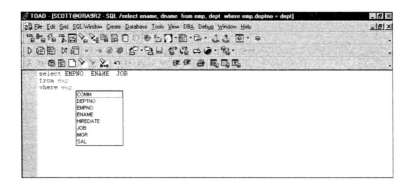

FIGURE 3.16   Automatic column select lists.

Using Aliases and Autoreplacement Substitutions

TOAD supports the use of its own alias names. Aliases are convenient to shorten keystrokes, using short names instead of rather long table names. TOAD also allows the automatic replacement of text, or in this case, these aliases. The purpose of the alias is to shorten keystrokes. The purpose of the automatic replacement is to automatically resolve the TOAD alias to the full table or column name.

TOAD aliases are used to shorten the number of keystrokes to develop SQL. TOAD aliases are not to be confused with Oracle RDBMS table aliases, which are used in qualifying columns in a multitable SQL statement.

TOAD aliases enable you to

- Access the Column Name Select drop-down list

- Type the alias as a shortcut rather than typing the full table name

Aliases are easy to set up with any text editor. Make sure TOAD is not running (on network installations, make sure all users are off TOAD) and edit the ALIASES.TXT file found in the TOAD installation directory under the TEMPS subdirectory.

 DO NOT edit this file with TOAD running. When TOAD exits, it rewrites this file and any changes you make will be lost!

Figure 3.17 illustrates the format of this file. The format is <table name>=<alias name>.

You will learn a method of quickly creating this file in the "Scripts That Write Scripts" section later in this chapter.

TOAD aliases are easy to use. Figure 3.18 shows a simple SQL statement using an alias to get to the Column Name Select drop-down. Notice that the user typed in 'inv.'. The '.' signaled the Column Name Select drop-down and the alias was resolved to the INVENTORY table.

[ic:Keyboard]The '.' signals TOAD to see if this is an alias.

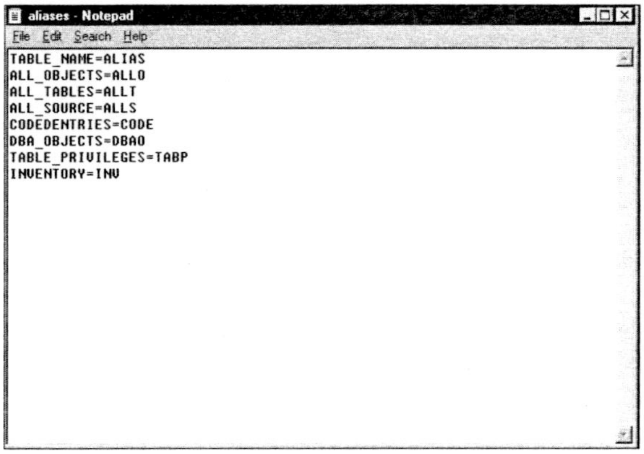

FIGURE 3.17　TOAD alias setup.

 Notice in Figure 3.19 that there is both an INVENTORY table and an INV table. The alias INV was resolved in Figure 3.18 to the INVENTORY table, not the INV table. Notice the column names in Figure 3.19 compared to those in Figure 3.18. Granted, this is a poor naming convention, but bear with the example. To get the INV table displayed, use Shift+Ctrl+T (or Edit, Columns drop-down no alias) to ignore the alias and get the correct list of columns. See Figure 3.20.

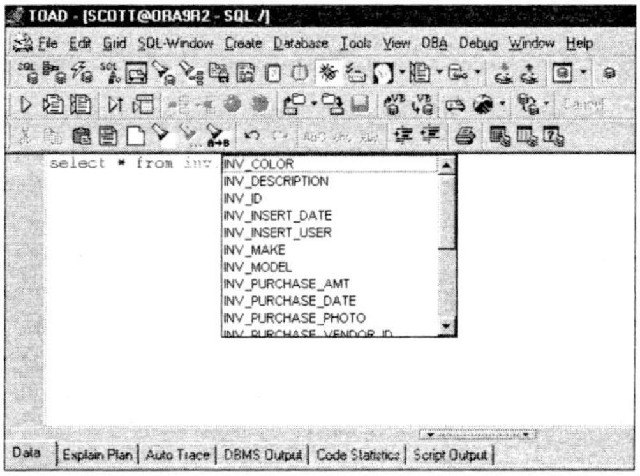

FIGURE 3.18　TOAD alias usage.

Shift+Ctrl+T ignores the alias request.

If an alias is identified in the SQL statement, and a Column Select is activated, the alias is automatically added to ALIASES.TXT.

TOAD scans only the first FROM clause in any SQL statement, so any TOAD aliases in complex SQL statements that have subqueries, for example, will not be found and resolved.

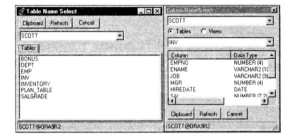

FIGURE 3.19   Available tables in the SCOTT schema.

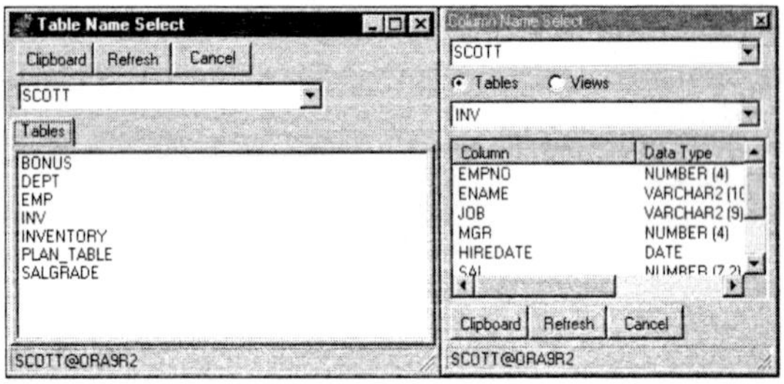

FIGURE 3.20   Ignore the alias in action.

Autoreplace substitution replaces a short string with the full name. This differs from TOAD aliases because aliases make reference to a different name but do not change the text of the SQL statement. When autoreplace substitution is defined, it happens automatically when you press the spacebar. Autoreplace substitution is activated by typing the short sequence (illustrated in Figure 3.21) and pressing the spacebar (the autoreplace delimiter key defaults to the spacebar). This will then automatically substitute the predefined string in place of the short key sequence. See Figure 3.22.

 Replacement happens after pressing the spacebar.

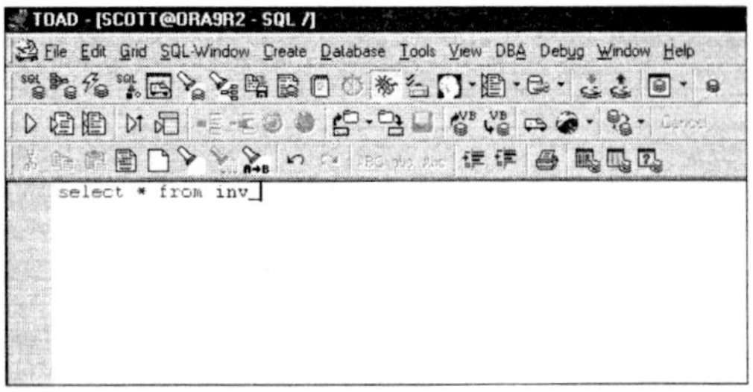

FIGURE 3.21   Autoreplace substitution key sequence.

There are two ways to create automatic replacement substitution strings. You can edit the PLSQLSUB.TXT file in the *<TOAD home directory>*\temps directory. The format is the same as the alias: *<short string>* = *<replacement string>*. The other way is to enter the substitution string by using the Edit, Editor Options, Auto Replace tab. See Figure 3.24.

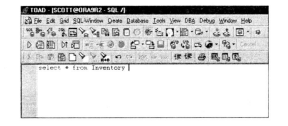

FIGURE 3.22   Autoreplace substitution in action.

Figure 3.23 illustrates the contents of this file. Notice the common typo 'teh' will automatically be converted to 'the' because this sequence will always be followed by pressing the spacebar. Also notice the 'inv' and 'Inv_' strings that were used in Figure 3.21 and Figure 3.22.

TOAD allows autosubstitution to be maintained by language type. You can edit and add to the list using the Editor Options, Auto Replace window. Supported languages for autoreplacement are HTML (*<TOAD home>*\temps\HTMLSUB.TXT), INI (*<TOAD home>*\temps\INISUB.TXT), JAVA (*<TOAD home>*\temps\JAVASUB.TXT), and TEXT (*<TOAD home>*\temps\TEXTSUB.TXT).

FIGURE 3.23   Editing the PLSQLSUB.TXT file.

 Be sure TOAD is NOT running when you are editing any of these files in the TEMPS directory. TOAD rewrites these files when closing, and any changes made to the files with TOAD running will be lost.

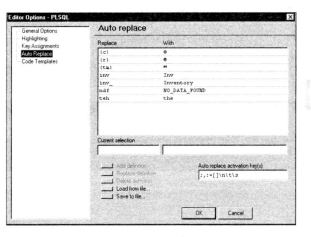

FIGURE 3.24   Adding autoreplace substitution in the Editor Options screen.

TOAD allows you to export and import these autosubstitution definitions. This is a convenient way to move them when setting up a new computer to use TOAD. It also might be convenient to have various autosubstitution files by application. This allows you to have specific substitutions for various applications, same alias but resolved to different names perhaps. See Figure 3.25.

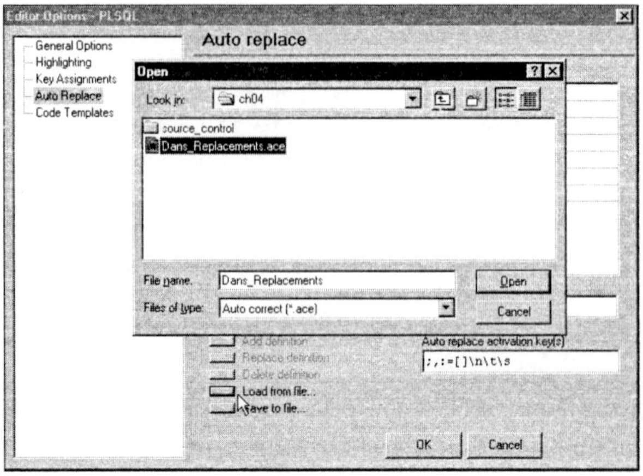

FIGURE 3.25   Saving and loading autoreplace definitions.

When loading autoreplace definitions in from a saved file, all previous substitutions currently in TOAD are lost and replaced with the new definitions.

These .ACE files are in a binary format and are only to be used with the TOAD Load facility (from the Editing Options menu).

SQL Templates

TOAD can easily format a SELECT or INSERT statement for any data-oriented object (view or table). Simply place the cursor on the object you want and press F4. This will perform a description on the object, as illustrated in Figure 3.26.

Notice in Figure 3.26 that everything you need to know about the object appears in this window.

It is particularly nice to have TOAD build a script that created the object. This information comes from the data dictionary and accurately reflects the object that you are working with.

Most of this information is covered in other chapters. To get to the SQL Templates, use the Columns tab and right-click on any of the column names. This brings up another menu of mostly administrative functions (most of these features are covered in other chapters); see Figure 3.27. Notice where the cursor is (Generate Statement); you have the choice of building a SELECT or INSERT statement for this particular object. When making a selection, TOAD will tell you that the "script copied to the clipboard." Figure 3.28 shows the code in the TOAD SQL Editor that was pasted from the clipboard. Both the SELECT and the INSERT are illustrated.

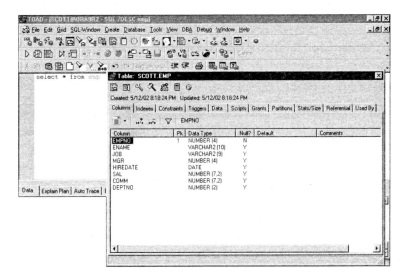

FIGURE 3.26   Object description.

 F4 to describe the object.

Right-click on a column in the Columns tab and select Generate Statement.

You can also use the Show SQL Template Window button (third toolbar, rightmost button) to paste in specific SQL templates while doing SQL coding. Figure 3.29 illustrates how to use these templates. Options include directly copying the template into the SQL window (as illustrated in Figure 3.29) or copying the template to the clipboard. Notice that there are all kinds of SQL templates. TOAD contains templates for row, group, and date functions. Also included are templates for PL/SQL coding, which will be covered in detail in the next chapter.

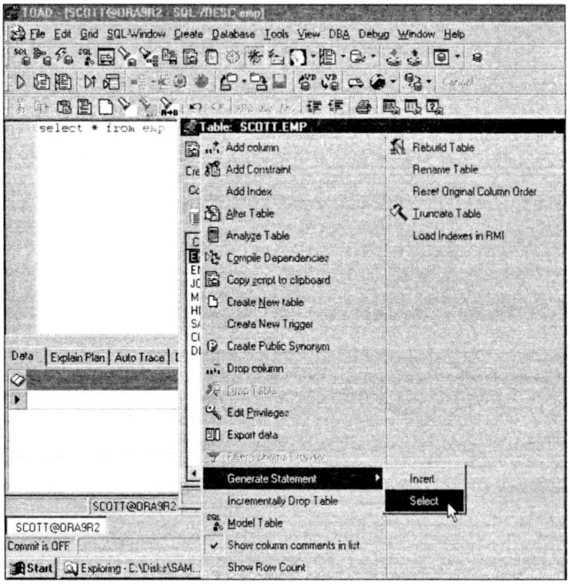

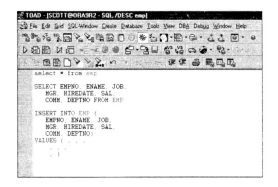

FIGURE 3.27   TOAD Generate Statement selection.

FIGURE 3.28   Generated SQL statements.

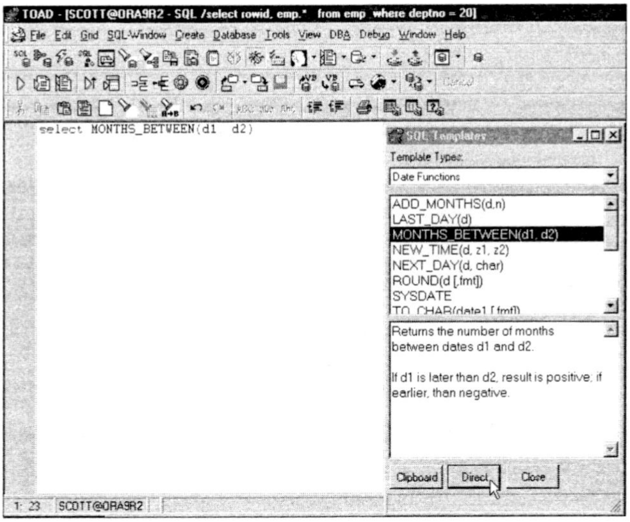

FIGURE 3.29   TOAD SQL templates in action.

Code Completion Templates

Code completion templates are boilerplate syntax where you type in the correct names, and so on, but the correct syntax with options is supplied.

Code completion templates work a lot like aliases except that they provide the entire syntax rather than just a word or object name. Figures 3.30 and 3.31 illustrate how this works. Instead of hitting the '.' to signal the replacement, you press Ctrl+Spacebar to signal the replacement.

    Ctrl+Spacebar signals code template.

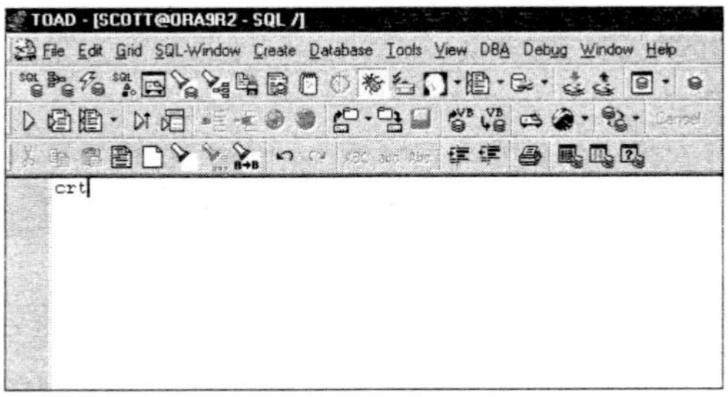

FIGURE 3.30   Code completion template key sequence.

Like the autoreplacement feature, additional code completion templates are easily added by using the Edit, Editor Options, Code Templates screen, as shown in Figure 3.32.

You can also edit the PLSQL.DCI file in *<TOAD Home Directory>*\temps and add additional templates with a text editor. See Figure 3.33 for the layout example.

Supported languages for code completion are HTML (*<TOAD home>*\temps\HTMLSUB.DCI), INI (*<TOAD home>*\temps\INISUB.DCI), JAVA (*<TOAD home>*\temps\JAVASUB.DCI), and TEXT (*<TOAD home>*\temps\TEXTSUB.DCI).

 Be sure TOAD is NOT running when you are editing any of these files in the TEMPS directory. TOAD rewrites these files when closing, and any changes made to the files with TOAD running will be lost.

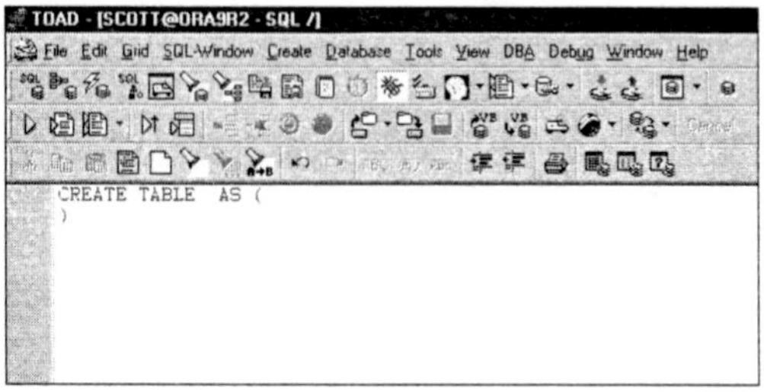

FIGURE 3.31 Code completion template in action.

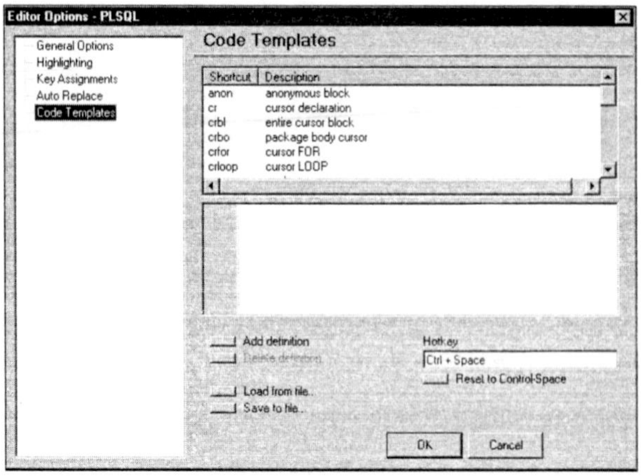

FIGURE 3.32 Adding code completion templates.

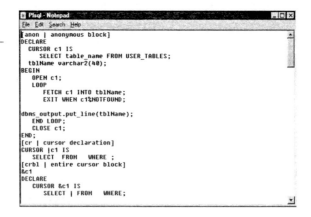

FIGURE 3.33 Code completion template file layout.

Executing SQL Statements

TOAD not only enables you to easily edit and create SQL and scripts containing SQL, but also to execute the SQL, review explain plans, and examine, edit, or change the result-set data.

The easiest way to execute SQL is with the Execute SQL button, the leftmost button on the middle toolbar. This executes the statement and returns the data when in full-view mode. Remember that F6 toggles between just the SQL Editor window and the results panel.

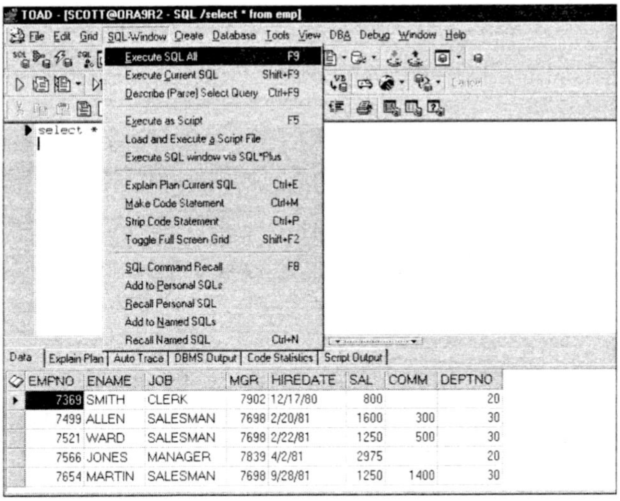

FIGURE 3.34   Executing SQL statements.

F9 executes all of the SQL statements in the SQL window, as does the Execute SQL All menu option, as in figure 3.34. Shift-F9 executes the SQL statement at the cursor, or the SQL statement that is highlighted.

    Shift-F9 executes the current SQL statement.

    If you are working with SQL in a script, highlight the SQL in the script and press F9 to execute the single SQL statement only.

Executing SQL Scripts

TOAD allows you to execute SQL and SQL scripts as scripts. This will display the output of the script in the Script Output tab in the results panel; see Figure 3.35. This might be convenient when working with scripts so you don't have to exit the TOAD environment to run scripts in SQL*Plus, for example.

F5 executes the current SQL statement as a script.

The script output gives you the output that the script will produce, not just the data. Figure 3.36 shows a short SQL*Plus script and its output with column headings. SQL*Plus compatibility with TOAD is discussed later in this chapter.

If there are any syntax errors, TOAD will highlight the syntax problem in the SQL text and display the Oracle error across the bottom of the output area.

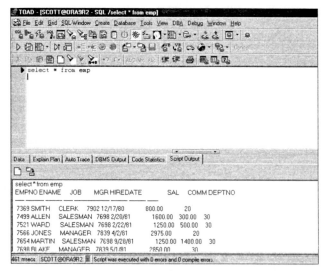

FIGURE 3.35   Executing a SQL statement as a script.

FIGURE 3.36   Executing a SQL*Plus SQL script as a script.

Editing Result-Set Data

TOAD allows you to change the data that appears in the Data tab of the results panel. The data columns being selected must include the ROWID column as well. Another way to select data from an object for update is by using edit *<object name>* syntax.

Figure 3.37 shows rows from the EMP table, demoting the manager Jones to a clerk and promoting the clerk Smith to manager.

To save the data changes, click the Commit button on the top toolbar (see mouse cursor in Figure 3.37).

 Make sure you exit the column you have edited before committing the data.

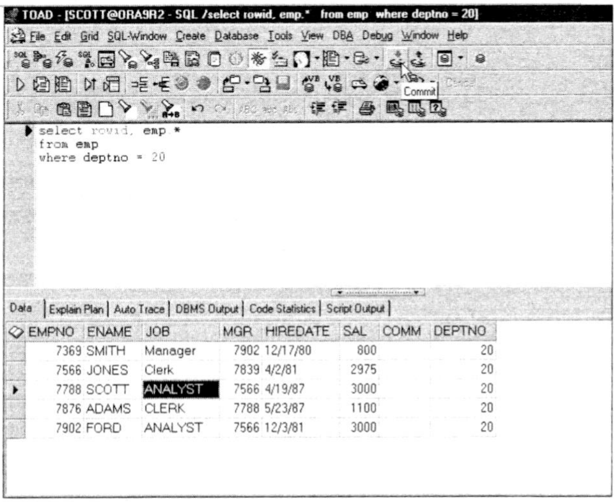

You can also sort the data in the data grid by simply clicking on the columns and making your sort-order selections.

TOAD allows you to view all the data for a particular row. Click on the button that looks like a book, and the current row in the data grid will appear in a pop-up box. Figure 3.38 shows the data in the pop-up. Notice the mouse cursor is pointing to the icon that makes the pop-up appear. Also notice that this data is for the first row in the data grid because it is marked as the current row.

FIGURE 3.37 Changing data values in the results panel.

Character, blob/long raw, and date fields all have a memo editor that can help visualize ad change the data in the field. Right-mouse click and select Memo Editor from the popup menu. This capability will continue to be enhanced in future releases of TOAD.

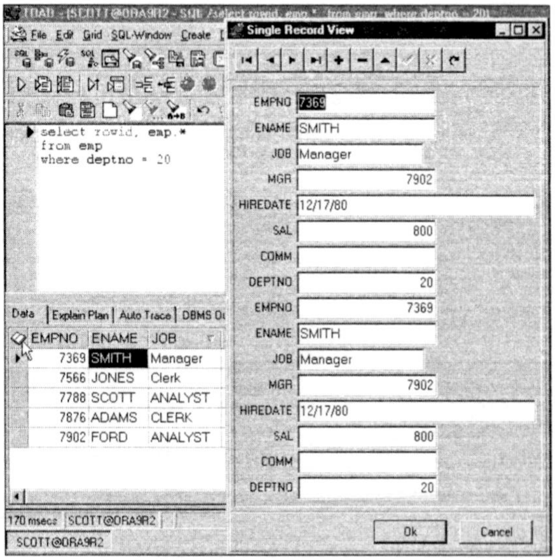

Saving Result-Set Data

The data in the results panel Data tab can easily be saved in a number of formats. Choose Grid, Save As and view the options available, as illustrated in Figure 3.39. You can create a delimited file, XML formatted file, and/or copy the results to the clipboard or to a named file.

FIGURE 3.38   Viewing and changing single-row data values in the results panel.

Printing Result-Set Data

TOAD makes it easy to format the data grid into an attractive report. Select the Print Grid by either choosing Grid, Print Grid from the menu bar or by right-clicking on the data grid and selecting Print Grid. Both options bring up the Report Link Designer, as shown in Figure 3.40.

 Right-clicking on the data grid gives many options including Print Grid.

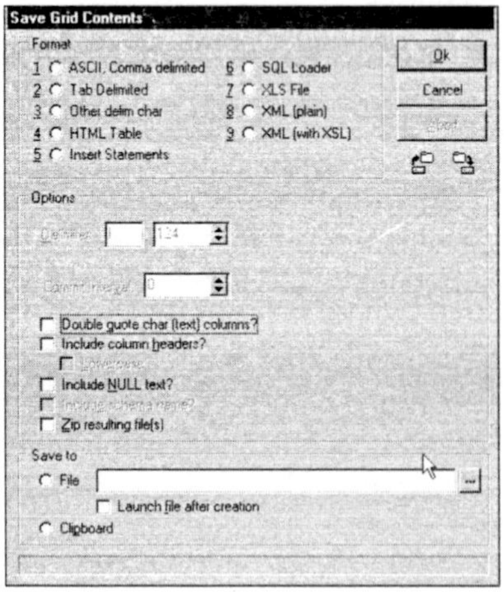

FIGURE 3.39   Saving data values in the results panel.

Change your data grid headings as desired for the report output. The Report Link Designer will allow you to add headers and footers, change the fonts, print only selected columns (right-click on the Data grid and check Preview Column or Remove Preview Column), and so on.

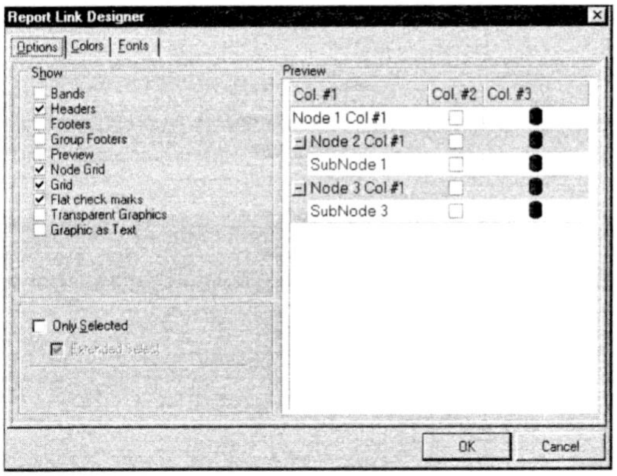

After selecting OK on this menu, you will be presented with the Print Options screen. From here, you can perform the standard print features, such as printing the whole report or only certain pages, and do page setup functions.

FIGURE 3.40   Toad Report Link Designer.

If you want column totals, choose Grid, Print Setup, select the column in the Columns tab, and then check the Total This Column check box. You can also change the column heading at this time.

Examining Explain Plans

TOAD allows you to easily see the explain plan for the currently executed SQL statement. This is visualized on the Explain Plan tab in the results panel. Figure 3.41 illustrates a rather simple explain plan.

 Ctrl+E also runs and displays an explain plan.

It is beyond the scope of this book to provide a basic explanation of explain plans and the various features of the rule- and cost-based Oracle optimizers. TOAD does support changing the Optimizer Mode by right-clicking on the SQL statement and selecting the Optimizer Mode option. Cost-based hints can easily be added by using the SQL Templates option (discussed earlier in this chapter).

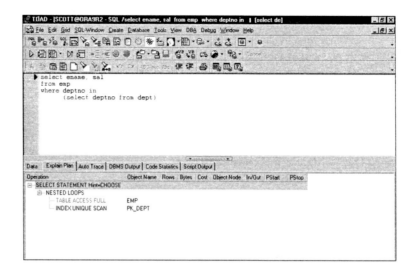

FIGURE 3.41   TOAD explain plans.

Problem Solving the Explain Plan Tab

If you get the error ORA-02404 Specified Plan Table Not Found as shown in Figure 3.42, you have two options.

The problem is that the TOADPREP.SQL script has not been run as described in Chapter 1, or the TOAD explain plan table has been renamed.

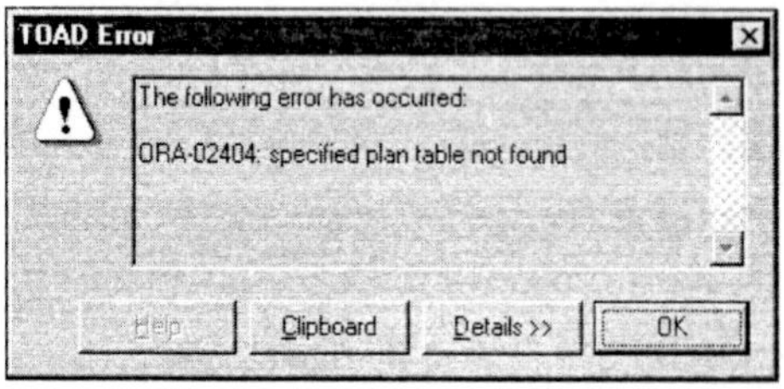

The solution is to run the script TOAD-PREP.SQL as defined in Chapter 1 and this, among other things, builds the TOAD_PLAN_TABLE. If you choose to use the Oracle RDBMS plan table (found in <Oracle Home>\RDBMS\admin) in file UTLXPLAN.SQL (this file is executed for

FIGURE 3.42   TOAD Explain Plan Not Found error.

each schema owner), click the TOAD Options button, and under the Oracle category, change the Explain Plan Table name to "PLAN_TABLE", removing the "TOAD_" from the beginning, as illustrated in Figure 3.43. This will allow TOAD to find the explain plan table for your schema.

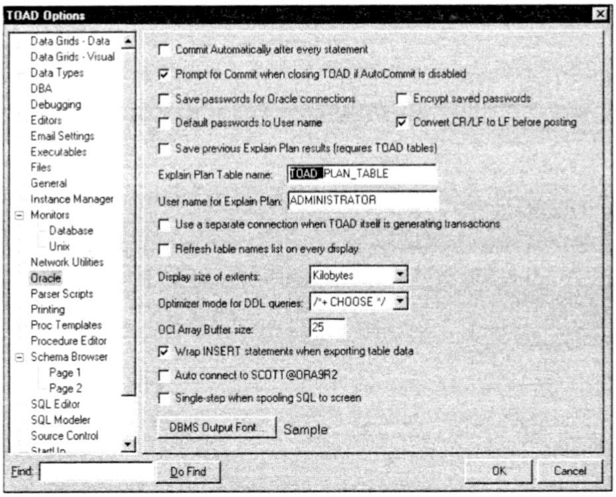

FIGURE 3.43　TOAD Explain Plan Definition window.

Examining Basic Performance Info

TOAD tracks basic information about the execution of the SQL statement or scripts. This information might be helpful in debugging certain issues with the SQL statement itself.

This information is on the results panel under the Code Statistics tab; see Figure 3.44.

FIGURE 3.44　TOAD Code Statistics tab.

Using Auto Trace

TOAD will run the Oracle trace function for you, run TKPROF and display the important information in the Auto Trace tab of the results panel; see Figure 3.45.

If the Auto Trace feature is not turned on for your login session, TOAD will tell you that it is disabled and ask you if you want it enabled.

It is beyond the scope of this book to discuss all the various fields in this tab's output, but here are several of the most important fields:

- Recursive calls: Oracle sometimes issues additional SQL statements on behalf of the running SQL statement. This is called recursive calls. Reasons include many extents on the object, dynamic space allocation (with an insert), and dictionary cache

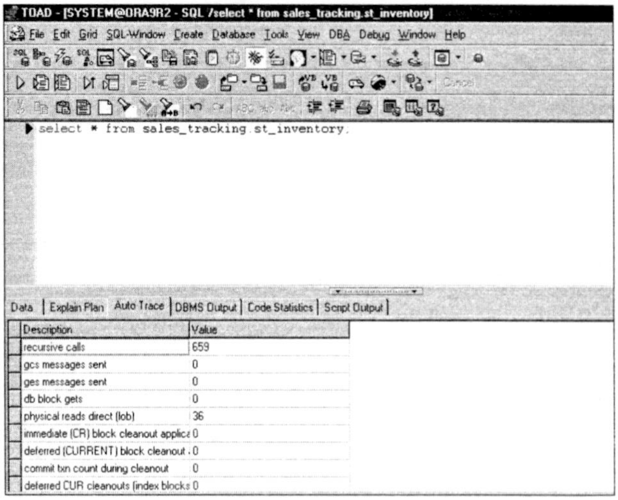

FIGURE 3.45   TOAD Auto Trace tab.

misses. The trace facility also generates recursive calls.

- Db block gets: This is the number of database block gets; it can be either physical or logical reads.

- Physical reads direct: This is the number of block fetch requests issued by Oracle.

It is beyond the scope of this book to go into great depth as to the meaning and interpretation of these various statistics.

The user running Auto Trace will need access to the V$STATNAME and V$SESSTAT dictionary views as illustrated in Figure 3.46.

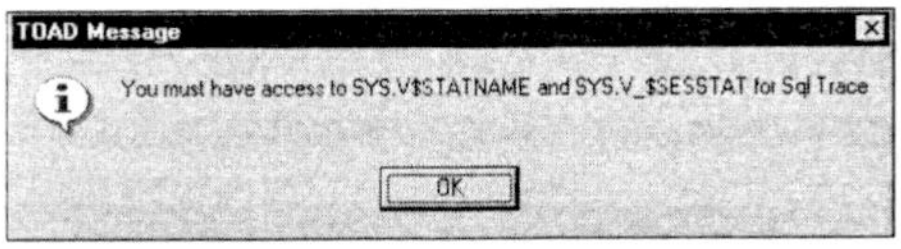

FIGURE 3.46   TOAD Auto Trace required permissions.

SQL*Plus Compatibility

SQL*Plus is used for a variety of things in the Oracle environment. In the early days (version 5 and before), SQL*Plus was also used as an administrative tool. Today, SQL*Plus has taken back the Server Manager role. SQL*Plus has always been a good character-mode reporting tool, a tool used to create SQL-creating-SQL (next topic in this chapter), and so on. It is quite powerful with its formatting and file creation (spool commands) to perform a variety of tasks in the Oracle environment.

TOAD is an excellent tool for creating and maintaining these SQL*Plus scripts. The Script Output tab in the results panel is powerful in that you can see what the script has produced without having to leave TOAD and run the script in a separate window with SQL*Plus.

TOAD primarily supports the reporting features of SQL*Plus and not the administrative functions that have been given back to SQL*Plus.

Make sure to run any SQL*Plus script as a script!

TOAD supports these SQL*Plus commands:

@ ("at" sign)

@@ (double "at" sign)

/ (slash)

BREAK (BRE) partial support

CLEAR

COLUMN (partial support, including: ALIAS, NOPRINT/PRINT, NEW_VALUE)

COMPUTE (partial support including: SUM, MIN, MAX)

DEFINE

DESCRIBE

HEADING

JUSTIFY

SPOOL *<Filename>*, SPOOL OFF, and SPO. Non-qualified files are created in the *<TOAD Home Directory>*\TEMPS\ directory. Relative-location file creation is supported.

SET AUTOTRACE

SET ECHO (ON/OFF)

SET ESCAPE (ON/OFF)

SET ESCAPE/ESC '\' (\ is any character)—defaults to \

SET HEADING/HEA (ON/off)

SET FEEDBACK (ON/off)

SET LINESIZE

SET SERVEROUTPUT/SERVEROUT (ON/OFF)

SET TERM (ON/off)

DEFINE/DEF and UNDEFINE/UNDEF

PAUSE

EXIT/QUIT

PROMPT/PRO

CONNECT/CON and DISCONNECT/DISC.

REM/REMARK

RUN

TOAD simply ignores the following SQL*Plus commands:

SET TAB

STORE SET

VERIFY

PAGESIZE

and any other SET commands not supported by TOAD.

The following SQL*Plus commands are NOT supported in TOAD:

ACCEPT	APPEND	ARCHIVE
LOG		
ATTRIBUTE	BTITLE/TTITLE	
CHANGE	COPY	DEL
EDIT	EXECUTE	GET
HELP	HOST	INPUT
LIST	PASSWORD	

RECOVER	REPHEADER / REPFOOTER	
SAVE	SHOW	SHUTDOWN
START	STARTUP	
TIMING	VARIABLE	
WHENEVER OSERROR	WHENEVER SQLERROR	

Scripts That Write Scripts

TOAD supports just about any kind of script. What makes Oracle so powerful is the ability to create scripts that actually build scripts!

 Make sure to run any SQL*Plus script as a script!

The most basic SQL-creating-SQL is the DROP TABLE script. This script can be used to clean up a schema from a departing employee, for example. Figure 3.47 illustrates this simple script. Notice the SPOOL command. The output from this command appears in the Notepad window.

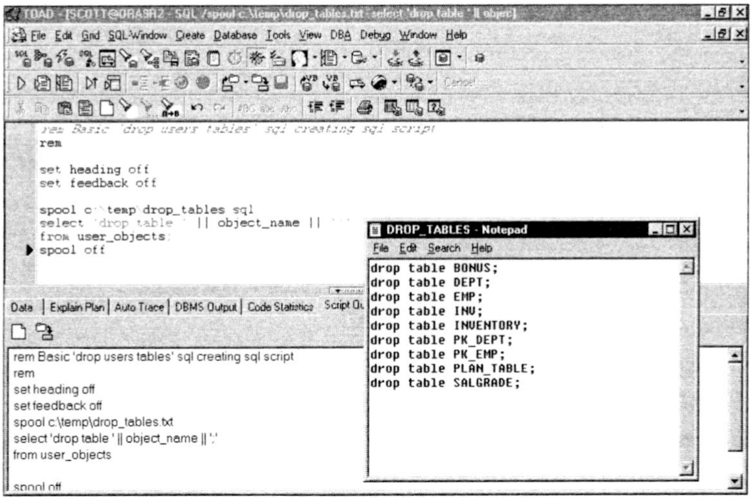

FIGURE 3.47   DROP TABLE SQL-Creating-SQL script.

TOAD can also use SQL-Creating-SQL to create most of the TOAD configuration files such as the ALIASES.TXT file. Figure 3.48 shows this script. Notice that it spooled ALIASES.TXT to the C:\TEMP directory. This file would have to be moved to the <TOAD home directory>\temps directory. The substr can be adjusted.

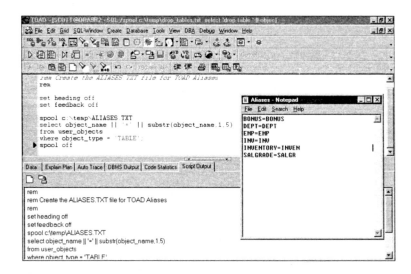

FIGURE 3.48   Creating the ALIASES.TXT file.

This technique of selecting data mixed with punctuation from USER_OBJECTS can be used to create most, if not all, of the TOAD configuration files.

Summary

This chapter covered using the TOAD SQL Editor, illustrating most of the features available. The real power in using TOAD is to get comfortable with the various keyboard shortcuts and to set up appropriate aliases and autoreplacements to aid the developer in the development cycle of SQL statements and SQL scripts.

The next chapter covers the TOAD Procedure Editor. Some of the features may appear similar to those features discussed in this chapter. In fact, some of the features are the same or similar. This book will make the distinction clear and use examples that are appropriate for the editor that the developer is using.

4

TOAD Procedure Editor

The Procedure Editor (or PL/SQL editor) is a better editing environment for PL/SQL procedures, functions, packages, and database triggers than the SQL Editor illustrated in Chapter 3. This editor contains a PL/SQL debugger, which is a full-featured symbolic debugger.

This editor enables you to develop, save, run, debug, and tune PL/SQL wherever it appears in applications or the database.

Overview

TOAD provides a number of features that make PL/SQL development easy:

- Keyboard shortcuts

- Table and column select lists

- PL/SQL templates

- Options for creating and executing PL/SQL procedures or parts of procedures

- Complete debugging capabilities

- Complete source code control

The Procedure Editor window gives you the ease and flexibility to create and edit PL/SQL no matter where it exists in the database. Figure 4.1 illustrates the Procedure Editor window, displaying a function stored in the database.

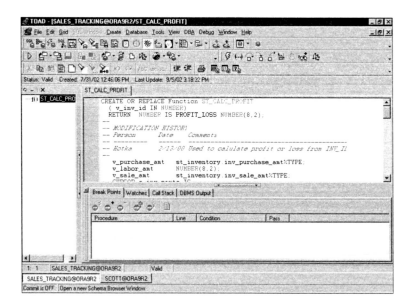

FIGURE 4.1   The TOAD Procedure Editor window.

This illustration shows the default Procedure Editor. The various buttons at the top perform just about any function (including executing the current SQL, saving the current SQL, and so on). There are three rows of buttons, or three TOAD toolbars. When you hover the mouse over a button, a balloon will appear with a description of its use.

A *shortcut* is a keystroke or keystrokes that perform a certain function. F1, for example, brings up the TOAD help facility. There is a button on the toolbar for about every shortcut. The savvy TOAD user makes extensive use of these shortcuts.

[ic:keyboard] F1 brings up the TOAD help facility.

Figure 4.2 illustrates the toolbars.

 The first and third toolbars are the same as the toolbars in the SQL Editor, discussed in Chapter 3. This chapter focuses on the Procedure Editor.

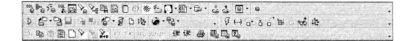

FIGURE 4.2   TOAD Procedure Editor window toolbars.

The second (middle) toolbar has buttons for actions that are specific to the Procedure Editor such as compiling, debugging features, and source-code check in/check out. This toolbar contains the following icons:

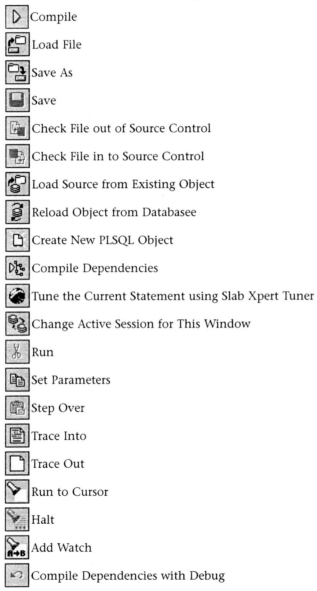

Compile

Load File

Save As

Save

Check File out of Source Control

Check File in to Source Control

Load Source from Existing Object

Reload Object from Databasee

Create New PLSQL Object

Compile Dependencies

Tune the Current Statement using Slab Xpert Tuner

Change Active Session for This Window

Run

Set Parameters

Step Over

Trace Into

Trace Out

Run to Cursor

Halt

Add Watch

Compile Dependencies with Debug

The first shortcut is F2. This toggles on the error message panel. Figure 4.3 shows the Procedure Editor with error message panel toggled on. This is helpful when working on longer SQL statements or SQL scripts.

F2 Toggles Error Message Panel

F9 Compile

Ctrl+S Save

F11 Run

Shift+F9 Set Parameters

F8 Step Over

F7 Trace Into

Shift+F8 Trace Out

F12 Run to Cursor

Ctrl+F5 Add Watch

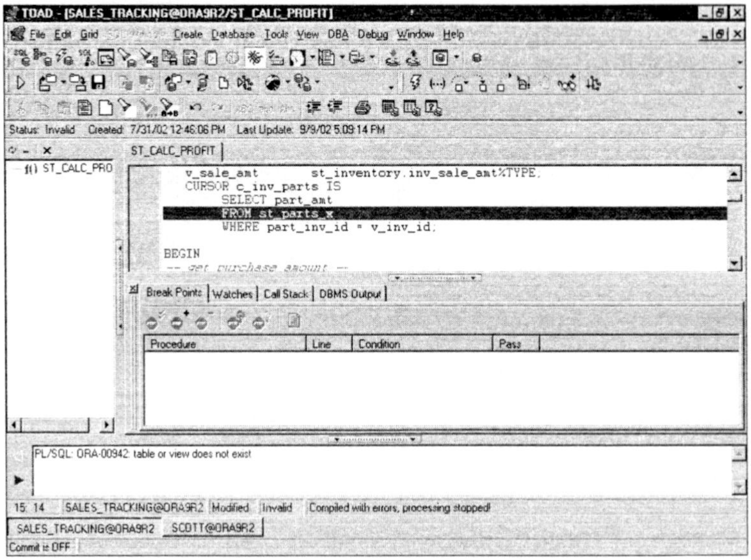

FIGURE 4.3   TOAD Procedure Editor window with error grid.

This editor has several parts. The main edit window enables you to edit multiple PL/SQL objects at a time. Each object will have its own tab along the top of this section. See the ST_CALC_PROFIT tab in Figure 4.3.

To the left of this section is the object navigator. This enables you to easily navigate to parts of the object, convenient for those code blocks with dozens or hundreds of lines of code.

The lower section is tabbed and enables you to set and see the breakpoints for the debugger, the debugger watches, the call stack (what objects have called other objects), and the DBMS_Output.

The F2 key toggles on/off the syntax error messages panel (see bottom of Figure 4.3). This panel automatically toggles on when you compile your code and you receive an error. F2 would then hide the panel.

[ic:keyboard] F2 toggles on/off error message line.

Figure 4.4 illustrates the Highlighting options in the Editor Options window. You can see that you have complete control over the editor environment (such as autoreplacement of words, general layout and text wrapping in the edit window, key assignments, and code templates).

TOAD has three editors: the SQL Editor (covered in Chapter 3), the Procedure Editor, and a text editor of your choice. The editor environment applies its options

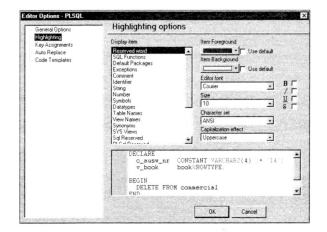

FIGURE 4.4   TOAD Procedure Editor Options.

to both TOAD editors. Additional editors can easily be added to TOAD. Choose View, Options from the menu bar, and then select Editors (or use the Configure TOAD Options button) to add your editor of choice. Figure 4.5 illustrates how to add the Notepad editor, for example. Be sure to use the variable %s to pass this editor the SQL that you are currently working on. If your current session has not been saved, you will be prompted to save it. Also, upon exiting your external editor, you will be prompted to reload your work from the saved file. You then use this external editor from the menu bar by choosing Edit, Load in External Editor or by using the short-cut Ctrl+F12. Figure 4.6 shows some work in the Notepad editor.

Ctrl+F12 accesses a previously defined external editor.

There are several ways to get PL/SQL code into the Procedure Editor. You can simply type in a new SQL statement, or create a new work area for a new SQL or PL/SQL block using the Create New PLSQL Object button. You can load SQL or PL/SQL from a file using the Load File button. This button has a drop-down menu that contains the history of loads. You can also check out code from the source code using the Check File Out of Source Control button. You can also load the code from the database using the Load Source from Existing Object button. This button also has a drop-down menu that contains the history of selected objects. You can also load code with a cut-and-paste from other applications.

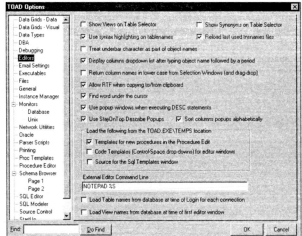

FIGURE 4.5   Defining external editors in TOAD.

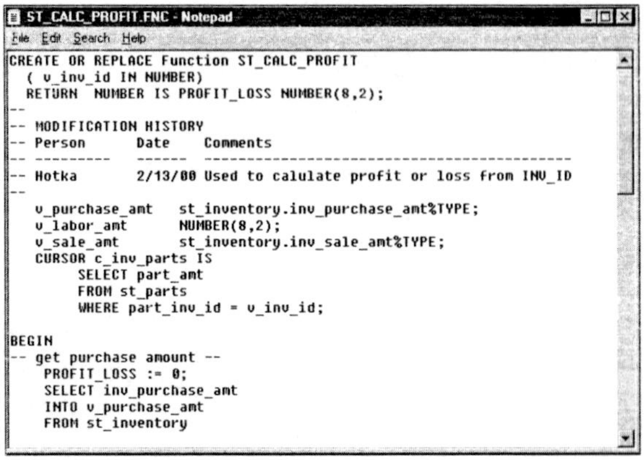

Figure 4.7 illustrates loading code from a file. Notice that the drop-down menu from the Load File button shows a history of files accessed by TOAD. Loading code from the database is just as easy using

FIGURE 4.6   Using Notepad as editor in TOAD.

the Load Source from Existing Object button. It has a similar drop-down menu of a history of objects accessed by TOAD. You can also create new code from the default code template by using the Create New PLSQL Object button. Notice that TOAD easily handles multiple objects at the same time, giving each its own tab.

TOAD will also easily format your PL/SQL into an easy-to-read format.

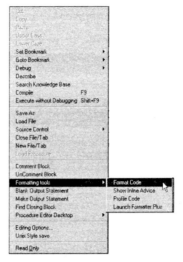

FIGURE 4.7 Loading code into the Procedure Editor.

Figure 4.8 shows how to access the formatter by right-clicking in the edit window and selecting Formatting Tools, Format Code from the context menu. Figure 4.9 shows how TOAD formats the SQL.

This overview covered some of the basic concepts and features of the Procedure Editor. The remainder of this chapter will cover specific topics in the Procedure Editor.

FIGURE 4.8 Accessing PL/SQL Formatter.

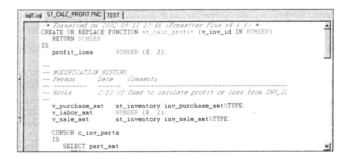

FIGURE 4.9 TOAD formatted PL/SQL.

Predefined Shortcuts

Keyboard shortcuts are one of the features that makes TOAD so powerful and easy to use. TOAD comes with a host of predefined shortcuts. These shortcuts save keystrokes and mouse actions and perform a variety of tasks such as issuing a describe on the current highlighted object, or find (find next, find previous, and so on). The shortcuts differ slightly between the Procedure Editor and the SQL Editor (covered in Chapter 3). This section focuses on the shortcuts for the Procedure Editor only.

Tables 4.1 and 4.2 are handy cross references for all of the Procedure Editor short-cuts. Table 4.1 shows the shortcuts arranged by keystroke, and Table 4.2 shows the shortcuts arranged by description. The third column refers you to the figure in this chapter where the shortcut is illustrated.

F2 or Shift+F2 Toggles output window

F9 Compile

Ctrl+S Save

F11 Run

Ctrl+F9 Set Parameters

F8 Step Over

F7 Trace into

Shift+F8 Trace out

F12 Run to cursor

Ctrl+F5 Add watch

TABLE 4.1   Procedure Editor Shortcuts by Keystroke

Shortcut	Description	Illustrations
F1	Windows Help File	
F2	Toggle Error Message Panel	Figure 4.3
F3	Find Next Occurrence	
Shift+F3	Find Previous Occurrence	
F4	Describe Table, View, Procedure, Function	Figure 4.23
F5	Set/Delete Break Point	Figure 4.54
F7	Trace Into While Debugging	Figure 4.52
F8	Step Over While Debugging	Figure 4.52
F9	Compile	Figure 4.35
Ctrl+F9	Set Code Execution Parameters	Figures 4.36, 4.50
Shift+F9	Execute Current Source Without Debugging	
F10 or right-click	Pop-up Menu	Figure 4.4
F11	Execute Current Source with Debugging	Figure 4.36
F12	Execute Current Source to Cursor With Debugging	
Ctrl+F12	External Editor, Pass Contents	
Ctrl+A	Select All Text	
Ctrl+Alt+B	Display Breakpoint Window	

TABLE 4.1   Continued

Shortcut	Description	Illustrations
Ctrl+C	Copy	
Ctrl+D	Display Procedure Parameters	
Ctl+Alt+D	Display Debugger in DBMS Output Window	
Ctrl+F	Find Text	
Ctrl+G	Goto Line	
Ctrl+L	Convert Text to Lowercase	
Ctrl+M	Make Code Statement	
Ctrl+N	Recall Named SQL Statement	
Ctrl+O	Open a Text File	
Ctrl+P	Strip Code Statement	
Ctrl+R	Find and Replace	
Ctrl+S	Save File	
Shift+Ctrl+S	Save File As	Figure 4.38
Ctrl+Alt+S	Display Call Stack Window	
Ctrl+T	Columns Drop-down	Figure 4.16
Shift+Ctrl+R	Alias Replacement	
Shift+Ctrl+T	Columns Drop-down no alias	Figure 4.18
Ctrl+Spacebar	Code Templates	Figure 4.27
Ctrl+U	Convert Text to Uppercase	
Ctrl+V	Paste	
Ctrl+Alt+W	Display Debugger Watches Window	
Ctrl+X	Cut	
Ctrl+Z	Undo Last Change	
Ctrl+.	Display Pop-up List Of Matching Table Names	Figure 4.16
Shift+Ctrl+Z	Redo Last Undo	
Ctrl+Tab	Cycles Through the Collection of MDI Child Windows	

TABLE 4.2   Procedure Editor Shortcuts by Description

Description	Keystroke	Illustration
Alias Replacement	Shift+Ctrl+R	
Code Templates	Ctrl+Spacebar	Figure 4.27
Columns Drop-down	Ctrl+T	Figure 4.16
Columns Drop-down no alias	Shift+Ctrl+T	Figure 4.18
Compile	F9	Figure 4.35
Convert Text to Lowercase	Ctrl+L	
Convert Text to Uppercase	Ctrl+U	
Copy	Ctrl+C	
Cut	Ctrl+X	

TABLE 4.2   Continued

Description	Keystroke	Illustration
Cycle through the Collection of MDI Child Windows	Ctrl+Tab	
Describe Table, View, Procedure, Function, or Package	F4	Figure 4.23
Display Breakpoint Window	Ctrl+Alt+B	
Display Call Stack Window	Ctrl+Alt+S	
Display Debugger in DBMS Output Window	Ctl+Alt+D	
Display Debugger Watches Window	Ctrl+Alt+W	
Display Pop-up List of Matching Table Names	Ctrl+.	Figure 4.16
Display Procedure Parameters	Ctrl+D	
Execute Current Source to Cursor With Debugging	F12	
Execute Current Source with Debugging	F11	Figures 4.4, 4.36
Execute Current Source Without Debugging	Shift+F9	Figure 4.36
External Editor, Pass Contents	Ctrl+F12	
Find and Replace	Ctrl+R	
Find Next Occurrence	F3	
Find Previous Occurrence	Shift+F3	
Find Text	Ctrl+F	
Goto Line	Ctrl+G	
Make Code Statement	Ctrl+M	
Open a Text File	Ctrl+O	
Paste	Ctrl+V	
Pop-up Menu	F10 or right-click	
Recall Named SQL	Ctrl+N	
Redo Last Undo	Shift+Ctrl+Z	
Save File	Ctrl+S	Figure 4.38
Save File As	Shift+Ctrl+S	Figure 4.38
Select All Text	Ctrl+A	
Set Execution Parameters	Ctrl+F9	Figure 4.36
Set/Delete Break Point	F5	Figure 4.54
Step Over While Debugging	F8	Figure 4.52
Strip Code Statement	Ctrl+P	
Trace Into While Debugging	F7	Figure 4.52
Toggle Error Message Panel	F2	Figure 4.3
Undo Last Change	Ctrl+Z	
Windows Help File	F1	

User-Defined Shortcuts

TOAD is completely configurable. You can easily add your own shortcuts to TOAD. It is easy to change the shortcut keystrokes for existing shortcuts, and it is just as easy to add your own shortcuts.

> For those readers who are either already familiar with short cuts, table and column select lists, aliases, and auto replacement substitutions can skip to "Using the PL/SQL Navigator found on page 23. This information is common (and already covered in chapter 3) to both the SQL Editor and the PL/SQL Editor.

Access the Editor Options menu with a right-click or by pressing the F10 key and selecting Editing Options.

To change an existing keystroke assignment, select Key Assignments, locate the particular assignment to change, and click on the Edit Sequence button as illustrated in Figure 4.10.

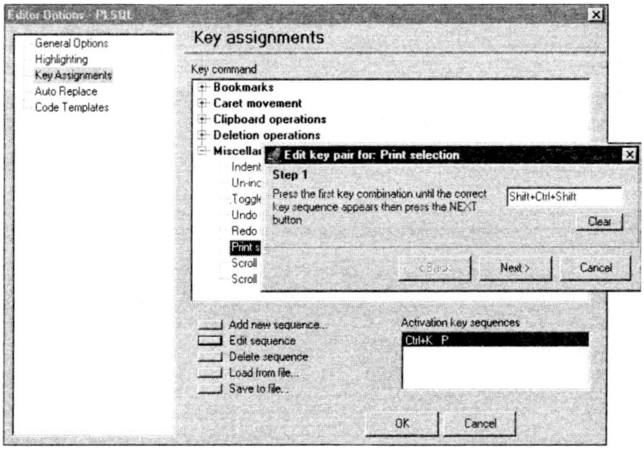

FIGURE 4.10 Changing shortcut keystroke assignments in TOAD.

To add additional keystroke assignments, select Key Assignments, locate the particular assignment to change, and click on the Add New Sequence button. Type the sequence desired to perform the key assignment task. In Figure 4.11, notice that Shift+Ctrl+D was added by pressing and holding down the Control key while pressing Shift and d.

Using Variables

TOAD supports all kinds of SQL from all kinds of applications. If you were to bring in SQL, for example, from a SQL*Forms application, it will contain bind variables. Bind variables are used to supply SQL with data at execution time. This allows applications to use the same SQL statement to select and manipulate different data, depending on the data supplied to the bind variables.

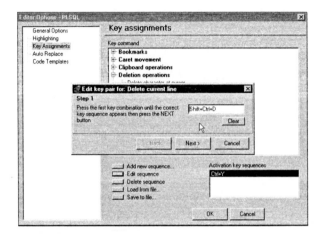

FIGURE 4.11   Adding shortcut keystroke assignments in TOAD.

Using the same SQL statement makes efficient use of the Oracle RDBMS SQL pool as the SQL will not be reparsed when using bind variables. The text of the SQL remains the same, so Oracle will reuse the same execution plan, making for a better-performing database environment.

Table and Column Name Select Lists

TOAD makes it easy to find and work with tables and columns. Figure 4.12 illustrates using the Show Table Select Window button (mouse cursor is pointing to this button). This brings up the Table Name Select window, with a list of available tables for this particular user. If the user has privileges to other schemas, the drop-down list in this window can be changed to the schema owner and those objects will then appear in the select list. Double-clicking on the selected object adds the selected table to the Procedure Editor at the current cursor location.

Similarly, columns can be added to the Procedure Editor by using the Show Column Select Window button. Figure 4.13 illustrates using this window to add the columns INV_MAKE and INV_TYPE to the SQL in the Procedure Editor. Notice the cursor is pointing to the Show Column Select Window button.

TOAD will automatically give a column select list if you type or select a valid schema table name followed by a '.'. Wait a second and the column select list will appear as illustrated in Figure 4.14!

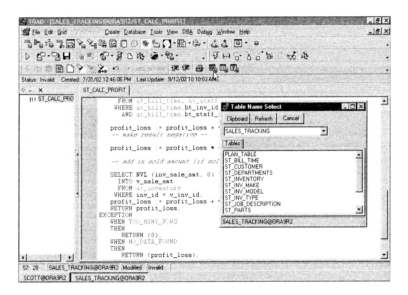

FIGURE 4.12   Table Name Select list.

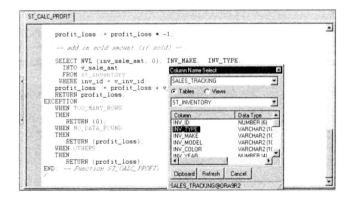

FIGURE 4.13   Automatic column select lists.

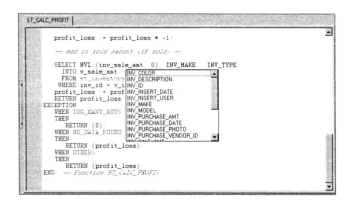

FIGURE 4.14   Column Name Select list.

Using Aliases and Auto Replacement Substitutions

TOAD supports the use of its own alias names. Aliases are convenient to shorten keystrokes, using short names instead of rather long table names. TOAD also allows the automatic replacement of text, or in this case, these aliases. The purpose of the alias is to shorten keystrokes. The purpose of the automatic replacement is to automatically resolve the TOAD alias to the full table or column name.

> TOAD aliases are used to shorten the number of keystrokes to develop SQL. TOAD aliases are not to be confused with Oracle RDBMS table aliases, which are used in qualifying columns in a multitable SQL statement.

TOAD aliases enable you to

- Access the Column Name Select drop-down list
- Type the alias as a shortcut a shortcut rather than typing the full table name

Aliases are easy to set up with any text editor. Make sure TOAD is not running (on network installations, make sure all users are off TOAD) and edit the ALIASES.TXT file found in the TOAD installation directory under the TEMPS subdirectory.

FIGURE 4.15   TOAD alias setup.

DO NOT edit this file with TOAD running. When TOAD exits, it rewrites this file and any changes you make will be lost!

Figure 4.15 illustrates the format of this file. The format is `<table name>=`
`<alias name>`.

 In Chapter 3, the section "Scripts That Write Scripts" discusses a method of quickly creating this file.

TOAD aliases are easy to use. Figure 4.16 shows a simple SQL statement using an alias to get to the Column Name Select drop-down. Notice that the user typed in 'inv.'. The '.' signaled the Column Name Select drop-down and the alias was resolved to the INVENTORY table.

 The '.' signals TOAD to see if this is an alias.

```
ST_CALC_PROFIT

        profit_loss := profit_loss * -1;

        -- add in sold amount (if sold) --

        SELECT NVL (inv_sale_amt, 0)  INV_MAKE    INV_TYPE
         INTO v_s INV_COLOR
         FROM inv INV_DESCRIPTION
        WHERE inv INV_ID
        profit_los INV_INSERT_DATE              _amt;
        RETURN pro INV_INSERT_USER
    EXCEPTION    INV_MAKE
        WHEN TOO_M INV_MODEL
        THEN       INV_PURCHASE_AMT
          RETURN   INV_PURCHASE_DATE
        WHEN NO_DA INV_PURCHASE_PHOTO
        THEN       INV_PURCHASE_VENDOR_ID
          RETURN (profit_loss);
        WHEN OTHERS
        THEN
          RETURN (profit_loss);
    END;  -- Function ST_CALC_PROFIT
```

FIGURE 4.16   TOAD alias usage.

 Notice in Figure 4.17 that there is both an INVENTORY table and an INV table. The alias INV was resolved in Figure 4.16 to the INVENTORY table, not the INV table. Notice the column names in Figure 4.17 compared to those in Figure 4.16. Granted, this is a poor naming convention, but bear with the example. To get the INV table displayed, use Shift+Ctrl+T (or Edit, Columns drop-down no alias) to ignore the alias and get the correct list of columns; see Figure 4.18.

 Shift+Ctrl+T ignores the alias request.

If an alias is identified in the SQL statement, and a Column Select is activated, the alias is automatically added to ALIASES.TXT.

TOAD scans only the first FROM clause in any SQL statement, so any TOAD aliases in complex SQL statements that have subqueries, for example, will not be found and resolved.

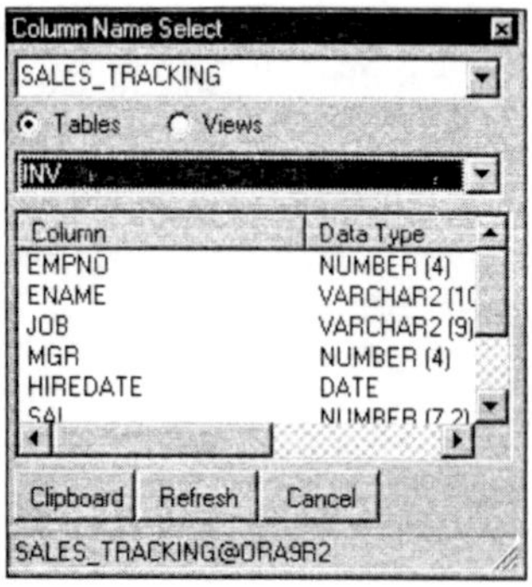

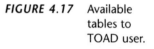

FIGURE 4.17   Available tables to TOAD user.

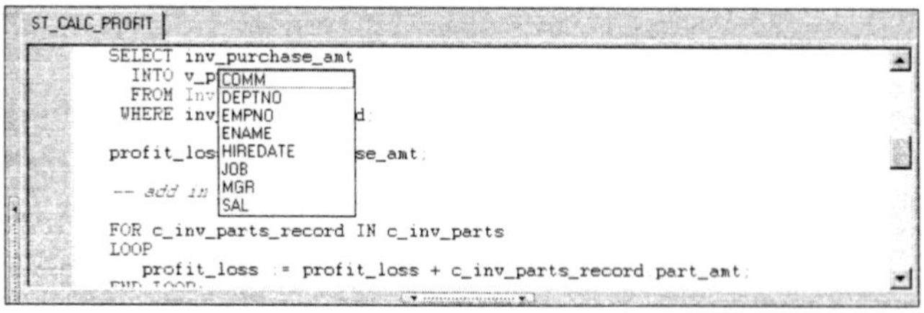

FIGURE 4.18   Ignore the alias in action.

Autoreplace substitution replaces a short string with the full name. This differs from TOAD aliases because aliases make reference to a different name but do not change the text of the SQL statement. When autoreplace substitution is defined, it happens automatically when you press the spacebar. Autoreplace substitution is activated by typing the short sequence (notice the "INV_" string illustrated in Figure 4.19) and pressing the spacebar (the autoreplace delimiter key defaults to the spacebar). This will then automatically substitute the predefined string in place of the short key sequence; see Figure 4.20.

Replacement happens after pressing the spacebar.

FIGURE 4.19   Autoreplace substitution key sequence.

```
ST_CALC_PROFIT |

    SELECT inv_purchase_amt
      INTO v_purchase_amt
      FROM Inventory
     WHERE inv_id = v_inv_id;

    profit_loss := v_purchase_amt;

    -- add in parts --

    FOR c_inv_parts_record IN c_inv_parts
    LOOP
        profit_loss := profit_loss + c_inv_parts_record.part_amt;
    END LOOP;
```

FIGURE 4.20   Autoreplace substitution in action.

There are two ways to create automatic replacement substitution strings. You can edit the PLSQLSUB.TXT file in the *<TOAD home directory>*\temps directory. The format is the same as the alias: *<short string>* = *<replacement string>*. The other way is to enter the substitution string by using the Edit, Editor Options, Auto Replace tab. See Figure 4.22.

Figure 4.21 illustrates the contents of this file. Notice the common typo 'teh' will automatically be converted to 'the' because this sequence will always be followed by pressing the spacebar. Also notice the 'inv' and 'Inv_' strings that were used in Figure 4.19 and Figure 4.20.

TOAD allows autosubstitution to be maintained by language type. You can edit and add to the list by using the Editor Options, Auto Replace window. Supported languages for autore-placement are HTML (*<TOAD home>*\temps\HTMLSUB.TXT), INI (*<TOAD home>*\temps\INISUB.TXT), JAVA (*<TOAD home>*\temps\JAVASUB.TXT), and TEXT (*<TOAD home>*\temps\TEXTSUB.TXT).

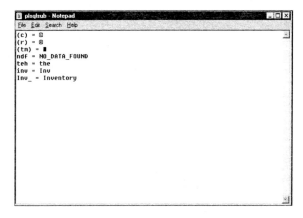

FIGURE 4.21   Editing the PLSQLSUB.TXT file.

Be sure TOAD is NOT running when you are editing any of these files in the TEMPS directory. TOAD rewrites these files when closing, and any changes made to the files with TOAD running will be lost.

TOAD enables you to export and import these autosubstitution definitions. See Figure 4.22. This is a convenient way to move them when setting up a new computer to use TOAD. It also might be convenient to have various autosubstitution files by application. This allows you to have specific substitutions for various applications, same alias but resolved to different names perhaps.

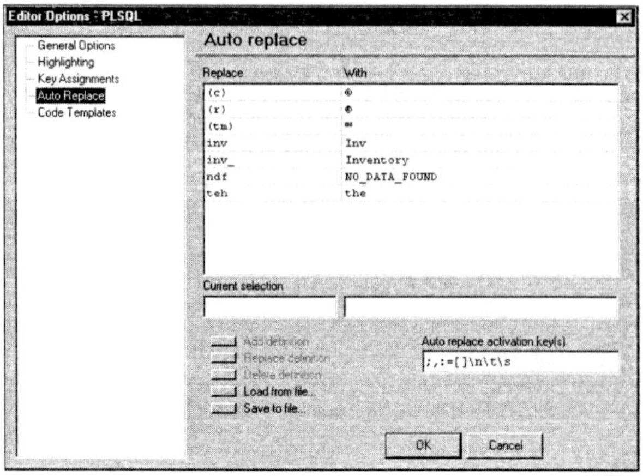

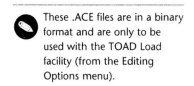

FIGURE 4.22   Adding autoreplace substitution using the Editor Options screen.

When loading autoreplace definitions in from a saved file, all previous substitutions currently in TOAD are lost and replaced with the new definitions.

These .ACE files are in a binary format and are only to be used with the TOAD Load facility (from the Editing Options menu).

SQL Templates

TOAD can easily format a SELECT or INSERT statement for any data-oriented object (view or table). Simply place the cursor on the object you want and press F4. This will perform a describe on the object, as illustrated in Figure 4.23.

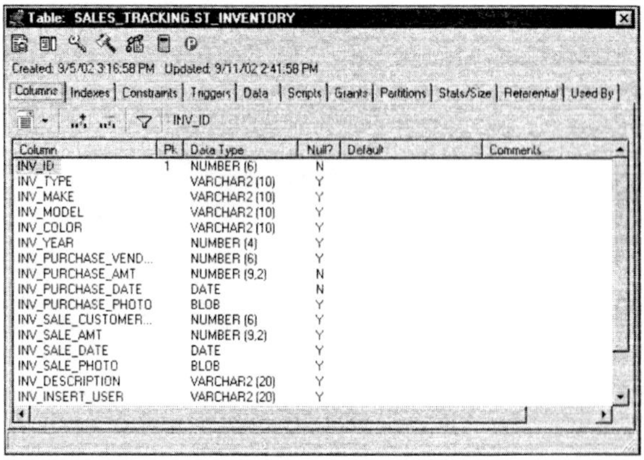

FIGURE 4.23   Object description.

Notice in Figure 4.23 that everything you need to know about the object appears in this window.

It is particularly nice to have TOAD build a script that created the object. This information comes from the data dictionary and accurately reflects the object that you are working with.

Most of this information is covered in other chapters. To get to the SQL templates, use the Columns tab and right-click on any of the column names. This brings up another menu of mostly administrative functions (most of these features are covered in other chapters), as shown in Figure 4.24. Notice where the cursor is (Generate Statement); you have the choice of building a SELECT or INSERT statement for this particular object. When making a selection, TOAD will tell you that the "script copied to the clipboard." Figure 4.25 shows the code in the TOAD Procedure Editor that was pasted from the clipboard.

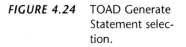

FIGURE 4.24   TOAD Generate Statement selection.

F4 to describe the object

Right-click on a column in the Columns tab and select Generate Statement

You can also use the Show SQL Template Window button (third toolbar, rightmost button) to paste in specific SQL templates while doing PL/SQL coding. Figure 4.26 illustrates how to use these templates. Options include directly copying the template into the Procedure Editor (as illustrated in Figure 4.26) or copying the template to the clipboard. Notice that there are all kinds of SQL templates. TOAD contains templates for row, group, and date functions.

```
ST_CALC_PROFIT
        SELECT inv_purchase_amt
          INTO v_purchase_amt
          FROM st_inventory
       WHERE inv_id = v_inv_id;

        SELECT INV_ID, INV_TYPE, INV_MAKE,
       INV_MODEL, INV_COLOR, INV_YEAR,
       INV_PURCHASE_VENDOR_ID, INV_PURCHASE_AMT, INV_PURCHASE_DATE,
       INV_PURCHASE_PHOTO, INV_SALE_CUSTOMER_ID, INV_SALE_AMT,
       INV_SALE_DATE, INV_SALE_PHOTO, INV_DESCRIPTION,
       INV_INSERT_USER, INV_INSERT_DATE, INV_UPDATE_USER,
       INV_UPDATE_DATE FROM ST_INVENTORY
```

FIGURE 4.25   Generated SQL statements.

FIGURE 4.26   TOAD SQL templates in action.

PL/SQL Object Templates

Code completion templates are boilerplate syntax where you type in the correct names, and so on, but the correct syntax with options is supplied.

Code completion templates work a lot like aliases except that they provide the entire syntax rather than just a word or object name. Figures 4.27 and 4.28 illustrate how this works. Instead of hitting the '.' to signal the replacement, you press Ctrl+Spacebar to signal the replacement.

    Ctrl+Spacebar signals code template.

FIGURE 4.27   Code completion template key sequence.

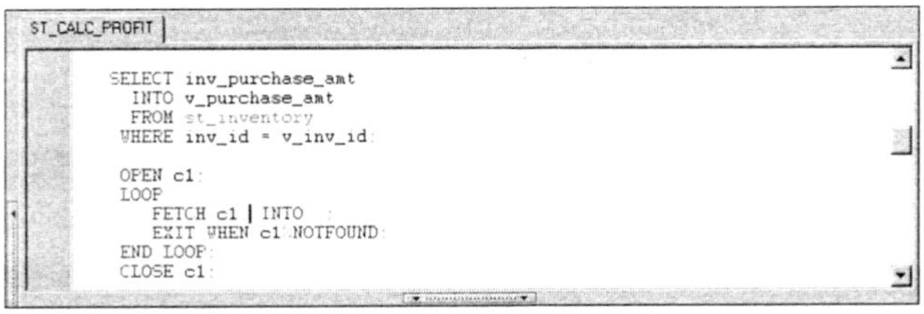

FIGURE 4.28   Code completion template in action.

Like the autoreplacement feature, additional code completion templates are easily added by using the Edit, Editor Options, Code Templates screen, as in Figure 4.29.

You can also edit the PLSQL.DCI file in *<TOAD Home Directory>*\temps and add additional templates with a text editor. See Figure 4.30 for the layout example.

Supported languages for code completion are HTML (*<TOAD home>*\temps\HTMLSUB.DCI), INI (*<TOAD home>*\temps\INISUB.DCI), JAVA (*<TOAD home>*\temps\JAVASUB.DCI), and TEXT (*<TOAD home>*\temps\TEXTSUB.DCI).

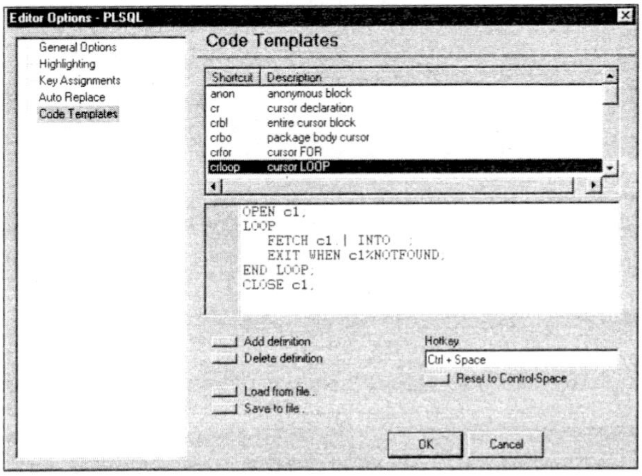

FIGURE 4.29   Adding code completion templates.

Be sure TOAD is NOT running when you are editing any of these files in the TEMPS directory. TOAD rewrites these files when closing, and any changes made to the files with TOAD running will be lost.

The author uses code templates to help with options in packages, such as the DBMS_OUTPUT package. Notice in Figure 4.31 that typing in the package and then pressing Ctrl+Spacebar gives the additional options available.

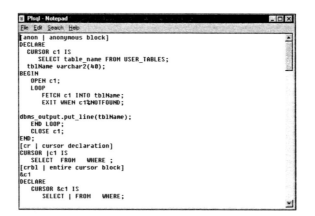

FIGURE 4.30 Code completion template file layout.

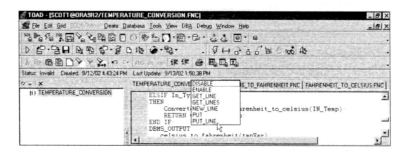

FIGURE 4.31 Code completion in action.

Creating a New PL/SQL Object

TOAD enables you to easily create new PL/SQL procedures. Figure 4.32 illustrates how to access the wizard, and Figure 4.33 shows the default PL/SQL code that is automatically generated. Notice in Figure 4.32 that the mouse cursor is on the Create New PL/SQL Object button.

FIGURE 4.32 Creating a new PL/SQL object.

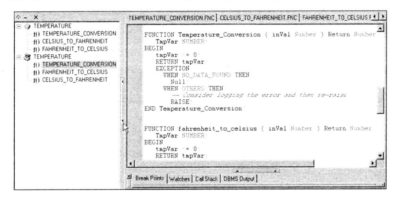

FIGURE 4.33 New PL/SQL object template.

Using the PL/SQL Navigator

TOAD makes it easy to move around large code files such as packages. Notice in Figure 4.34 that the left window features the package 'TEMPERATURE' and if you click on each of the headings, TOAD instantly jumps to that part of the package in the main edit window. This navigator window can be closed or resized by clicking and dragging the bar that the cursor is pointing to in Figure 4.35.

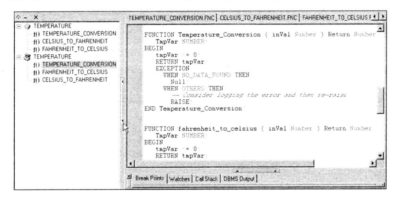

FIGURE 4.34 The Procedure Editor's navigator window.

Compiling PL/SQL Code

Compiling code in the current Procedure Editor window is easy. Click on the Compile button (leftmost button on middle toolbar) or press F9.

  F9 = Compile

Notice the compiled code in Figure 4.35. The error window at the bottom will highlight any errors found. In this example, the previous line is missing a semicolon ';'. Sometimes the problem is not on the current line but on lines around the highlighted line.

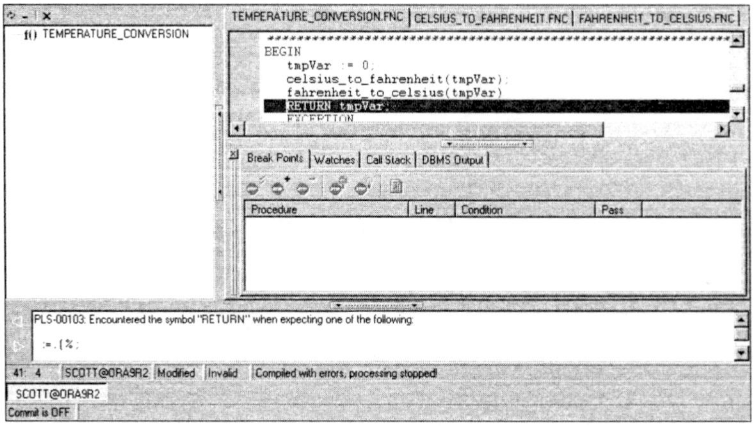

FIGURE 4.35   Compiling code.

Executing PL/SQL Code

TOAD enables you to develop and run code without having to leave one environment and go to another (as you would using an editor and SQL*Plus, for example). Code can easily be run by clicking the Run button or pressing the F11 key. Figure 4.36 illustrates the parameter screen as TOAD noticed that this procedure has input variables. The TEMPERATURE_CONVERSION procedure calls two functions. After these parameters are set, use the '(...)' button or Ctrl+F9 to change any of the variables (brings up this same interface). Figure 4.37 shows the completion of the procedure. Notice the output in the DBMS_OUTPUT tab.

F11 = Run

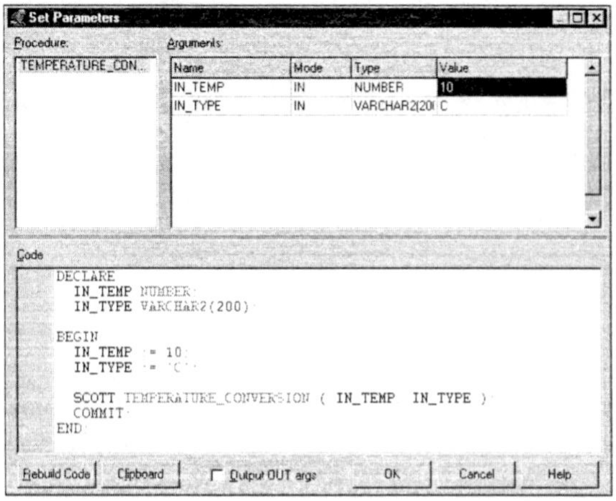

FIGURE 4.36   The Set Parameters input screen.

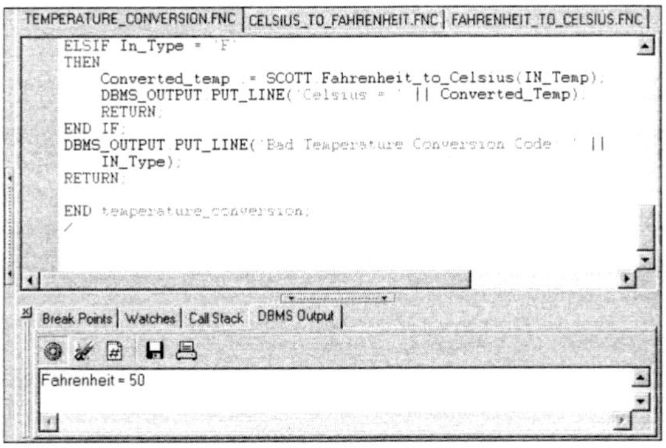

TEMPERATURE_CONVERSION.FNC
CELSIUS_TO_FAHRENHEIT.FNC
FAHRENHEIT_TO_CELSIUS.FNC
ELSIF In_Type = 'F'
THEN
Converted_temp := SCOTT.Fahrenheit_to_Celsius(IN_Temp);
DBMS_OUTPUT.PUT_LINE('Celsius = ' || Converted_Temp);
RETURN;
END IF;
DBMS_OUTPUT.PUT_LINE('Bad Temperature Conversion Code: ' ||
IN_Type);
RETURN;
END temperature_conversion;
/
Break Points
Watches
Call Stack
DBMS Output
Fahrenheit = 50

FIGURE 4.37 Executing code.

Saving PL/SQL Code to Files

Saving your work to operating-system files is easy. Use the Save As button (see the mouse cursor in Figure 4.38) and pick the location where you would like the code to be created. When you get a clean compile on the code, it is also stored in the database in the schema that you are currently connected to. Figure 4.38 shows the Save to File function. Ctrl+S will save the code in the original file it was created as. Shift+Ctrl+S will perform the same task as the Save As button.

You can also right-click on the tab of the item you want to save or close and if it contains changes, you will be prompted to save the file before TOAD closes the tab.

Ctrl+S = Save file to current name

Shift+Ctrl+S = Save As

Save File
Save in: ch04
CELSIUS_TO_FAHRENHEIT.FNC
FAHRENHEIT_TO_CELSIUS.FNC
ST_CALC_PROFIT_2
ST_CALC_PROFIT_3
TEMPERATURE.PKB
TEMPERATURE_CONVERSION.FNC
File name: TEMPERATURE_CONVERSION
Save as type: PLSQL (*.sql;*.qry;*.prc;*.spc;*.bdy;*.trg;*.plb
Save
Cancel

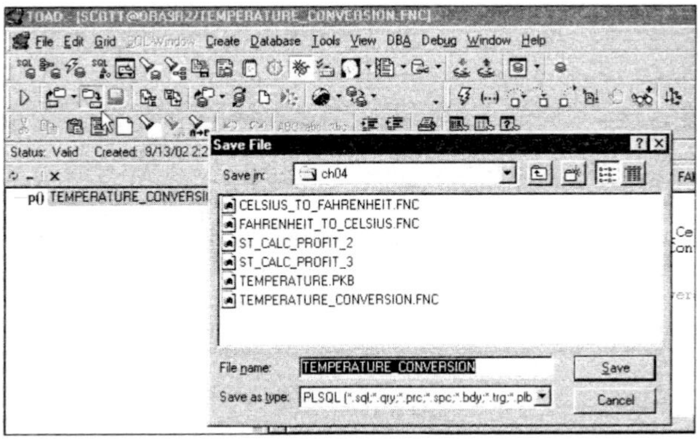

FIGURE 4.38 Saving code to a file.

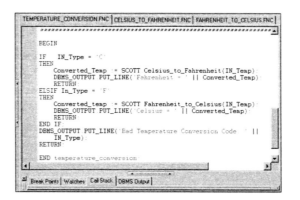

FIGURE 4.39   Code before formatting.

Formatting PL/SQL Code

TOAD can easily format the PL/SQL code into an easy-to-read format. Figure 4.39
shows the code block before formatting, and Figure 4.40 shows the code block after
formatting. TOAD will put a comment line in the header that this code has been
reformatted. Right-click in the code block and select Formatting Tools, Format Code
to access. See Figure 4.41.

 This option is available only if the formatting option was purchased from Quest
Software, Inc.

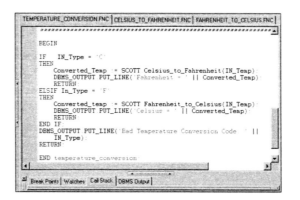

FIGURE 4.40   Code after formatting.

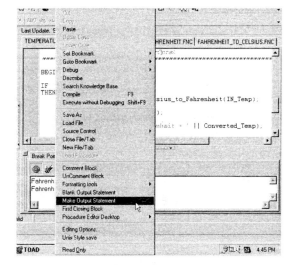

FIGURE 4.41   Accessing the Code Formatter.

Using DBMS_OUTPUT

DBMS output is the main output from PL/SQL. You can use DBMS_OUTPUT to format print lines, display data (as we did with the TEMPERATURE_CONVERSION procedure), and display error conditions. This was a popular technique to display information when debugging code. It is referenced here to illustrate how easy it is to add these statements for debugging or other purposes.

Right-click on the code and select Make Output Statement (as illustrated in Figure 4.42). Put the cursor in the code where you want to put the DBMS_OUTPUT statement and paste (Ctrl+V). Fill in the text that you would like to see in the DBMS_OUTPUT tab after execution as illustrated in Figure 4.43.

FIGURE 4.42   Accessing the DBMS_OUTPUT blank statement.

To see the DBMS_OUTPUT, you will need to make sure this option is checked in the Debugging category of the TOAD Options screen; see Figure 4.44. This is the equivalent of setting `serveroutput` on in SQL*Plus.

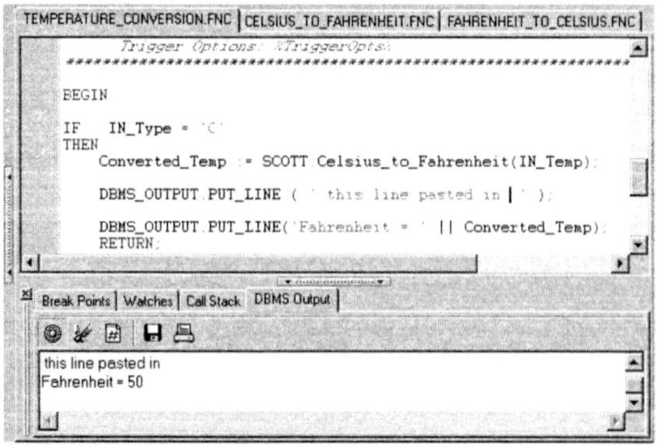

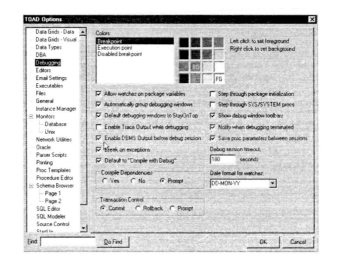

FIGURE 4.43   DBMS_OUTPUT in action.

FIGURE 4.44   TOAD DBMS.OUTPUT settings.

Debugging Setup, Requirements, and Parameters

TOAD contains a powerful debugger that enables you to traverse code, view variable content, start or stop execution of code, and step in/out of called procedures. This is known as *symbolic debugging*.

You must have a valid Quest Software license key to use the debugger. To check the options available in your version of TOAD, click on Help, About and make sure Debugger appears in the Options line; see the mouse cursor position in Figure 4.45. To add a license key, click on Help, Register TOAD.

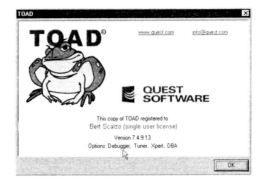

There are also some important settings to enable the debugging feature. In the TOAD Options screen, under the Procedure Editor category, make sure that Enable Compiling Multiple Objects from a Single File is NOT checked on, as illustrated in Figure 4.46.

FIGURE 4.45   TOAD license options.

TOAD relies upon the Oracle Probe API to get the debug information. Run the Oracle Probe API Version script in a SQL Editor window as seen in Figure 4.47. TOAD requires this API to be at least at the level of 2.2 (major=2, minor=2).

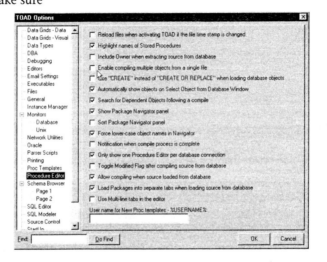

This script as well as the Temperature scripts are available on the Web site for this book.

FIGURE 4.46   TOAD Options settings for debugging.

If you are using TOAD against an Oracle 7 database, make sure that BLANK_TRIMMING is set to TRUE in the INIT.ORA parameter file for the call stack to display properly.

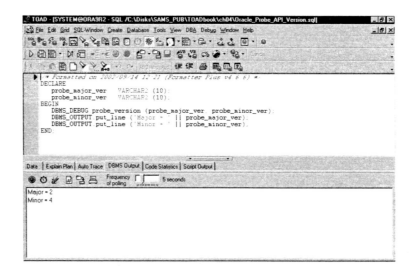

FIGURE 4.47   Oracle Probe API Version.

> If you are using TOAD against an Oracle 7 database, and you get the error Debugger is
> not responding, you will have to comment out all the DBMS_OUTPUT statements and
> uncheck Enable DBMS Output Before Every Debugging Session in the TOAD Options
> screen under the Debugging category.

Basic Debugging PL/SQL Code

The TOAD debugger is easily accessed by using the nine
buttons on the right side of the Procedure Editor toolbar
(middle toolbar). See Figure 4.48. These same functions are
also accessible from the Debug menu (see Figure 4.49), and
all of the functions have a shortcut keystroke as well.

FIGURE 4.48   The Debug toolbar.

Debug	
(...) Set Parameters	Ctrl+F9
⚡ Run	F11
▶ Run to Cursor	F12
Step Over	F8
Trace Into	F7
Trace Out	Shift+F8
Halt Execution	
Set Breakpoint	F5
Add Watch at Cursor	Ctrl+F5
Evaluate/Modify	Ctrl+Alt+E
▶ Breakpoints	Ctrl+Alt+B
Call Stack	Ctrl+Alt+S
Watches	Ctrl+Alt+W
DBMS Output	Ctrl+Alt+D

FIGURE 4.49   The
Debug drop-down
menu.

The following keystrokes access many of the Debug features.

F11 = Run

Ctrl+F9 = Set Parameters

F8 = Step Over

F7 = Trace Into

Shift+F8 = Trace Out

F12 = Run to Cursor

Ctrl+F5 = Add Watch

The TOAD debugger relies heavily upon certain functions. These functions, described in the following list, are used throughout this section.

- Set Parameters: Allows you to set any input variables.

- Run: Executes the procedure/function.

- Run to Cursor: Executes the procedure/function until the line containing the mouse cursor is reached.

- Step Over: Executes one line of code at a time but does not go into any called procedures or functions.

- Trace Into: Executes one line of code at a time and does go into any called procedure or function, executing its code one line at a time as well.

- Trace Out: Returns execution to the calling routine, stopping on the next line of code after the call statement.

- Halt Execution: Stops debugging or stepping through the lines of code.

- Set Breakpoint: Stops the debug process at the line with the breakpoint.

- Add Watch at Cursor: Watches allow for the contents of specific variables to be monitored during the debug process. This key allows you to add additional variables to be monitored.

- Evaluate/Modify: Allows for "watched" variables to be visualized and changed on the fly.

- Breakpoints: A breakpoint stops execution at the line with the breakpoint. This key allows you to add, change, or delete breakpoints.

- Call Stack: Displays the call stack, or an ordered list of procedures/functions that were called to get to this particular procedure/function.

- Watches: Displays the variables currently being monitored. This window also allows you to add, change, or delete watched variables.

- DBMS Output: Displays any DBMS_OUTPUT generated by the procedure/function.

Please note that DBMS_OUTPUT is not displayed until the procedure/function completes execution or the Halt button is used.

Let's walk through a simple debugging session using TEMPERATURE.PKG, which contains a procedure and its related functions.

These procedures and functions are available on the Web site for this book.

The debugging process relies heavily upon the Oracle Probe API. With this in mind, the TOAD debugger cannot see any of the code variables until the code is executing.

The two main buttons to go through the code are the Trace Into and Step Over buttons/functions. Trace Into stops on each line of code. Step Over does the same thing except it will not follow the lines of code into a called procedure or function; the code will be executed and the debugger will simply stop on the next line of code in the current procedure.

The author speaks of named buttons, but often in TOAD there is a shortcut and/or keystroke available for the same function. For simplicity, the author will speak of the named button.

You can set "watches" to see and edit the content of variables. These watches allow you to see the changes in the contents of the variables as the code is being debugged, in the tab at the bottom of the screen (see Figure 4.52). You can also hover over a variable with the mouse and it will display the contents as well.

To begin a debugging session, load TEMPERATURE.PKG and click the Compile Dependencies with Debug button (or simply click the Compile button after clicking the Toggle Compiling with Debug button, in the middle of top toolbar). This puts the necessary debug information into the procedures/functions. If you do not use this function, you might get the message No Debug Information Available.

Click the Trace Into button. The parameter screen will pop up; see Figure 4.50. Ignore the Celsius_to_Fahrenheit and the Fahrenheit_to_Celsius functions for now. Click on the Temperature_Conversion procedure and set IN_TEMP to 10 and IN_TYPE to C. Click on OK.

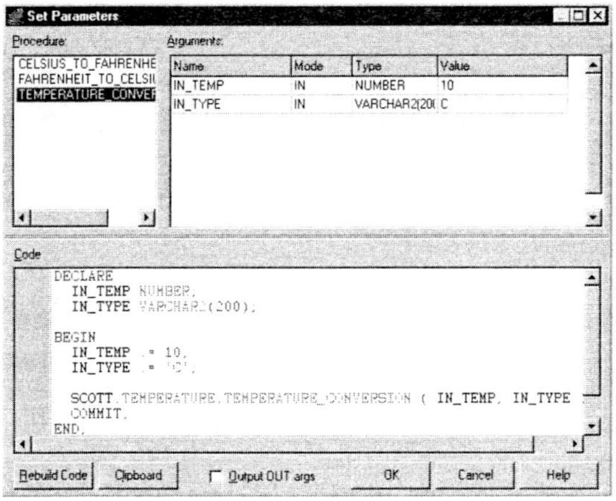

Now set a watch on Converted_Temp. The debugger should have stopped on this first line. You can do this in one of three ways:

- Use the Watches tab line and the '+' button.

- Right-click on the variable name, select the Add Watch button from the toolbar, and then select Debug, Add Watch at Cursor (see Figure 4.51).

- Press Ctrl+F5.

FIGURE 4.50   TOAD runtime parameter input.

Notice in the Watches tab (see Figure 4.52) that it added the variable and that it is NULL. TOAD has not executed this first statement yet, so the variable is not set to 0 yet. Press F7 or click the Trace Into button and watch it change.

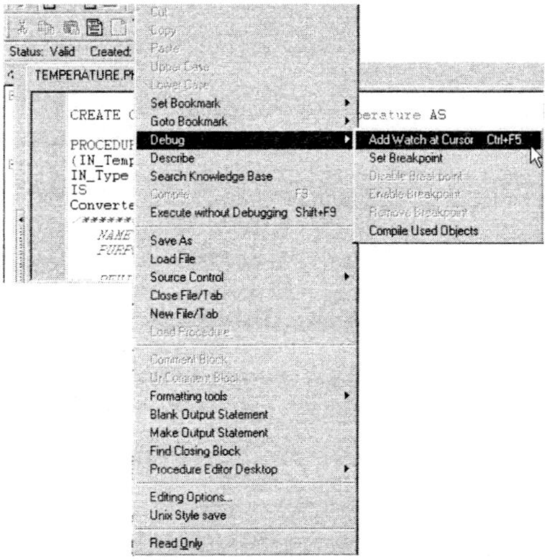

FIGURE 4.51   Setting a watch.

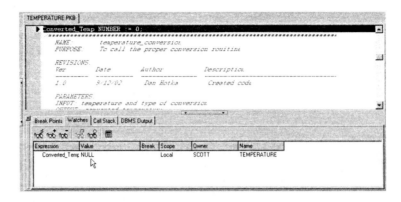

FIGURE 4.52   Watching a variable.

The Halt button will stop execution of the code at any time. You can walk through the code, see the content of variables anywhere they appear, and change the contents of the variables on the fly by selecting the variable in the Watch tab and clicking the Evaluate/Modify button (see Figure 4.53). This enables you to change the contents of a variable right before a critical check or procedure for testing purposes.

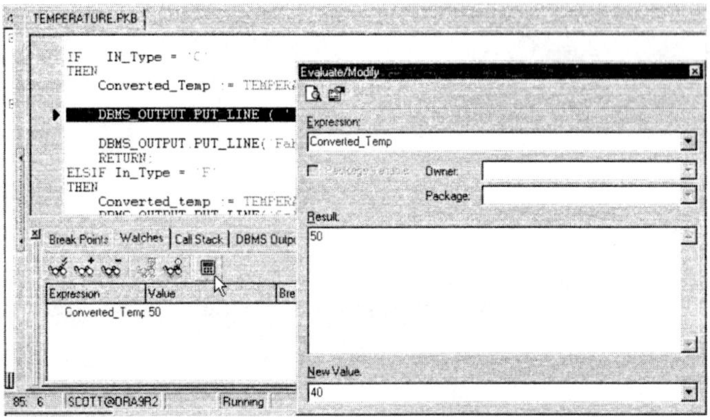

FIGURE 4.53   Changing variable content.

Rather than stepping through code one line at a time, you might want to run a bunch of code and either stop at a designated point (a breakpoint) or where the cursor is in the code. You can use the Run to Cursor button or press F12 to execute the code until it gets to the line with the mouse cursor. You can set a breakpoint in a number of ways (by clicking just to the left of the line where you want the break-point, as shown in Figure 4.54, or by using the Break Points tab with the '+', or by pressing F5). This allows you to execute the code by clicking the Run button or pressing F11, and the debugger will stop when it gets to this line. Later in this chapter, you will learn how to set conditional breakpoints, or the debugger will stop on a line only when certain conditions exist (such as looped ten or more times, and so on). Stopping the code at convenient times is how you evaluate variable content at critical points in the code.

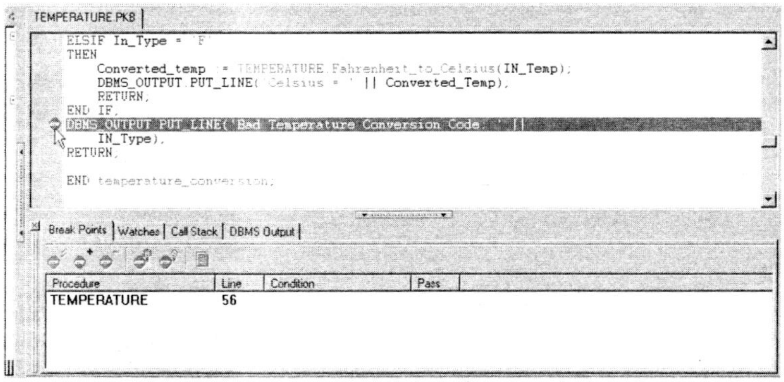

FIGURE 4.54   Setting breakpoints.

Debugging triggers are different from debugging procedures. The INSERT INTO, UPDATE .. SET, and DELETE trigger code is not available to the debugger until the values have been entered.

When debugging something like FOR LOOP_COUNT IN 1..500 LOOP ..., set a watch on the LOOP_COUNT variable and use Evaluate/Modify to change 500 to a much smaller number so that you don't have to loop 500 times to see it exit the routine.

Debugging Breakpoint Options

The previous section showed how to set breakpoints to stop the code at predetermined lines of code. TOAD also allows "conditional" breakpoints.

Figure 4.55 illustrates how to set a breakpoint so that execution stops after 10 times though the loop. Press F11 to execute the procedure. Notice in Figure 4.56 that a watch was placed on the loop_counter variable and that the loop_counter is at 9. This is because the loop is on its tenth iteration and the variable loop_counter (where the breakpoint is set) has not been incremented yet.

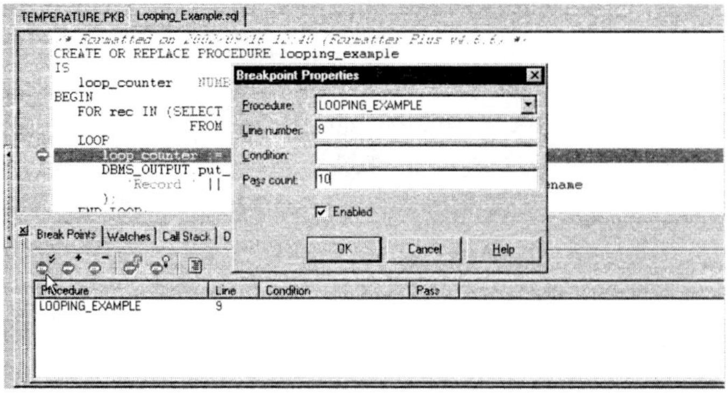

FIGURE 4.55   Setting a conditional breakpoint.

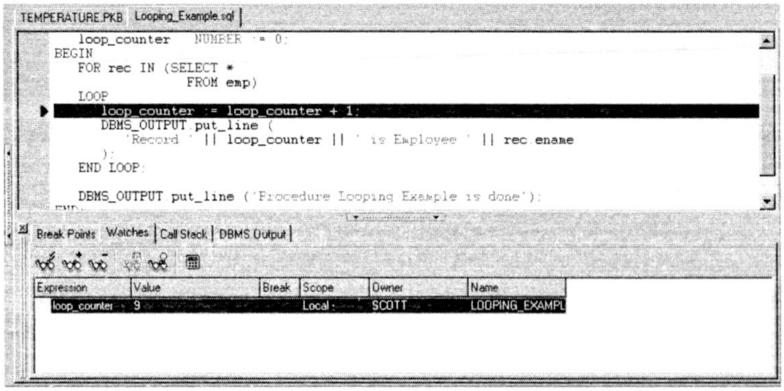

FIGURE 4.56   Conditional breakpoint in action.

Figure 4.57 illustrates how to set a conditional breakpoint on a particular condition such as 'ENAME = SMITH'. When running the procedure, position the mouse over the 'rec.name' on line 11 and you will see that the code did stop executing when the ENAME of SMITH was located. If you check the `loop_counter` variable, you will notice that it is at 0, so SMITH just happens to be the first row returned.

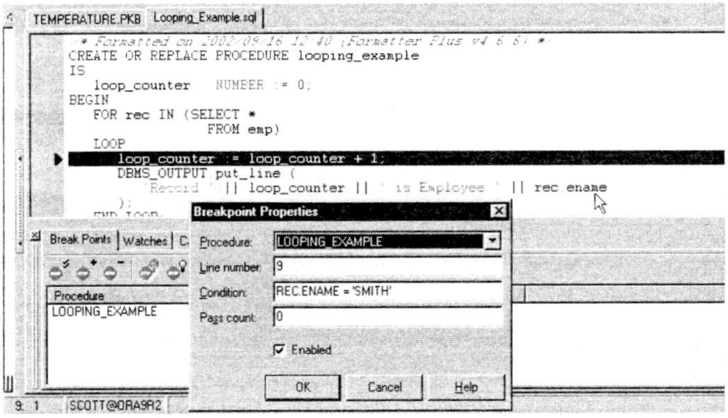

FIGURE 4.57 Conditional breakpoint in action (2).

Advanced Debugging PL/SQL Code

The Call Stack tab is handy to see which routine you are in and at what line number. Notice that Figure 4.58 names the Temperature package twice. This is because at line 44, you entered the Celsius_to_Fahrenheit function (at line 78). This call stack allows you to see the tree structure of called routines based on code execution.

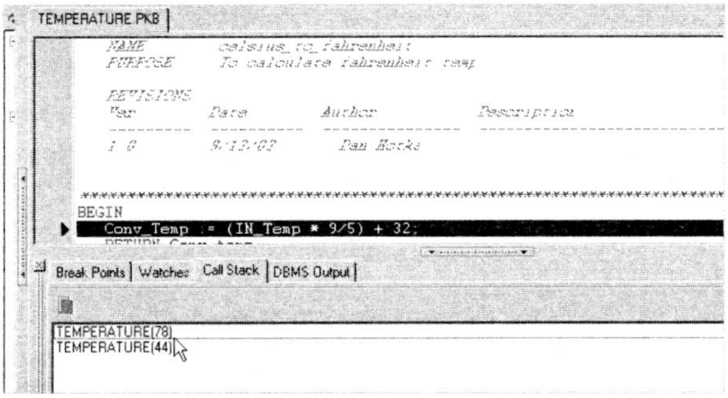

FIGURE 4.58 Call stack information.

TOAD also allows watches to be set on implicit variables and even record types. Notice in Figure 4.59 that a watch placed on the rec implicit variable (implicit variables are not defined other places in the procedure) displays all of the columns in the EMP table for the row for the conditional breakpoint! You can also position the mouse over the rec variable type, and it will display all the current column data as well.

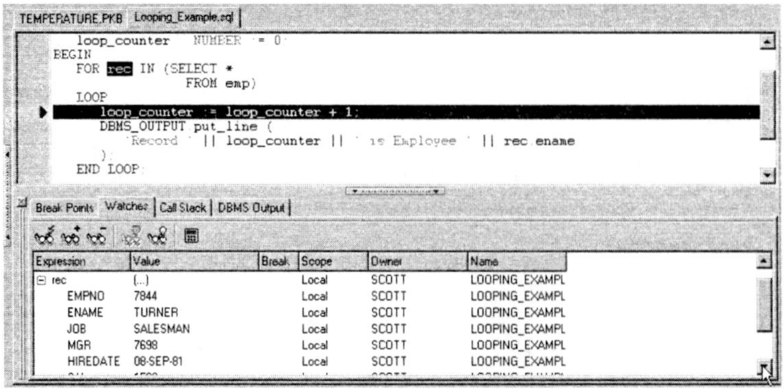

FIGURE 4.59   Implicit variable watch.

Profiling PL/SQL Code

Starting with version 8i, Oracle can track statistics on the execution of SQL, including procedures and functions. TOAD interfaces with the DBMS_PROFILE package, giving you an easy way to track and compare your program statistics.

If the Stop Watch button on the top toolbar, or the PL/SQL Profiling and Profiler Analysis buttons (on the Database menu) are greyed out, run the script *<Oracle Home>*/RDBMS/admin/profload.sql as SYS. You will also then need to run the TOAD script TOADProfiler.sql found in the *<TOAD Home>*/Temps directory. Be sure to exit and restart TOAD.

The Stop Watch button on the top toolbar is a toggle. Turn it on and the Profiler will ask you for a run name after the procedure has completed execution, as illustrated in Figure 4.60.

When you want to see how your code executions compare, select Profiler Analysis from the Database menu (see Figure 4.61), and it will display all kinds of useful information about your code execution as seen in Figure 4.62. Double-clicking on any of the functions in the lower panel will further break down the timings. You can easily see what part of your code is taking the longest to execute, for example. You can easily filter out particular Unit Types and you can change the graphic to a bar chart.

If you are debugging a package or procedure that appears to have performance issues, use the PL/SQL profile to help indicate exactly which called procedure or function has the performance issue.

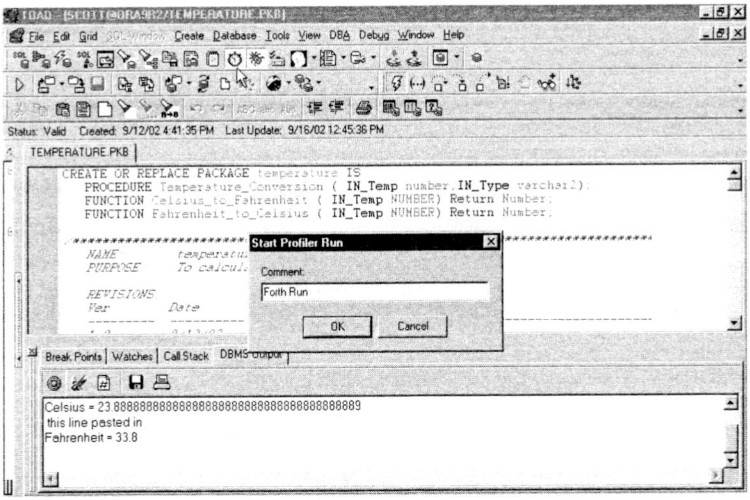

FIGURE 4.60   Oracle Profiler Collection.

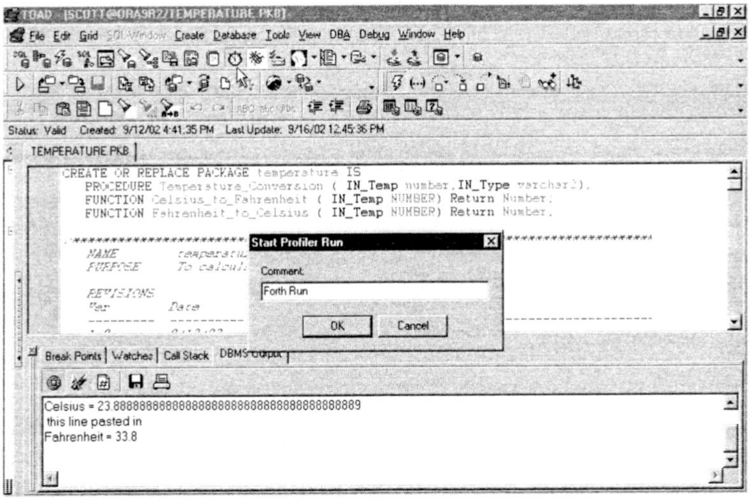

FIGURE 4.61   Accessing profile analysis.

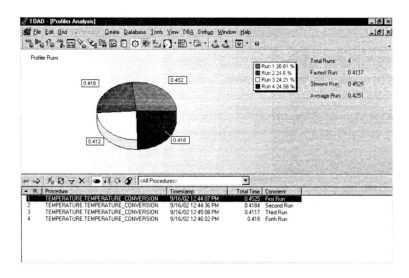

FIGURE 4.62   Profile analysis.

Setting Up Source Control

Source code control allows for a systematic approach to ensure that only one person is making changes to the code at a time. These systems also provide other benefits such as security (only certain people can access certain code), code change tracking, and so on.

TOAD supports many source code control systems. Check the TOADSoft.com site for a complete list of source code control systems supported.

It is easy to set up source code control with TOAD. Make sure your source code control software is installed and working properly. Then go to the Source Control category of the TOAD Options screen and fill in your options as illustrated in Figure 4.63.

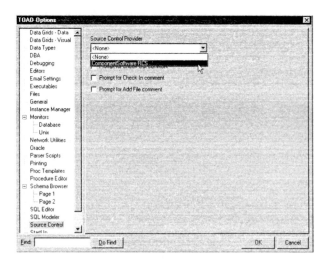

FIGURE 4.63   Source code control setup.

Using Source Control

TOAD allows you to check code into and out of any supported Source Code Control package. Notice in Figure 4.64 that the source code control buttons (Check File Out and Check File In) are not greyed out. Many source code control systems use "projects" to organize code. In this example, pick the project that you would want to associate the code with, and TOAD will then check it in. When checking out code, if someone else has it checked out, the source control package you are using will issue a message that TOAD will display saying who has the code checked out and typically when they checked it out.

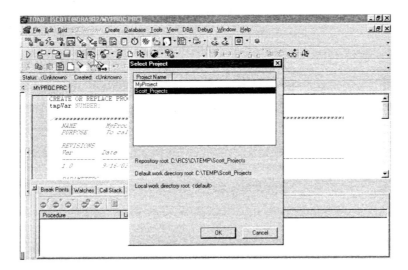

FIGURE 4.64   Source code control in action.

This book does not cover the specifics of using various software programs for source code control.

Summary

This chapter covered using the TOAD Procedure Editor, illustrating most of the features available. This editor in TOAD not only enables you to easily create and work with packages, procedures, triggers, and functions, but gives you the full power of a symbolic debugger as well.

The next chapter dives into newer features of TOAD for the DBA. The developer who has to do occasional DBA administrative functions will find this chapter very useful as well.

5

Using TOAD for Routine DBA Tasks

Although TOAD has historically been known as the Tool for Oracle Application Development, it is nonetheless a robust and capable database administrators' tool—especially with the addition of the optional DBA module. In fact, through informal polls done at TOAD user group meetings, Quest has found that more than 40% of existing TOAD users are in fact DBAs or perform varying levels of DBA tasks. Thus TOAD has indeed become much more than just a SQL and PL/SQL developers' tool. It is now a legitimate DBA tool as well, competing with and often surpassing offerings such as Oracle's Enterprise Manager (OEM) and Embarcadero's DBArtisan.

Regardless of whether your job title includes the three letters DBA, you can and should use TOAD to perform any database administrative tasks that are necessary for your organization. For example, some companies hire database consultants and expect them to do everything, but other shops may have developer and DBA as separate job titles. From TOAD's perspective, it really does not matter. If you need to do any database administrative tasks, TOAD is the tool of choice. Thus any references that follow the term DBA really mean anybody who's doing database administrative tasks, regardless of their actual job title.

TOAD offers its numerous DBA capabilities through various menus and toolbars, which are organized by relative function and in conformance with Windows standards. But in practice, DBAs perform these tasks based upon need and often by scheduled interval. So to cover them based upon their menu or toolbar placement would be counterproductive. Therefore, all the DBA tasks are categorized into two simple groupings: routine and non-routine. This chapter covers those database administrative tasks that are considered routine.

Checking Status of All Your Instances

One of the most important and routine tasks any DBA does is to check the status of their databases. In fact, what they really want to visually and very quickly ascertain is which:

- Servers are down

- Listeners are down

- Instances are down

Of course, you could wait for the phone to ring or your pager to go off. But it is infinitely more desirable to have a compact and focused way to easily verify all this information. So TOAD provides the Instance Manager screen, which is located on the main menu at DBA, Instance Manager and depicted in Figure 5.1.

FIGURE 5.1   TOAD Instance Manager screen.

With this one screen, the DBA can quickly see the status of all their database servers, listeners, and instances. If all is well, the Node, Listener, and Database (that is, database instance) cells in the grid displayed on the Status tab will all contain green check marks. If there are any problems, the cells will contain red X's. While the screen is checking for the first time, the cells will contain a red question mark inside a yellow circle. Of course, the goal is to always see all green check marks, as shown in Figure 5.1, meaning that all is well.

One option on this screen that seems to cause minor confusion is the Polling Priority drop-down list. Contrary to common and incorrect belief, polling priority has absolutely nothing to do with your database server. TOAD performs Instance Manager monitoring by creating a Windows background execution thread on your client PC. This drop-down list merely enables you to assign that thread's execution priority. The valid priorities include idle (will only refresh when no other Windows task is running), lowest, lower, normal, higher, highest, and time-critical. If you intend to keep an Instance Manager screen up at all times, the recommendation is to choose a setting of normal or below (the default is lower).

This screen also offers two other very useful DBA functions. First, you can create an INIT.ORA text file with the actual parameter values currently set for that database instance by using the Build Init.Ora button. This would be very useful if you've modified parameter values that are session-modifiable. And second, you can start up, alter, or shut down a database instance by using the Startup, Shutdown, and Alter buttons. So in essence, you can both monitor and control all your database instances from the Instance Manager screen.

Note that there are many options within TOAD related to using the Instance Manager screen, shown in Figures 5.2, 5.3, and 5.4. The TOAD Options screen can be opened either by using the Toolbox icon on the main toolbar or from the main menu at View, Options.

Figure 5.1 shows the options category for Instance Manager. You can select which servers to poll and also which servers to post alerts for when they are down. Alerts exhibit themselves in one of two ways: by animating the TOAD tray icon and/or through e-mail messages. Did you notice in Figure 5.1 the TOAD tray icon, which appeared in the lower right-hand corner of the screen? When this option is enabled and a database selected for alerts has problems, the TOAD tray icon will animate. Likewise, if the Enable Email Alerts check box is checked, TOAD will e-mail an appropriate alert message. However, for this to work, you must visit the

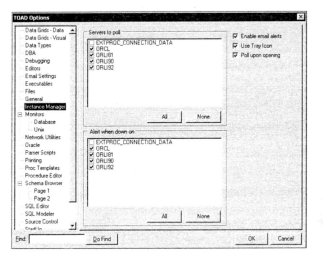

FIGURE 5.2   TOAD General Options for Instance Manager.

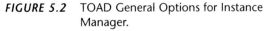

FIGURE 5.3   TOAD Email Settings options for Instance Manager.

options category for Email Settings and define all the appropriate information as depicted in Figure 5.3.

One of the most important and routine tasks any DBA does is to check the status of their databases. So this is most likely one of the first things a DBA would want to do when they start their daily, morning routine. Therefore, wouldn't it be useful if TOAD would automatically open this screen when it launched? You can choose that option in the TOAD Options category for DBA as shown in Figure 5.4. You just need to check the box for Open an Instance Manager at Startup. Now TOAD will automatically launch this window, as well as any others indicated under the options category for Startup.

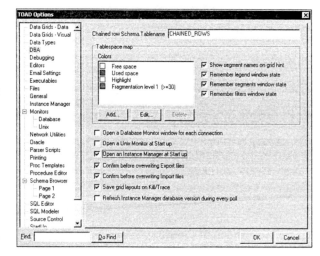

FIGURE 5.4   TOAD Startup Options for Instance Manager.

Notice that in Figure 5.4, the check box for Refresh Instance Manager Database Version During Every Poll is not checked. Because it's very unlikely that your database version will change between refresh intervals, it's entirely unnecessary to perform this additional database operation. You'll notice a definite decrease in the refresh performance if you have more than a few database servers to check and leave this one option turned on. Therefore, the recommendation is to keep it turned off at all times.

Checking an Instance's Alert Log File

Just because the DBA's database servers, listeners, and instances are up does not mean that all is perfectly well. Problems might very well exist that should be addressed. For example, one of the Oracle background processes may have improperly terminated, yet people can still successfully connect to the database. Thus the Instance Manager screen gives the Oracle DBA a fifty-thousand-foot view, for it merely performs simple tests such as `ping` and `tnsping` and connects to the database. So the DBA should dig a bit deeper to be sure that all is really well.

Unfortunately, there is no quick and easy screen within TOAD to perform such detailed checks. Nonetheless, you still can utilize TOAD to find out where that information is and even possibly to access it.

Oracle creates and maintains an alert log file in the background dump destination directory, pointed to by the database instance parameter BACKGROUND_DUMP_DEST. Although you could reference the INIT.ORA file to determine this setting, TOAD offers at least three other ways to easily discover the same information:

- Inspect data for the Oracle Parameters window, opened from the main menu at DBA, Oracle Parameters and depicted in Figure 5.5.

- Perform a SELECT against table V$PARAMETER in a TOAD SQL Editor window.

- Inspect the data for view SYS.V_$PARAMETER by using a TOAD Schema Browser window.

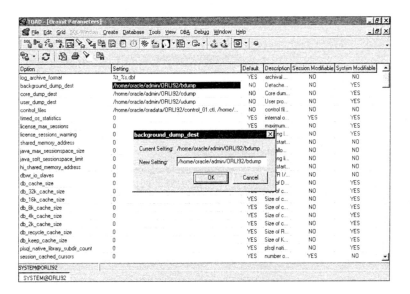

FIGURE 5.5   TOAD Oracle Parameters screen.

After you have the information for where the alert log file is located, it depends on your database server's operating system as to what you do next. For Windows-based Oracle database servers, you can simply use Windows Explorer and Notepad to locate and examine the file (assuming that you can either map the network drive or log in to the proper Windows database server). For UNIX-based Oracle database servers, you should use TOAD's telnet interface on the Network Utilities screen, located on the main menu at File, Network Utilities.

Figure 5.6 shows an example of logging into a Linux database server and examining the alert log file using the `tail` command. As you can see, there are no hidden or otherwise unobserved database errors. Of course, the smart DBA would probably do a more sophisticated command with a larger portion of the log file, such as `tail -100 alert.log | grep ORA-`.

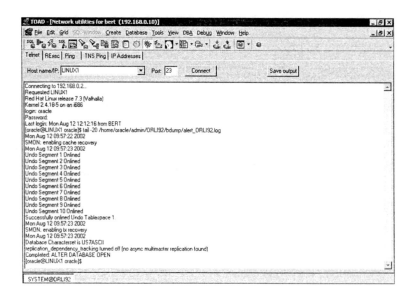

FIGURE 5.6   Checking the alert log file using TOAD's telnet.

Examining Tablespace Usage and Projections

Probably the least disputed purely DBA job function is database space management, meaning the creation, monitoring, and overall administration of tablespaces and their associated data files. Even "do it all" consultants and senior developers who perform DBA tasks prefer to leave space management to someone else. One reason is that space has a tendency to reach some threshold or limit during normal sleeping hours, when batch jobs execute and pagers going off irritate spouses the most. Welcome to the world of production support!

Thus many DBAs performing database space management generally attempt to fulfill two goals. First, to avoid short-term space issues such as failure to allocate an extent for any permanent or temporary database object. And second, to possess sufficient disk space available for both short-term and mid-term database needs. It's this second objective that poses the greatest challenge, as anyone can pre-allocate all the storage in order to avoid "unable to allocate extent" messages. But it takes careful planning and attention to growth patterns in order to avoid running out of disk space before new disks arrive (or are even ordered).

Monitoring Tablespaces

TOAD offers two primary interfaces for space management: one for overall monitoring and another for administrative needs. Figure 5.7 shows the Tablespaces screen, which is used for overall monitoring and is located off the main menu at DBA, Tablespaces.

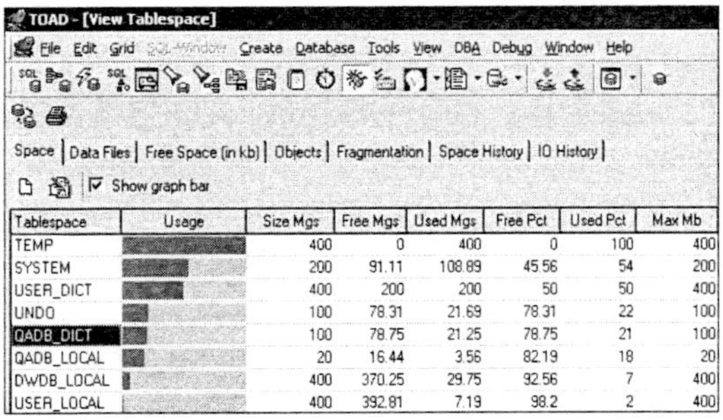

Note that the Tablespaces screen provides a single interface for viewing all your tablespace information at once. Note that each tab displays different detailed information across all the tablespaces in the database. However, it's the Space tab, shown in Figure 5.7, which is the most eye-appealing. It's the only place in TOAD where you can graphically view space usage across all your tablespaces at once.

FIGURE 5.7   TOAD Tablespaces screen.

Of special interest are the last two tabs on the Tablespaces screen: Space History and IO History. These tabs permit you to graphically display space and IO usage over time, assuming that this historical information is being collected. This is exactly that second and more critical space monitoring and planning step discussed earlier. Figure 5.8 shows the Space History tab.

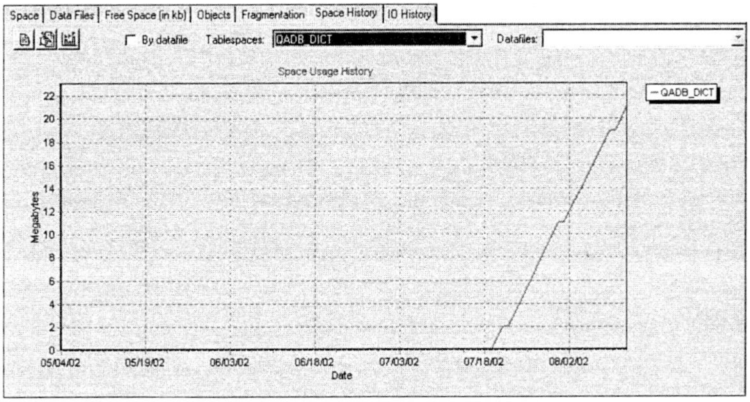

FIGURE 5.8   TOAD Space History tab.

Note in Figure 5.8 that the QA database's dictionary-managed tablespace has grown very rapidly over the past month. Although it's only 22 megabytes now, it has grown from nothing to this size in less than a month. Look at the slope of the line. This tablespace is worth careful monitoring. But how big will it be next month, or better yet over the next three months? TOAD can predict this for you using sound statistical methods (assuming that you have sufficient history for TOAD to make an accurate projection). The rightmost icon in the upper left corner, which looks like a bar chart, will launch TOAD's Database/Tablespace Forecasting screen. Here you merely enter how far out to project and TOAD does the rest. Figure 5.9 shows that our QA database's dictionary-managed tablespace from Figure 5.8 will grow to nearly 105 megabytes over the next three months.

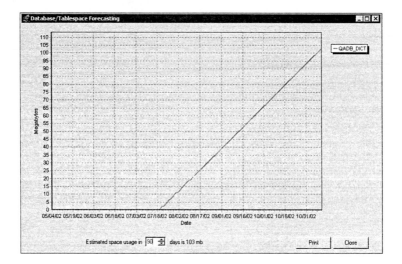

FIGURE 5.9   TOAD Database/Tablespace Forecasting screen.

When you open the Tablespaces screen, TOAD verifies whether your TOAD schema contains the necessary repository tables and data collection package, and whether it has been scheduled by using DBMS_JOBS. If the check fails and you are not connected as the TOAD user, you will see a warning that you must create these objects while connected as the TOAD user. But if the check fails and you are connected as the TOAD user, you will enter the Space Manager Setup screen, shown in Figure 5.10, to define and create all the required components (which you also can do manually when on either of these last two tabs by clicking the very first icon in the upper-left corner of the Tablespaces screen).

You have three very simple selections to make on this screen. First, how often should TOAD collect the information? Second, how long should TOAD keep that information? And third, should TOAD start with empty tables (that is, with no history) or should it try to project some data backwards? The recommendation is to collect data every day (preferably just after a typical batch cycle), keep at least a year's worth of data (for more accurate projections), and to start with empty tables (no need for fake data being backfilled; it would just skew any short-term projections until sufficient history is collected).

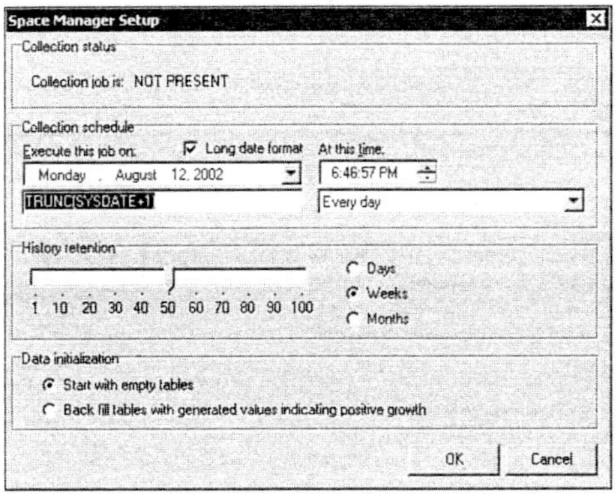

FIGURE 5.10   TOAD Space Manager Setup screen.

Managing Tablespaces

TOAD's other primary interface for space management, which addresses more administrative needs, is the Schema Browser's Tablespaces tab, shown in Figure 5.11. The Schema Browser is launched by either selecting its icon on the main toolbar (second icon from the top left by default) or from the main menu at Database, Schema Browser. In fact, for many DBAs the Schema Browser may actually be their default initial screen, as defined in the TOAD Options for Startup.

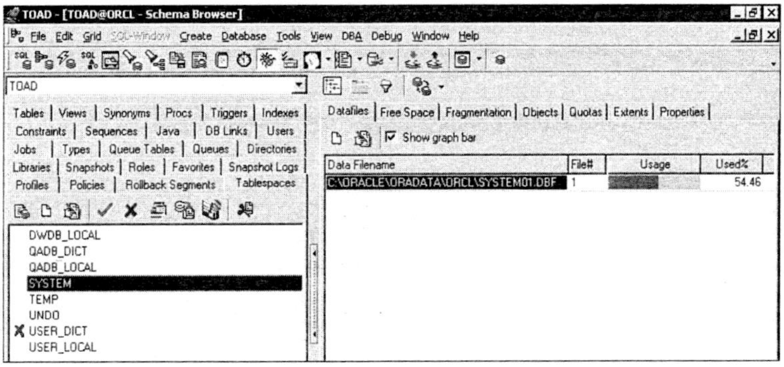

FIGURE 5.11   TOAD Schema Browser Tablespaces tab.

The Schema Browser's Tablespaces tab provides much of the same detailed information about tablespaces and their data files as does the Tablespaces screen discussed in the preceding section, but more importantly, it provides numerous features for managing these resources as well. The left-hand side (LHS) of the Schema Browser's Tablespaces tab provides toolbar icons for the most common tablespace administrative tasks:

- Create Script, which copies the selected tablespace's DDL to the Window's clipboard.

- Create New Tablespace, which launches a modal window for creating a new tablespace.

- Alter Tablespace, which launches a modal window for altering an existing tablespace.

- Place Online, which alters the selected tablespaces to the online status.

- Take Offline, which alters the selected tablespaces to the offline status and displays a red X next to the LHS display as shown in Figure 5.11 for the USER_DICT tablespace.

- Show Tablespace Map, which launches the Tablespace Map screen for the selected tablespace (this screen is found on the main menu at DBA, Tablespace Map and is covered later in this chapter in the section "Checking the Level of Tablespace Fragmentation").

- Export Tablespace Using Export Wizard, which launches the Export Utility Wizard (this wizard is found on the main menu at DBA, Export Utility Wizard).

- Coalesce Tablespace, which coalesces the selected tablespaces in order to reduce fragmentation.

- Drop Tablespace, which drops the selected tablespaces and their associated data files (where possible depending upon the Oracle version).

Moreover, the right-hand side (RHS) of the Schema Browser's Tablespaces tab provides toolbar icons for the Datafiles, Fragmentation, and Quotas tabs. The Datafiles tab toolbar icons are probably the most useful, and include:

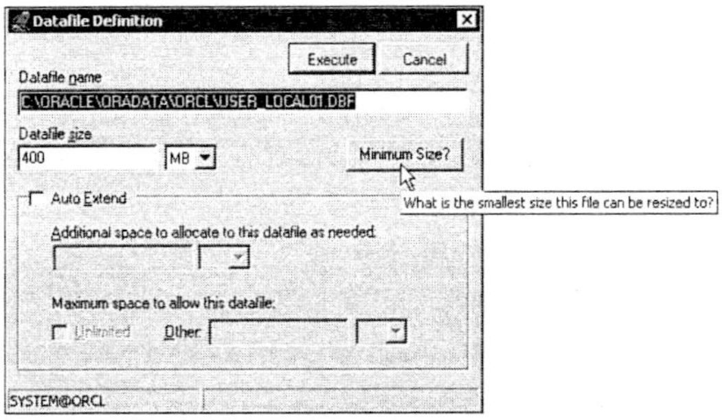

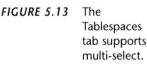

- Add Data File, which launches a modal window for creating a new data file.

FIGURE 5.12   TOAD Datafile Definition window, for size estimation.

- Alter Data File, which launches a modal window for altering an existing data file—and includes a handy utility for calculating the minimum size the data file can be resized down to, shown in Figure 5.12.

However, arguably the most useful aspect of the Schema Browser's Tablespaces tab is the multi-select capability, which enables you to select one or more tablespaces upon which to perform an administrative operation. For example, Figure 5.13 shows just how simple it now is to coalesce all the tablespaces in the entire database at once. You merely need to multi-select the desired tablespaces, right-click to activate the context menu, and then pick an operation. That's all there is to it.

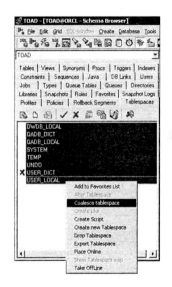

FIGURE 5.13   The Tablespaces tab supports multi-select.

Checking Tablespaces for Free Space Deficits

Another space management task that many DBAs routinely perform is to check which tablespaces contain objects whose next extent allocation request would exceed the current available contiguous free space. In other words, it checks which tablespaces are candidates for the infamous "unable to allocate extent" error message. The idea is to locate those tablespaces and allocate more space in order to avoid any such messages. For just this purpose, TOAD has the Identify Space Deficits screen shown in Figure 5.14, which is located on the main menu at DBA, Identify Space Deficits.

So what exactly is the screen in Figure 5.14 pointing out? The USER_DICT tablespace contains four tables and three indexes, each of whose next extent allocation request size is larger than the tablespace's currently available free space. Let's assume that only the CITY table is likely to grow over time (that is, both STATE and COUNTRY tables are static and JUNK is only temporary). The space management problem is actu-

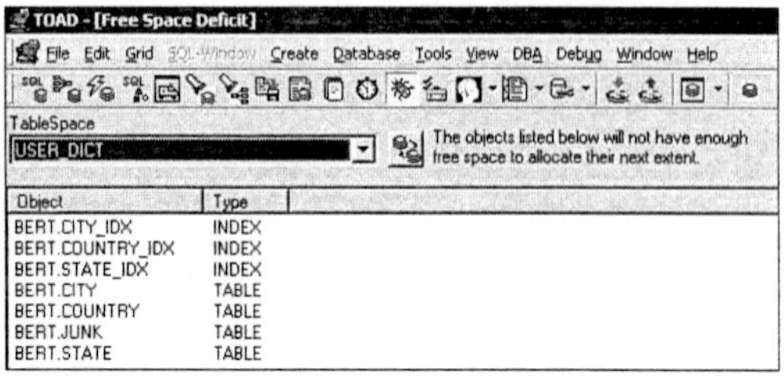

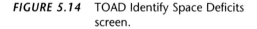

FIGURE 5.14   TOAD Identify Space Deficits screen.

ally twice as bad as you may initially suspect. If the CITY table now adds rows that require an extent allocation, it's also quite likely that the CITY_IDX index will grow as well and thus also need more space. The point is that although this screen identifies space management problem areas, it does not really indicate just how big a problem you may have. So you should carefully review this screen's output before acting (that is, altering the tablespace to add a data file, increasing the size of a data file, or making a data file auto incremental in terms of its file size based upon need).

Reviewing Schema Object Extent Allocations

A routine task that some DBAs perform is monitoring schema object extent allocations. However, today this task has become somewhat less important than it has been historically. With the great reduction in disk costs during this past decade, database sizes have increased greatly. Today, a 100GB database is not uncommon or considered especially large. And today's data warehouses are often tens to hundreds of terabytes in size. Add to that locally managed tablespaces with the option for uniform extent sizes, and extent counts become much less of a hot issue. So tables and indexes with hundreds, thousands, or even tens of thousands of extents may well be a non-issue for some databases.

TOAD provides two ways to review object extent allocations. The quickest and easiest way to monitor extents is by using the Schema Browser's Tablespaces tab and using the Extents tab on the right-hand side, shown in Figure 5.15. The Schema Browser is launched by either selecting its icon on the main toolbar (second icon from the top left by default) or from the main menu at Database, Schema Browser. Remember that the Schema Browser may actually be the default initial screen, as defined in the TOAD Options for Startup.

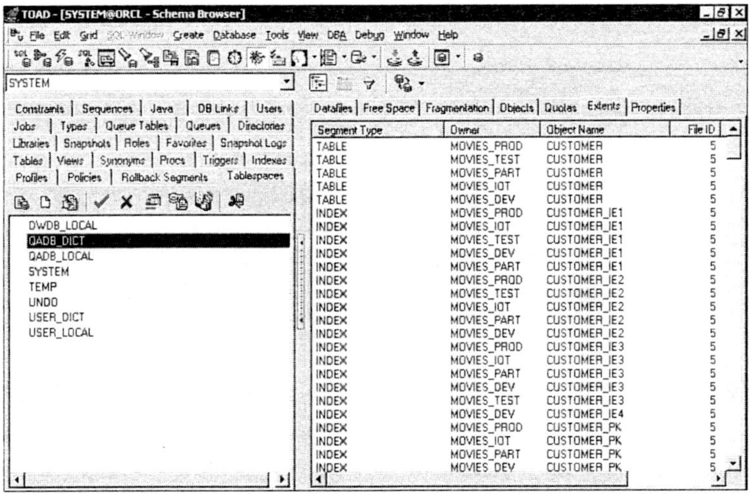

FIGURE 5.15   TOAD Schema Browser Tablespace tab for viewing extents.

However, this interface does not provide any capabilities other than column sorting. Plus, the query to populate the data grid in this tab can take a very long time to run. So what if you wanted to look across all tablespaces and filter the results based upon the object type or owner? You cannot do so by using this interface. You would need to use TOAD's View Extents screen shown in Figure 5.16, which is located on the main menu at DBA, Extents. Also note that this screen offers a Print Extents Report button for a hardcopy report of the results. With all these additional capabilities, the View Extents screen is the recommended method for reviewing object extent allocations.

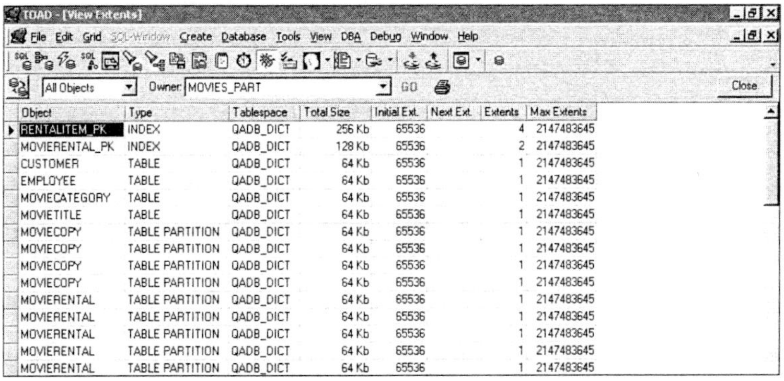

FIGURE 5.16   TOAD View Extents screen.

Checking the Level of Tablespace Fragmentation

A routine task many DBAs perform is monitoring tablespace fragmentation. But ask DBAs what they mean by tablespace fragmentation, and you'll most likely get at least several different answers. The reason is twofold. First, there is both confusion and disagreement on what the general term means. And second, there are several kinds of Oracle database fragmentation often referred to when referencing the general term. A quick review of the Oracle fragmentation terminology follows:

- Tablespace Free space Fragmentation (TFF) occurs when a tablespace contains more than one extent of free space.

- Segment Fragmentation (SF) occurs when a segment is so large as to consume multiple extents.

- Data Block Fragmentation (DBF) occurs when rows are deleted from data blocks and leave holes of unused space.

- Index Leaf Block Fragmentation occurs when rows are deleted, thus creating partially or completely empty leaf blocks in the index B-tree.

- Row Fragmentation (RF) or chaining occurs when an update increases a row length such that it cannot fit in its current data block and must migrate to a new data block that has sufficient room for the entire row.

TOAD offers screens for examining tablespace free space and segment fragmentation, which will be covered next. TOAD doesn't offer anything for Data Block Fragmentation, and TOAD's offerings for both Index Leaf Block Fragmentation and Row Fragmentation are covered in the next chapter.

For viewing Tablespace Free space Fragmentation (TFF), you should use the TOAD Schema Browser's Tablespaces tab and look at the Fragmentation tab on the right-hand side of the window, shown in Figure 5.17. The Schema Browser is launched by either selecting its icon on the main toolbar (second icon from the top left by default) or from the main menu at Database, Schema Browser. Remember that the Schema Browser may actually be the default initial screen, as defined in the TOAD Options for Startup.

Note that the screen in Figure 5.17 breaks this information down into nice, digestible pieces. It shows that there are two free space extents over 100 megabytes and six of them from 1 and 10 megabytes. Of course, one of those free space extents that's over 100 megabytes is probably our free space extent above the high water mark (for example, never been utilized yet). Naturally this free space information is provided by data file, because new extent allocations cannot span across them.

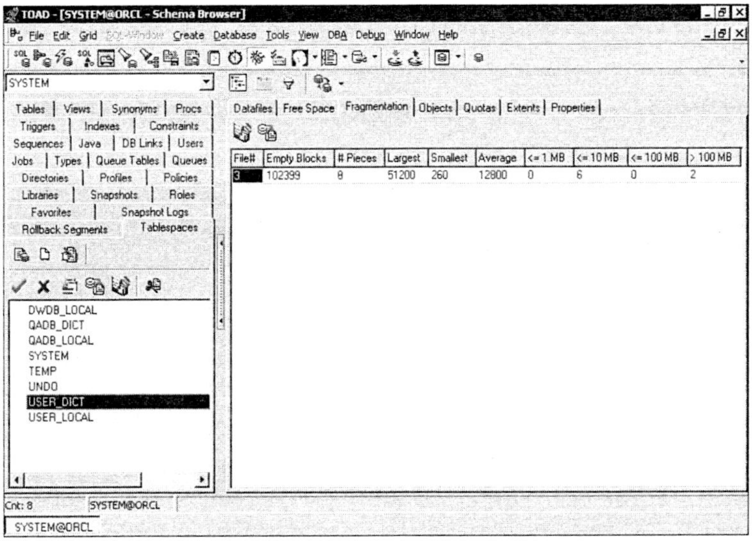

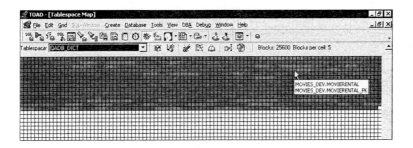

FIGURE 5.17   TOAD Schema Browser Tablespace tab for viewing TFF.

For viewing Segment Fragmentation by tablespace, you should use the TOAD Tablespace Map screen, which is located on the main menu at DBA, Tablespace Map and shown in Figure 5.18. The basic formula used to calculate the map's coloring scheme is:

- 100 - ROUND((SUM OF the BLOCKS FOR that SEGMENT - LARGEST BLOCK IN that SEGMENT) / SUM OF the BLOCK FOR that SEGMENT * 100))

FIGURE 5.18   TOAD Tablespace Fragmentation Map.

Note that as you hover your mouse over cells in the map, it displays which segments consume data blocks represented by that cell. In Figure 5.18, the map shows that a table and its primary key share data blocks in that cell. But that cell might represent hundreds of actual data blocks if this were a large tablespace. Thus they may not overlap at all. Of course, having a table and its indexes in the same tablespace is a bad idea (although not with regard to fragmentation, but for spreading IO to avoid hot disks). So keep in mind that red cells really represent segments that consume a high percentage of blocks for their overall size. Thus they are candidates for object rebuilds (a topic covered in the next chapter).

Note that the Tablespace Fragmentation Map screen offers some very useful capabilities through its toolbar icons. You can coalesce the selected tablespace, display a graphical legend, display a pop-up window for showing the pointed-to cell's segments (rather than relying on the bubble help format shown in Figure 5.18), and display a pop-up window for filtering the displayed segments by data file, object type, owner, and object. So look at Figure 5.19 where these last three options have been turned on. Notice that some of the cells are now shown in yellow. These represent cells containing the data blocks for the filter selection of the index MOVIES_PROD.MOVIERENTAL_PK. Note too that the Filters window has a toolbar icon for Rebuild Table/Index, which allows rebuilding those objects that the connected schema owns.

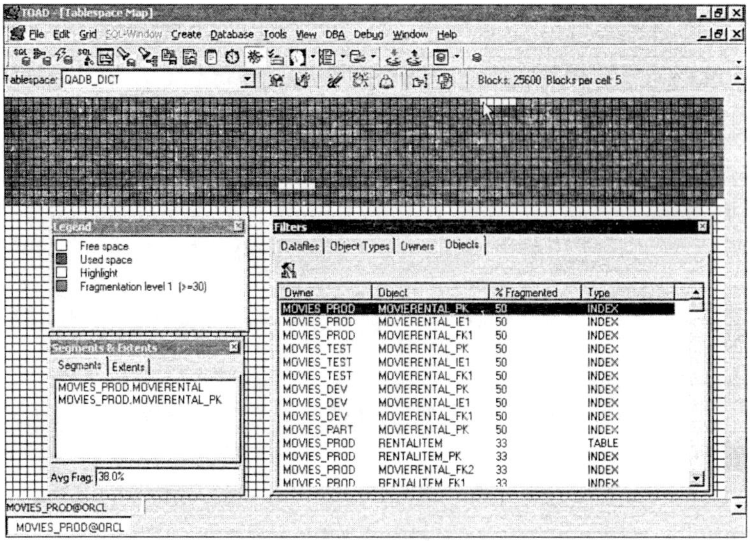

FIGURE 5.19   TOAD Tablespace Fragmentation Map pop-up windows.

Finally, note that there are a few options within TOAD related to using the Tablespace Map screen, depicted in Figure 5.20. The TOAD Options screen can be opened either by using the Toolbox icon on the main toolbar or from the main menu at View, Options. Probably the most useful feature is the ability to define new threshold percentages and colors for highlighting on the tablespace map.

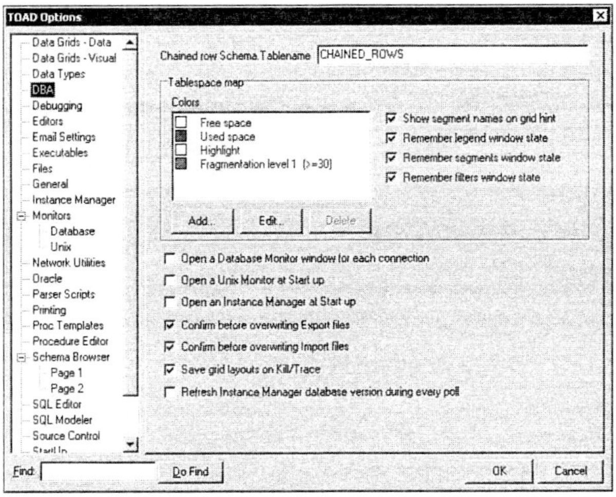

FIGURE 5.20   TOAD Tablespace Fragmentation Map options.

Checking the Overall Health of a Database

Probably the most important and routine task that any DBA could do is to check on the relative health of their databases. What they want is a one-stop shop report that details exceptions to normal thresholds. In short, they want to click a button and see simple output of only those things that require their attention. Moreover, many DBAs would also like to automate such exception reporting. They would like to receive such reports automatically every morning by e-mail, so that they can start their day with a cup of coffee and a clean review of all their databases' health.

TOAD offers this capability through its Database Health Check screen, shown in Figure 5.21 and launched from the main menu at DBA, Health Check. Keen observers will notice that the Database Health Check offers many features either similar to or the same as some of the screens covered in this chapter. That is correct. In fact, this utility is so valuable that many DBAs now use the Database Health Check in lieu of these other screens. You'll have to judge for yourself whether to use one or the other—or possibly both.

The Database Health Check screen enables users to run such an exception report for one or more databases and up to 41 health check options. Some of these options are checked by default and others are not, and some offer users the ability to customize the threshold value. For example, option #9 would find tables with more than six indexes. You can change that value merely by clicking the Adjust text next to its check box, which then launches a pop-up window for customizing the threshold value. After you've selected your databases, options, and thresholds, you merely click the Generate Report toolbar icon and then view the output on the Report Output tab.

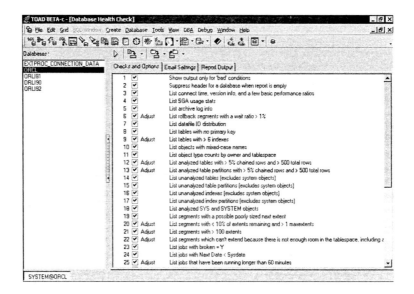

FIGURE 5.21   TOAD Database Health Check screen.

Note that running this report creates a background thread to run the report so that you can continue to work within TOAD. So you will see a message that the report is running, and the output will scroll by in the Report Output tab while the report runs. You can cancel the report by simply clicking the Cancel button, which will only display on the screen's toolbar when reports are running. Also note that the Database Health Check creates new and separate database connections rather than using the current TOAD connections. So you will see these additional connections and their associated Oracle processes when monitoring your database server.

To receive the Database Health Check Report Output results by e-mail is a simple, two-step process. First you must select the Email Settings tab in the Database Health Check screen and select when the message should be sent and in what format, as shown in Figure 5.22. The recommendation is to

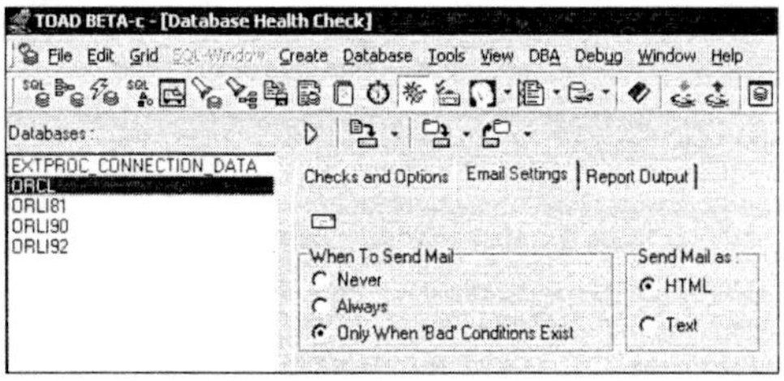

FIGURE 5.22   TOAD Database Health Check Email Settings.

choose Only When 'Bad'
Conditions Exist (that is,
true exception reporting)
and to send the output as
HTML. The reason for
HTML is because TOAD
highlights and color-codes
the output in a manner
conducive to easy reading
and focusing on key prob-
lems. Second, and only if
the When To Send Email
option is enabled, you must
visit the TOAD Options
category for Email Settings
and define all the appropriate information as depicted
in Figure 5.23. Remember
that the TOAD Options

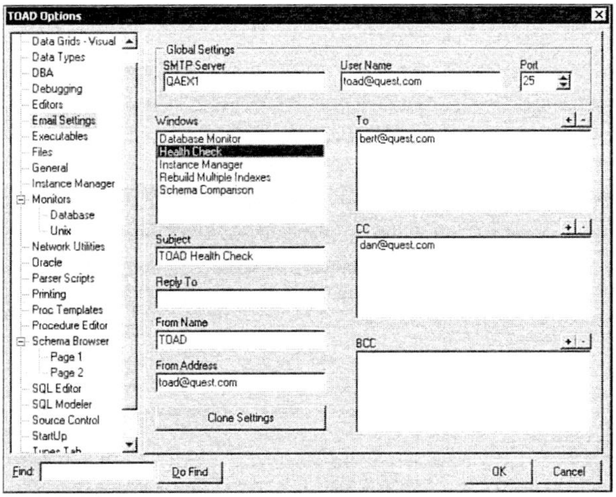

FIGURE 5.23   TOAD E-Mail Options for Database
Health.

screen can be opened either by using the Toolbox icon on the main toolbar or from
the main menu at View, Options.

The ideal scenario would be to have this report ready and waiting for you each
morning in your e-mail inbox. That way you could start your day by quickly checking the exception status of all your databases (of course, no e-mails would mean no
exceptions). To accomplish this, you must schedule this report to run on your
Windows machine by using the Microsoft Task Scheduler as shown in Figure 5.24.
For Windows 2000, this is located at Start, Settings, Control Panel, Scheduled Tasks,
Add Scheduled Task.

Note that you're simply scheduling Windows on your PC to run TOAD in command-
line mode, where you provide the connection information and a health check (HC)
command text file. To produce that file is very simple. You merely need to open the
Health Check screen, make all your selections, and then choose Save Options to File
under the Save Settings to File drop-down toolbar icon. The generated file will
contain everything necessary to start TOAD, connect to the database, and then run
this screen. The generated command file will also contain comments on some
commands you can add to tailor its behavior (for example, to close the screen and
also shut down when the report is complete).

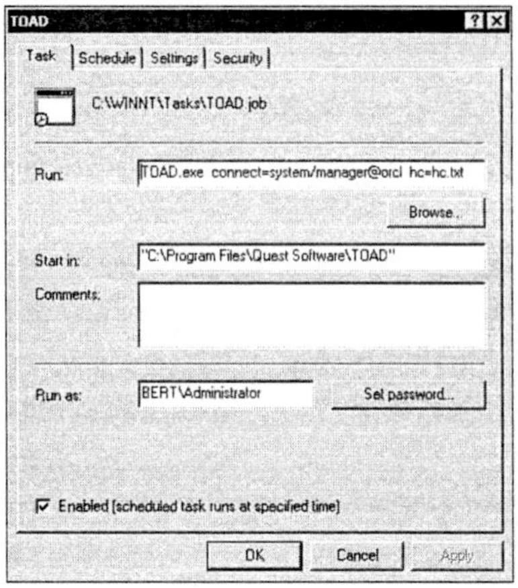

FIGURE 5.24   Windows Scheduling of TOAD Health Check report.

Monitoring SQL Currently in the Shared Pool

Another task many DBAs have to perform is sampling the SQL code being executed by the database for code review and potential tuning. Why would the DBA need a screen to do this? Why couldn't they just look at the code itself? If the end-users are doing ad-hoc queries or using tools that construct the SQL code on the fly, the DBA may have no real source code to inspect. This is becoming much more common with the plethora of SQL database end-user and developer tools now available. Thus the DBA often must peruse the SGA in order to see what's being done.

TOAD offers a screen perfectly tailored for this task, the SGA Trace/Optimization screen, shown in Figure 5.25 and located on the main menu at Tools, SGA Trace/Optimization. The top half of the screen shows the SQL statements in the SGA, although the bottom half shows the complete statement, its execution statistics, and its explain plan. Note that this screen offers drop-down boxes to restrict by SQL statement type and by the user executing (in Figure 5.25 only SELECT statements for the user MOVIES_PROD are shown). Moreover, the DBA is free to add additional, optional search constraints for requiring either a minimum number of executions or only SQL statements containing certain text.

After you locate SQL statements of interest, you can click the SQL toolbar icon to load that SQL into TOAD's SQL Editor. Now you can utilize TOAD's numerous coding and tuning features to optimize that code. And if you're having trouble locating the SQL code of interest due to the very large number of statements being held in the SGA, you can click the Flush the SGA button to clear the statements.

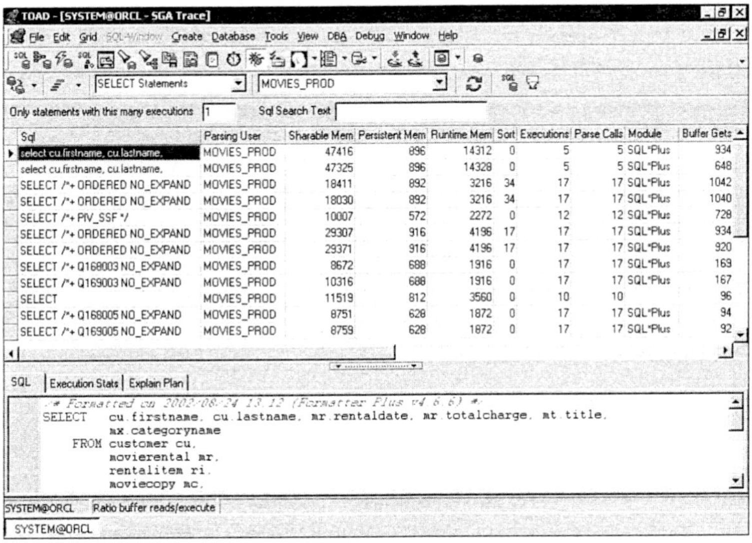

FIGURE 5.25   TOAD SGA Trace/Optimization screen.

Determining Resource-Intensive Sessions

No matter how hard the DBA tries, bad database performance can happen. A user walks into your cubicle looking for help because suddenly and without cause, database performance came to a grinding halt. Users always claim that no one changed anything or issued a questionable query.

Fortunately TOAD has a screen for finding out just exactly why database performance has tanked—it's the Top Session Finder screen, shown in Figure 5.26 and located on the main menu at DBA, Top Session Finder. This screen helps the DBA find those sessions that are consuming excessive database resources. And though TOAD ships with 11 predefined resource profiles to use as your search criteria, you may create custom profiles as well. In Figure 5.26, the search criteria shown was for all those sessions making heavy database sort usage.

When defining your own profiles, you can select either a single parameter or multiple parameters (controlled by this screen's options and accessed by using this screen's toolbar icon for options). When you select multiple parameters as in Figure 5.26, you can assign relative weights for each parameter. The screen will then sort the obtained results by the weighted sum. So in Figure 5.26 the disk sorts are 100 times more important than memory sorts, and thus should sort higher in the results so as to be more visible. It takes a little effort to get used to thinking this way, but this capability makes the screen very powerful and quite useful.

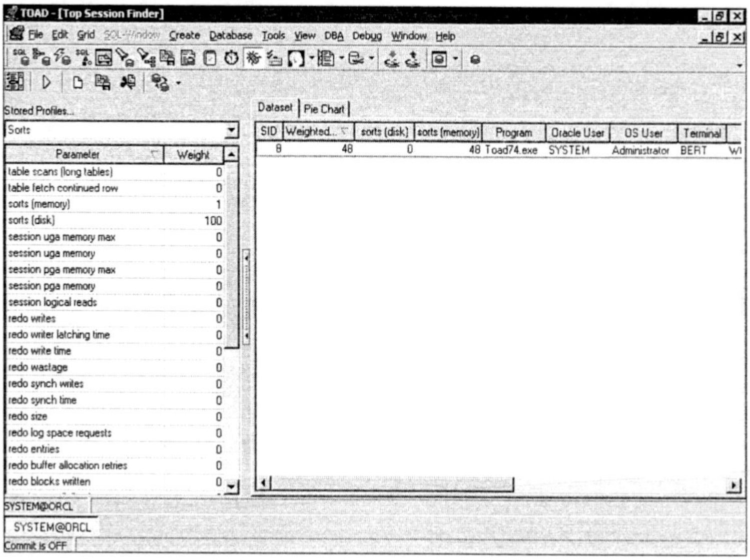

FIGURE 5.26   TOAD Top Session Finder screen.

Monitoring and Killing User Sessions

The Oracle process model is very complex and prone to problems. In the client/server world, process disconnects between client and server processes can leave Oracle in a questionable state. These disconnects can occur for many reasons, including network problems, abnormal client program terminations, client operating system crashes, client operating system reboots, and a host of other reasons. And although Oracle's SMON and PMON background server processes are supposed to detect and handle all of these situations, often database sessions and resources can reach a problem state when these server processes fail to detect and address such conditions. So the DBA must become involved.

But these connectivity issues are not the only kind of Oracle process problems that can occur. Sessions may issue statements that compete for resources, such as temporary space, rollback segments, or data file space. Moreover, sessions may also have statements that compete for access to the same rows of data. And in the worst-case scenario, this competition may cause a deadly embrace or deadlock. Again, Oracle is supposed to automatically handle or resolve many of these issues as well. And once again, the reality is that often the DBA must step in to assist Oracle.

When dealing with such session-related issues, probably the most utilized, practical, and indispensable feature within TOAD is the Kill/Trace Session screen, shown in

Figure 5.27 and located on the main menu at DBA, Kill/Trace Session. This do-it-all screen is the central console from which to see or do anything related to sessions. Not only can you see all the sessions, their SQL statements, cursors, explain plans, and DML progress as shown in Figure 5.27, but you can see the database locks, blocking locks (shown in Figure 5.28), database objects being accessed, and all activity related to rollback segment usage (shown in Figure 5.29). This one screen truly shows it all.

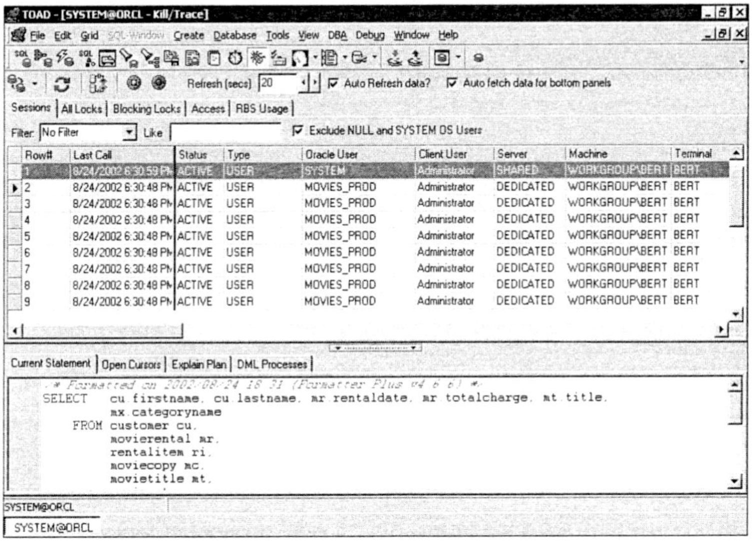

FIGURE 5.27   TOAD Kill/Trace Session screen.

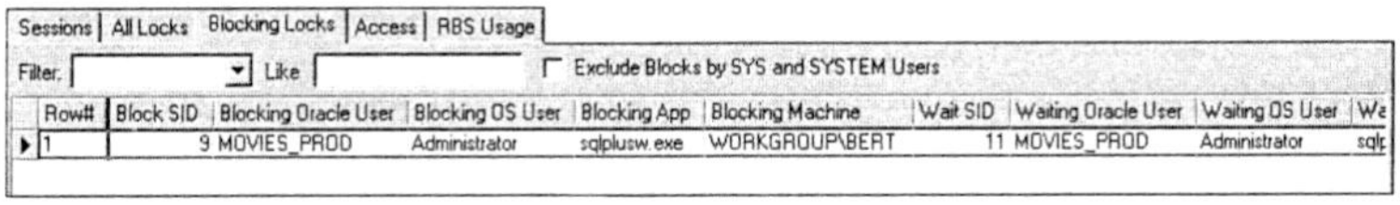

FIGURE 5.28   TOAD Database Blocking Locks.

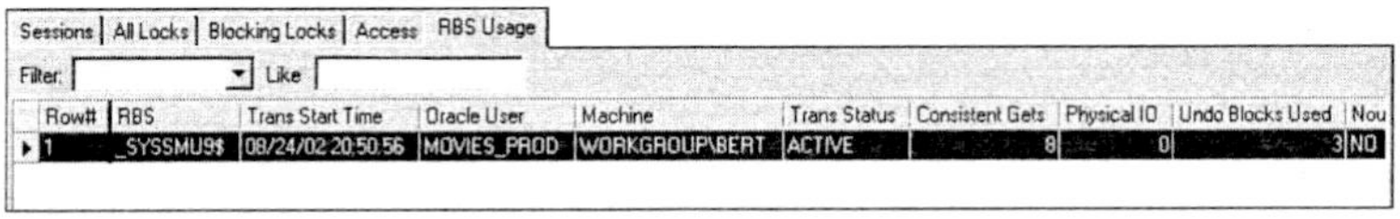

FIGURE 5.29   TOAD Rollback Segment Usage.

Of course, the Kill/Trace Session screen provides much more capability than to simply view all this detailed session data. The screen's toolbar icons enable you to start or stop a trace file for a session and to kill a session. The trace files are critical when either working with Oracle support to debug RDBMS problems, using TOAD's PL/SQL Profiler, or using TOAD's TKPROF interface. And killing a session is often necessary to circumvent the problems encountered with Oracle processes.

> The command TOAD issues to kill the process is of the form:
> ALTER SYSTEM DISCONNECT SESSION 'SID#, SERIAL#' IMMEDIATE

Note that killing Oracle server processes in this manner is not guaranteed to always work instantaneously. Sometimes Oracle will kill the server process immediately so that the operating system's command to see the process (for example, the ps command on UNIX) will show it as killed right away. Sometimes Oracle may internally mark the process as deleted, but yet not actually kill the OS process until much later. In fact, Oracle support documents that this can take hours depending on what the process was doing and which requires being rolled back. This is not a TOAD problem, but an Oracle process behavior beyond TOAD's control. Thus it's not unusual for people to kill the processes by OS commands instead of through Oracle. For manually killing processes on UNIX, you should use TOAD's telnet interface on the Network Utilities screen, located on the main menu at File, Network Utilities.

Remember that an important and routine task any DBA does is to monitor and kill sessions. So this is most likely one of the first things a DBA would want to do when they start their daily, morning routine and throughout the work day. Therefore, wouldn't it be useful if TOAD would automatically open this screen when it launched? It can do so if you use the TOAD Options category for Startup as shown in Figure 5.30. You just need to check the box for Kill/Trace Within Startup Windows Per Connection. Now TOAD will automatically launch this window at startup.

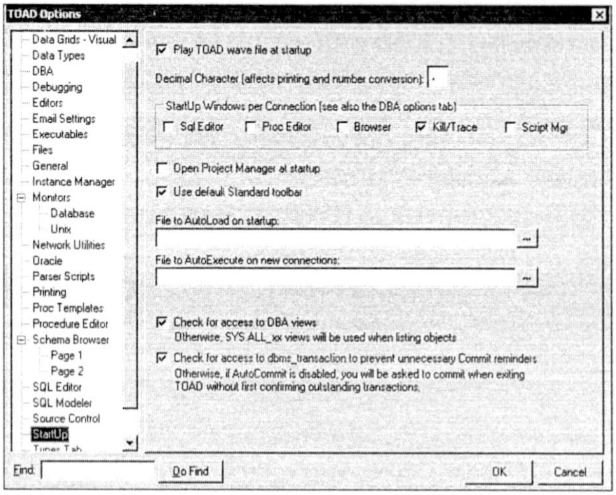

FIGURE 5.30   TOAD Startup Options for Kill/Trace Session.

Creating, Altering, and Managing Database Objects

Probably the most common task any DBA does is to create, alter, and otherwise manage database objects. For example, the typical DBA might perform daily routine tasks such as:

- Add a new data file to a tablespace

- Modify a data file to increase its size

- Create a new rollback segment

- Create a new database role

- Grant a role or privilege to a role

- Create a new database user

- Grant a role or privilege to a user

- Create a table and some indexes on it

- Add or drop columns from a table

- Add a new constraint to a table

- Add a new index to a table

- Create a new view definition

In fact, the complete list of routine DBA tasks is almost endless, such that the preceding list merely attempts to show the nature of such tasks. Basically the DBA performs nearly all the commands found in the Oracle SQL Reference manual. That means the DBA is issuing ALTER, ANALYZE, COMMENT, CREATE, DROP, GRANT, RENAME, and REVOKE commands for all database object types and in all their various syntactical formats. That's one heck of a lot of syntax to have to remember!

Fortunately for the DBA, TOAD nicely encapsulates and abstracts nearly 100% of these commands by using its Schema Browser, shown in Figure 5.31. You can launch the Schema Browser either by clicking its icon on the main toolbar (second icon from the top left by default) or from the main menu at Database, Schema Browser. Although Figure 5.31 shows the Users tab, the basic principles of user interaction and screen behavior are virtually the same across all tabs. The right-hand side of the window will show detailed information for the selected object, whereas the left-hand side of the window will show the objects and toolbar icons to work on the selected objects. Moreover, those options are also available by using the context menu. Plus, users can multi-select objects with either method. Note that the first three toolbar icons shown on all the tabs are Copy Script to Clipboard (that is, reverse-engineer the DDL), Create New Object, and Alter Existing Object.

Because the typical DBA needs to create, alter, and manage objects on a never-ending basis, wouldn't it be useful if TOAD could automatically open this screen when it launched? Well, it can, if you use the TOAD Options category for Startup as shown in Figure 5.32. You just need to check the box for Browser Within Startup Windows Per Connection. Now TOAD will automatically launch the Schema Browser at startup. It is also recommended that you check the box for Check for Access to DBA Views.

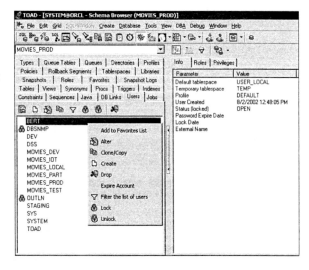

FIGURE 5.31   TOAD Schema Browser for routine DBA tasks.

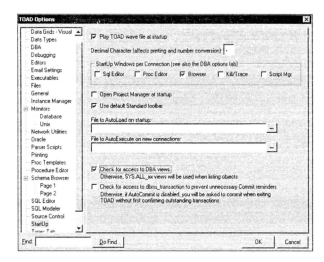

FIGURE 5.32   TOAD Startup Options for Schema Browser.

Scheduling DBA Tasks by Using UNIX Job Scheduler

For those DBAs managing Oracle on UNIX, TOAD offers the ability to schedule shell scripts that perform true server-side database administrative tasks. Plus, TOAD ships with over 50 very useful shell scripts that work on Linux, Solaris, HPUX, AIX, and Tru64 already provided. Moreover, TOAD provides a simple template for creating additional scripts. TOAD simply utilizes the server's cron daemon to schedule and run the tasks. The TOAD Unix Job Scheduler is shown in Figure 5.33 and is located on the main menu at DBA, OS Utilities, Unix Job Scheduler. Its tree view contains two basic node types at the first level: one entry for All Available Tasks and an entry for each database server.

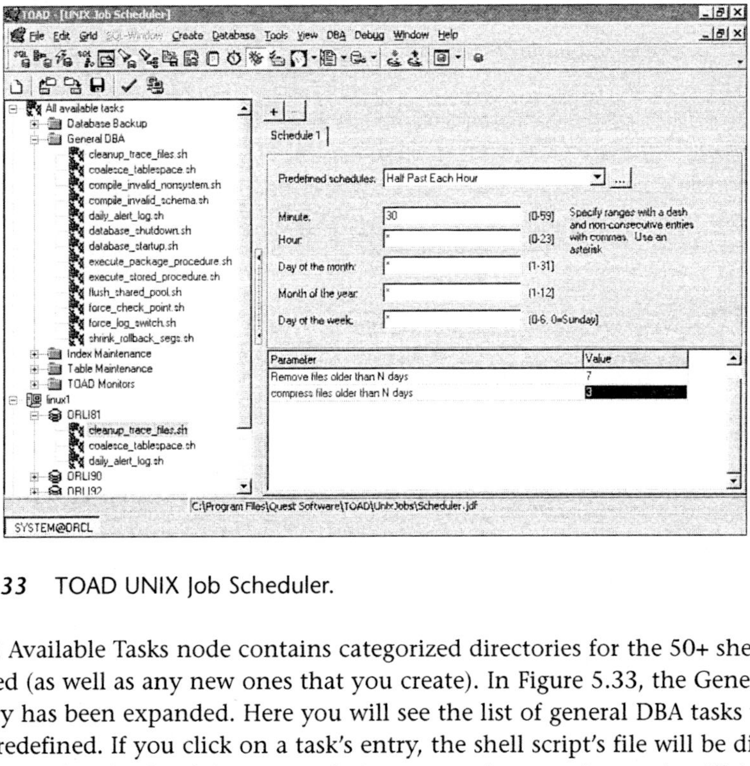

FIGURE 5.33 TOAD UNIX Job Scheduler.

The All Available Tasks node contains categorized directories for the 50+ shell scripts provided (as well as any new ones that you create). In Figure 5.33, the General DBA category has been expanded. Here you will see the list of general DBA tasks that have been predefined. If you click on a task's entry, the shell script's file will be displayed on the right-hand side of the screen. So in essence the tree view under All Available Tasks serves as a mini-explorer for viewing the shell scripts. These shell script files are located in the base TOAD directory under unixjobs\Base\Shell.

The individual server nodes contain each of the database SIDs for that server. Initially, TOAD scans the PC's local host file to construct the server list and the TNSNAMES.ORA file to create the SID list. You can, of course, customize the nodes in case the automatically discovered entries are incorrect. You just right-click to add servers and SIDs. To use these servers and their SIDs (regardless of whether manually or automatically created), you must perform a right-click edit operation to provide critical operational information, as described in the following two paragraphs.

For each server, you must provide the UNIX user id, password, and schedule deployment directory as shown in Figure 5.34. TOAD will log in to that UNIX user id when deploying the job schedule. It's also the user id that will be running all the jobs via cron. The UNIX user id does not have to be the Oracle account as shown. It could be any UNIX user id. But note that some DBA tasks, such as a backup, require that the user id be in the UNIX DBA group and thus have read access to the Oracle data files. The UNIX user id should also have access to sufficient disk space for the log files created by each job execution. Although TOAD keeps log files for just the past 10 days or 10 most recent executions, a server with lots of SIDs and jobs could still consume lots of space.

For each database SID, you must provide the correct Oracle home directory and various Oracle user ids and passwords as shown in Figure 5.35. The Oracle home directory is used to set an environment variable utilized by all the shell scripts to reference Oracle binary files (for example, $ORACLE_HOME/bin/sqlplus). If you set the wrong value here, the deployed schedule will not work. There are three types of Oracle user ids and passwords that must be provided. The first is a DBA user id for performing typical tasks requiring DBA privileges (for example, coalesce a tablespace). The second is the user id owning the TOAD objects for performing TOAD tasks (for example, gathering TOAD history for tablespace growth). And the third is a user id with SYSDBA rights for database startup and shutdowns (if used).

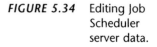

FIGURE 5.34 Editing Job Scheduler server data.

After the server and SID information are correct, it's time to schedule jobs. It's really very easy; you just drag and drop a job from the Available Tasks. If you drop it on a server, it adds that task to all the SIDs. If you drop it on a SID, it's only added to that SID. You can also drag and drop a task from one SID to another. That's all there is to it. Look back again at Figure 5.33. The ORLI81 SID has three scheduled jobs.

There is still one more critical step though, as all tasks have properties. When you select a scheduled task on the tree view, the right-hand side displays that job's properties. Look back once again at Figure 5.33. You must define how often you want each job to run. They come with reasonable defaults, but should be reviewed and set for your needs. Plus many jobs have optional parameters that control their behavior. Again sensible defaults are provided that should likewise be reviewed and set to your specific needs.

After all the server, SID and task information has been set, you are ready to deploy the job schedule. First you should click the Check Required Elements toolbar icon (the one with the green check mark) in order to verify that all your data entry is correct. Then you merely click the Deploy/FTP icon to copy the jobs and schedule to the server. The Deploy/FTP icon also activates the schedule with cron. It's all up and running at this point.

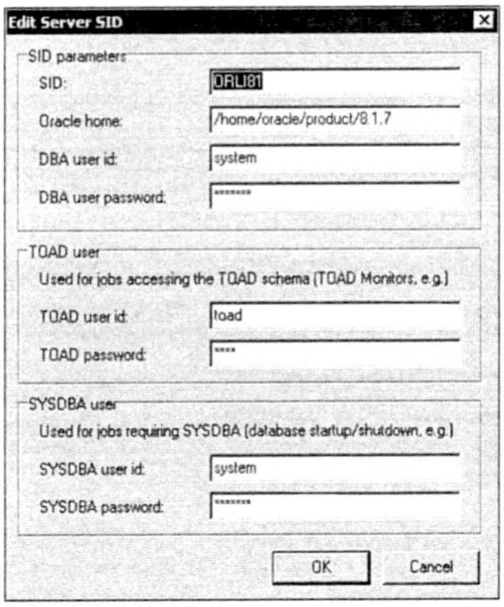

To monitor and control deployed jobs, you merely select a particular server node back on the job scheduler tree view and reference the Log tab as shown in Figure 5.36. Note that there are four options under the Refresh Log List button: All Log Files, Last Execution, Failures Only, and Failures Only/Last Execution. You can view the log files using either the View Log File toolbar button or by double-clicking on a log file entry (it FTPs the file to your machine and then opens it in Notepad). Plus you can delete log files on the server to control disk space usage. Finally, you view the crontab file and start or stop the cron schedule. In short, you should never have to log in to a UNIX box to work with anything related to the TOAD job scheduler. The GUI provides for every conceivable need.

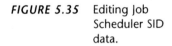

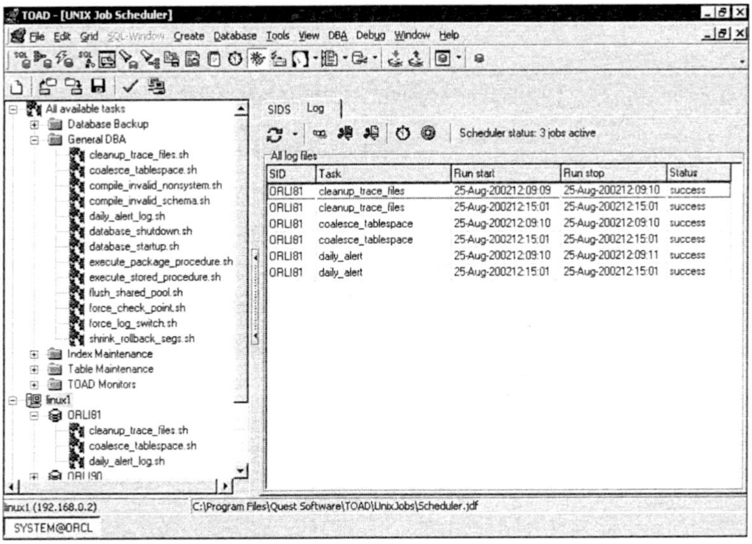

FIGURE 5.35   Editing Job Scheduler SID data.

FIGURE 5.36   Monitoring and controlling deployed jobs.

Summary

This chapter covered those database administrative tasks that are considered routine. These are the tasks that DBAs need to do every day or quite frequently. All these tasks are extremely important, such as monitoring all your instances, monitoring tablespace disk usage, checking for tablespace fragmentation, monitoring/killing sessions, and numerous other tasks. Without TOAD, these routine tasks would be very time-consuming for even the most experienced DBA.

The next chapter covers those database administrative tasks that are considered non-routine (that is, only performed weekly, monthly, and so on).

6

Using TOAD for Non-Routine DBA Tasks

TOAD offers its numerous DBA capabilities through various menus and toolbars. However, these menus and toolbars are organized by relative function and in conformance with Windows standards. But in practice, DBAs perform these tasks based on need and often by scheduled interval. So to cover them based on their menu or toolbar placement would be counterproductive. Therefore, all the DBA tasks are categorized into two simple groupings: routine and non-routine. This chapter covers those database administrative tasks that are considered non-routine.

Creating a New Database

Creating a new database sounds like a simple task. But as with any other complex endeavor, the foundation you lay at the start will determine your success. Many DBAs have scripts they've written over the years for creating databases that they can "hack upon" for current needs. Other DBAs prefer to use Oracle's Database Configuration Assistant (available with later versions of the database). But both these approaches suffer the same drawback; the DBA must be intimate with every single Oracle feature for the target database version and must explicitly define all the necessary information in Oracle terms. The problem is that you may well be a developer whose responsibilities include certain DBA functions. In that case, you may not be up to date on every single little Oracle tidbit. You just want to create a database as quickly as possible that meets your application's needs.

TOAD's New Database wizard was specifically designed with this scenario in mind. In fact, the guiding mantra was from Star Trek III, when Captain Kirk asks Mr. Scott if the Enterprise is fully automated yet and he replies, "A chimpanzee and two trainees could run her!" That's how easy this utility aims to be. Unlike Oracle's Database Configuration Assistant, which is more suited to DBAs, the TOAD New Database wizard was designed so that people with limited Oracle expertise could click a few buttons and create a database. The information requested by the wizard is more about the server hardware and application needs than about vague Oracle parameters and settings. The real-world test case for the New Database wizard was a group of Web consultants building Oracle applications but not having any DBAs because their project time spans were so short (that is, generally averaging under 90 days).

Note that TOAD's New Database wizard can be used to generate both UNIX and Windows scripts necessary to create the database. For UNIX, it will generate a shell script and an INIT.ORA file. For Windows, TOAD's New Database wizard will generate a batch script, a SQL file, and the INIT.ORA file. All scripts are generated such that the user can make customizations easily. In other words, the TOAD generated scripts can serve as their basic templates (similar to the way DBAs use scripts they've maintained over the years). Moreover, these scripts can be rerun at any time to re-create the database as well. TOAD offers all this functionality with little or no Oracle expertise required.

The TOAD New Database wizard takes you through five steps and is accessible from the main menu at DBA|New Database. Note that all the selections you make during these five steps will affect both the generated code and possibly some of the options presented in the windows themselves. There are both Next and Back buttons in this wizard, so you can easily move back and forth to try various settings and options. Plus you can save and load your selections to a file on your PC. That way, when you get some or all the settings the way you like, you can save them for future restoration.

In step 1, you must provide some very basic database information, as shown in Figure 6.1. If you're merely creating a local database, TOAD will offer the ability to run the generated scripts at the wizard's conclusion. If instead you're creating a remote Windows or UNIX database, TOAD will just generate all the scripts. You will need to find other methods with which to deploy and execute those scripts. For example, with a UNIX database, you could use TOAD's FTP and `rexec` abilities (accessible from the main menu under File). Note that the Oracle base and home directory settings on this screen are critical. The database files will be created in the `ORACLE_BASE`/`admin`/`SID` directory. And Oracle commands will be referenced in the `ORACLE_HOME`/`bin` directory. The scripts will not work if these settings are not 100% correct.

In step 2, you answer some basic server hardware and application requirements questions, as shown in Figure 6.2. How many users will the database have? How many CPUs on the server and at what speed? How much RAM? How many controller channels and with how much cache memory? These are all questions that should take little or no thought on your part. The answers, however, are very important because they will be utilized to calculate values for numerous Oracle parameters and settings in the generated scripts and INIT.ORA file. Thus TOAD enables you to focus and think in non-Oracle terms and translates the input into good Oracle configurations and settings. It's like having a DBA expert in the box for creating new databases.

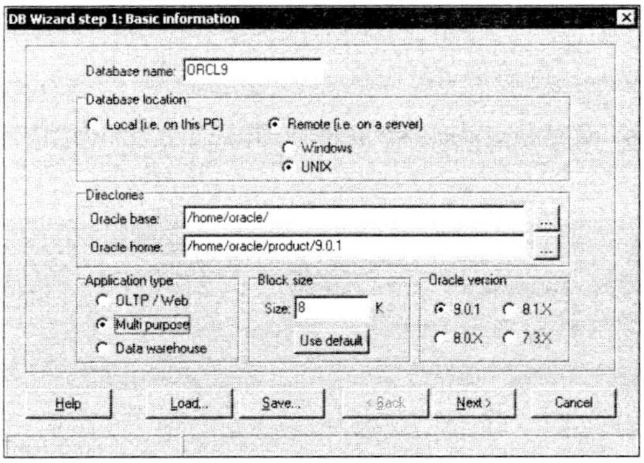

FIGURE 6.1   TOAD New Database wizard—step 1.

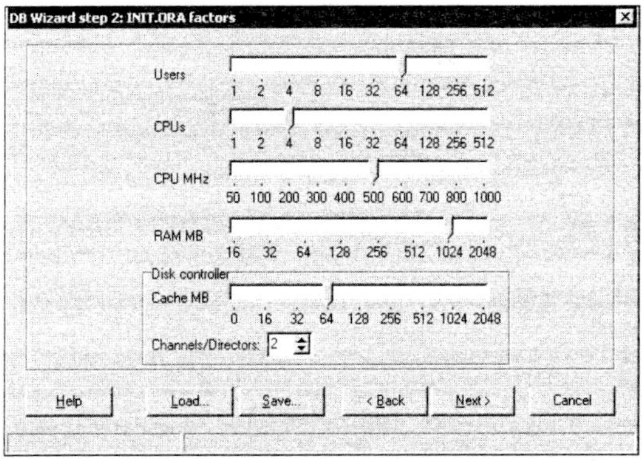

FIGURE 6.2   TOAD New Database wizard—step 2.

In step 3, you must decide on how you want to define your database's space allocation. In automatic mode, you continue working in the manner where you focus on non-Oracle responses and TOAD translates that into ideal Oracle selections. If instead you choose manual mode, you will be working in a more traditional mode where you must define tablespaces and allocate space to them yourself. Your selection here will decide which screen comes up next in the wizard. We'll examine both alternatives; however, the automatic mode is highly recommended.

In step 4 for automatic mode, you merely need to tell TOAD how big to make the database and where space exists on your server that can be used for creating that database. That's it, as shown in Figure 6.4. TOAD will then utilize expert rules to optimally place the data, redo, and control files. The only Oracle-related question on this screen is whether to use dictionary versus locally managed tablespaces via the

Extent Mgmnt button (the default is locally managed). Of course, this button is sensitive to the Oracle database version setting from step 1 and adjusts accordingly. And for those who are interested, you can preview how your available space will automatically map to tablespaces to handle your requested database size.

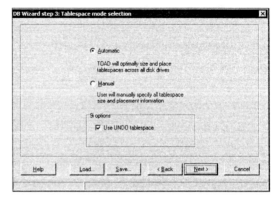

FIGURE 6.3   TOAD New Database wizard—step 3.

When you define your volume information, keep in mind that not everyone is using just simple disks—hence the term volume. If you have just simple disks, your volumes might be something like "C:\" and "D:\" for a Windows box. But more and more these days people are using volume managers to abstract away physical disks and instead deal with volumes. So a volume may have four disks and implement RAID as shown in Figure 6.5. The physical properties for the number of disks, RAID level, interface type, transfer rate, and rotation speed are critical to the rules that automatically lay out your database files. Note, too, that whether a volume contains operating system or swap files also helps

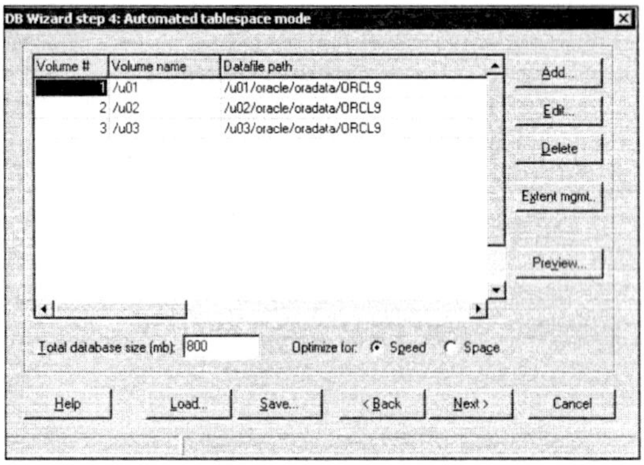

FIGURE 6.4   TOAD New Database wizard—step 4 automatic.

to decide where to place database files. Once again, TOAD's New Database wizard makes the job super easy. You let it know how much space, where it is, and some other hardware properties, and TOAD will calculate the best database layout for your needs.

In step 4 for manual mode, you must define all the tablespace information as shown in Figure 6.6. So instead of just saying give me a database of size x on the following volumes, you have to perform the more traditional work of defining each Oracle tablespace, its size and data file placement. That also means you need to know which tablespaces to create. For example, you'd need to decide between creating a rollback segment tablespace versus using an undo tablespace for an Oracle 9i database. But in automatic mode, all the best alternatives would have been automatically selected for you. This interface is provided for those DBAs who are comfortable with and accustomed to working this way. For non-experts or people just wanting the fastest way to create a database, the automatic mode is the better choice.

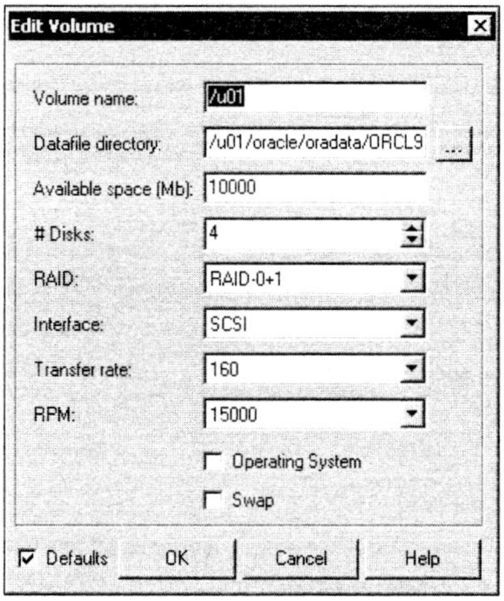

Finally in step 5, you get to select whether or not to run various advanced Oracle administrative scripts and where to create the generated output. And if you were creating a local database, you also would have been given the option to run the generated script as well. Plus there are buttons to view all the generated code. For UNIX, you can preview both the shell script (which also contains the SQL code as a here document) and the INIT.ORA file, which is shown in Figure 6.7. For Windows, you can preview the batch script, SQL file, and INIT.ORA file. When you click Finish, all these files are written to the location specified.

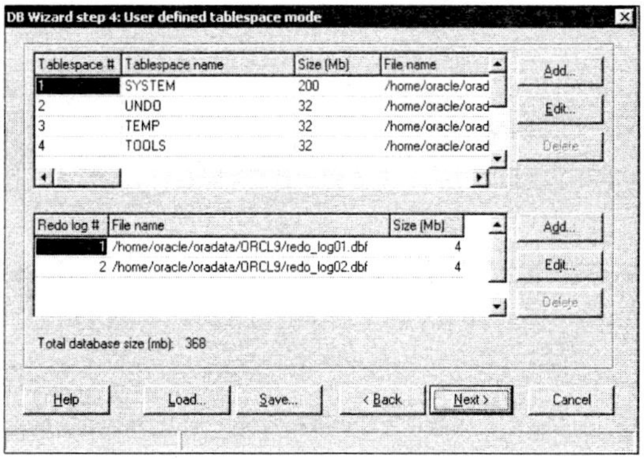

FIGURE 6.5   TOAD New Database wizard—Edit Volumes.

FIGURE 6.6   TOAD New Database wizard—step 4 manual.

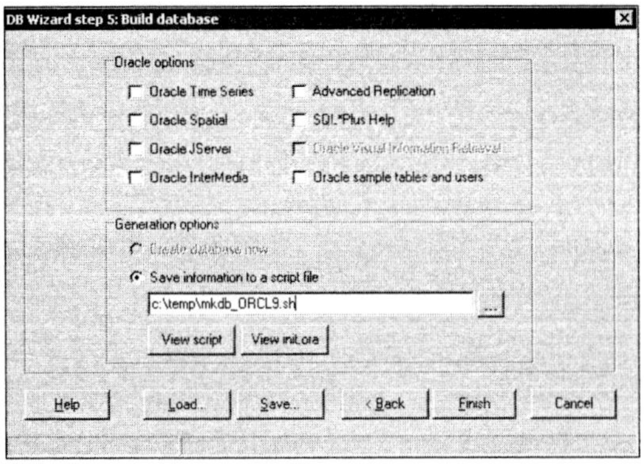

FIGURE 6.7   TOAD New Database wizard—step 5.

Starting and Stopping Databases

On occasion, DBAs may need to either start up or shut down their databases. Sometimes it's to forcibly clean up hung or locked server processes. Other times it's to simply effect INIT.ORA parameter file modifications. And some DBAs just like to cycle their databases every now and then because they believe it's good preventive medicine. Whatever the reasons, TOAD can do both database startups and shut-downs via the Instance Manager screen accessible from the main menu at DBA|Instance Manager (this screen was also covered in the preceding chapter for the monitoring of your databases).

Figure 6.8 shows TOAD being utilized to shut down a database. One thing happening behind the scenes that later seems to cause some confusion is that TOAD makes a copy of the current Oracle instance parameter settings in the TOAD install directory under the DBA subdirectory. Many TOAD users are only accustomed to working with local databases, and thus this step seems useless (because the INIT.ORA file for local database is already available). But TOAD must also work for DBAs who manage remote databases, whose INIT.ORA files are not on their local PC. So TOAD makes a copy of the settings so that it can start what it stops. By the way, this is exactly how Oracle's Enterprise Manager (OEM) works as well. OEM creates a file under the `sysman\ifiles` directory.

Figure 6.9 shows TOAD being utilized to start up a database. See the option to specify a parameter file? Again, for people working with local databases, you could use either the TOAD-created file or the actual INIT.ORA file on your PC. For people working with remote databases, the only option you have is the TOAD-created parameter file. Note that if you choose a startup level less than open, the Instance Manager screen's Alter button will enable. This would be useful if you wanted to do a startup mount in order to do some recovery tasks, and then later needed to open the database for normal operations.

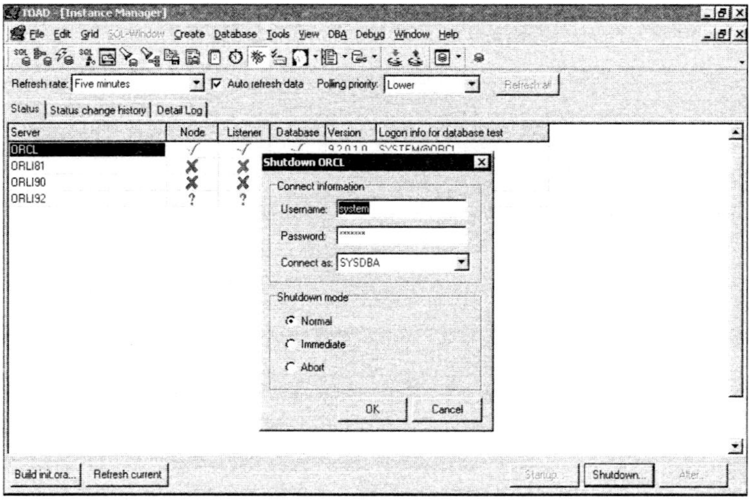

FIGURE 6.8   TOAD Instance Manager—Shutdown Database.

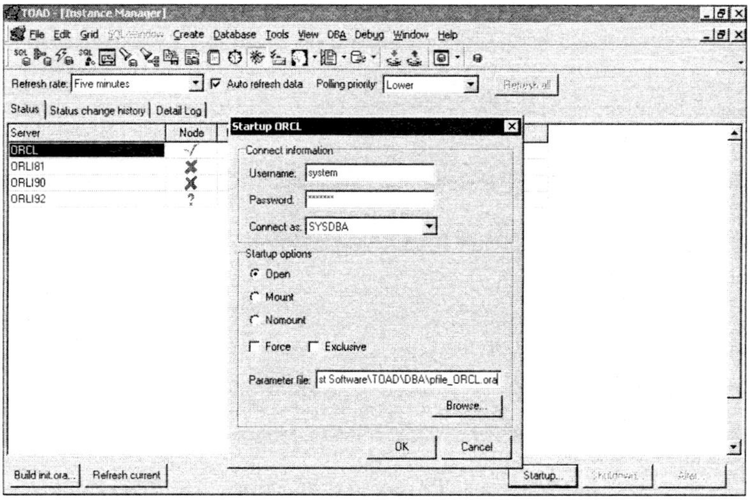

FIGURE 6.9   TOAD Instance Manager—Startup Database.

There is one final issue and it is important to consider when using TOAD for database startups and shutdowns. If you always use TOAD for all database startups and shutdowns, you should never have any problems where parameter settings are an issue. But if you mix methods and tools for doing database startups and shutdowns, you may well run into problems. For example, assume that the database is up, you change some dynamic parameters, and then use TOAD to shut down the database. If you now do a database startup using some other tool such as OEM or SQL*Plus, you'll lose the dynamic parameter modifications you made that were saved in the TOAD parameter file. This scenario would fail using OEM and then SQL*Plus in exactly the same way. Thus this is not a TOAD problem, but merely shows that doing database startups and shutdowns requires consistent methodology in order to avoid such problems. Of course, most DBA tasks should have consistent rules governing their execution for best results.

Examining Oracle and NLS Parameters

A relatively simple task that DBAs should consider on occasion is to review their database initialization and national language setting (NLS) parameters. Although both parameters play crucial parts in a database's behavior, after the ideal settings are ascertained they tend not to change very much. So while DBAs may use these screens a lot for limited durations (for instance, right after a new database is created), they do not generally use them often enough for them to be considered routine.

The INIT.ORA file referenced for the database startup defines the initialization parameters. The parameter settings can be reviewed and dynamically set using TOAD's Oracle Parameters screen shown in Figure 6.10 and accessible from the main menu at DBA|Oracle Parameters. This screen provides four very useful features that can be found on the screen's toolbar. First, you edit all those parameters that are session- or system-modifiable. With the newer versions of Oracle, more and more of these parameters can be dynamically set. Second, you can print the grid. This is very useful for reviewing a hard copy of all these settings. Third, you can search the parameters. And finally, you can save the parameters to a file in the following formats:

- ASCII (comma-delimited)
- Tab-delimited
- Other delimiting character
- HTML
- INSERT statements
- SQL Loader
- XLS
- XML (plain)
- XML (with XSL)

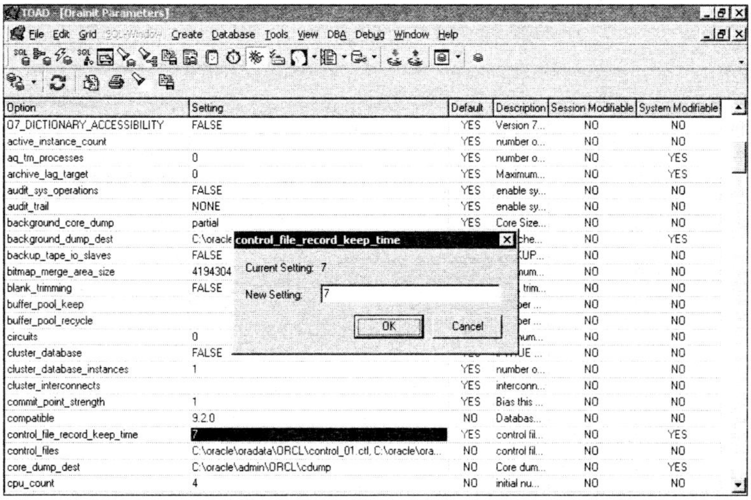

FIGURE 6.10   TOAD Oracle Parameters screen.

The NLS parameters are defined by the CREATE DATABASE command used to create the database and by the NLS_ parameters contained in the INIT.ORA file referenced for database startup. The parameter settings can be reviewed and dynamically set using TOAD's NLS Parameters screen, which is shown in Figure 6.11 and can be accessed from the main menu at DBA|NLS Parameters. This screen has three tabs in order to separate the various session-, instance-, and database-level NLS parameters. Note that only the session-level NLS parameters are dynamic and thus modifiable.

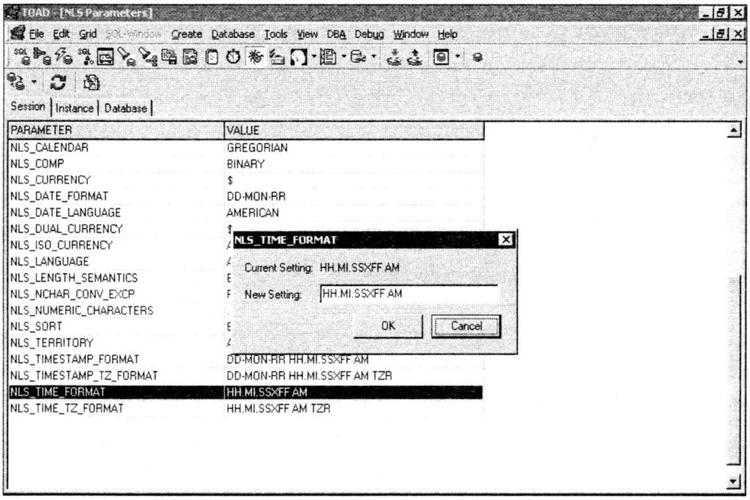

FIGURE 6.11   TOAD NLS Parameters screen.

Estimating Table and Index Sizes

As was pointed out in the preceding chapter, space management is a very critical issue and responsibility for DBAs. Although there are the very routine aspects of monitoring tablespace and disk space usage over time and making projections for the future based on that history, DBAs are also often asked to estimate how big an object will be merely based on the estimated row count. For example, how large will this table be if it had a million instead of ten thousand rows? TOAD provides estimate screens of just this nature for both tables and indexes.

FIGURE 6.12   TOAD Table Size Estimate—structural.

The TOAD Table Size Estimator is accessible from the main menu at Tools|Estimate Table Size and offers three methods for estimating table sizes. First and by default, TOAD can use the table's structural information to calculate the average row size and then multiply that by the desired row count as shown in Figure 6.12. Note that this method provides overly large estimates because it assumes each row will use the entire potentially variable length for each record. Second, TOAD can use any pre-existing analysis information on the table as shown in Figure 6.13. TOAD simply multiplies the analyzed average row length by the desired row count, which provides a significantly higher degree of accuracy. Finally, TOAD itself can calculate the average row size by examining actual table data as shown in Figure 6.14. However, this method can take an inordinately long time and produce results that are only marginally more accurate.

FIGURE 6.13   TOAD Table Size Estimate—analyzed.

The TOAD Index Size Estimator is accessible from the main menu at ToolsIEstimate Index Size and offers two methods for estimating table sizes. First and by default, TOAD can use the table's structural information to calculate the average row size and then multiply that by the desired row count as shown in Figure 6.15. Note that this method provides overly large estimates because it assumes each index column will use the whole potentially variable length. And second, TOAD itself can calculate the average row size by examining actual table data as shown in Figure 6.16. However, this method can take an inordinately long time and yet produces results that are only marginally more accurate.

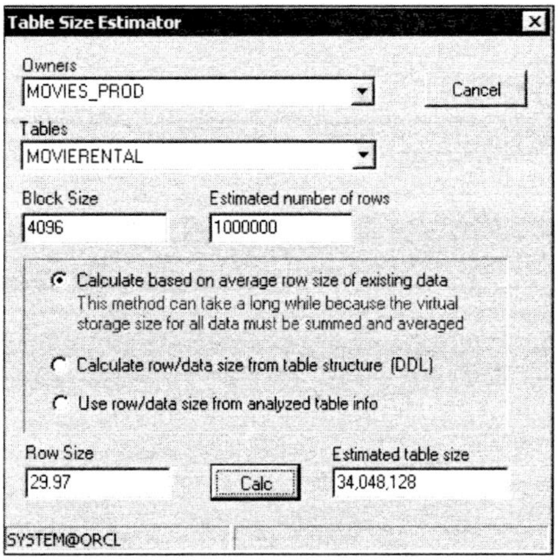

There is only one caveat for both these screens and all their various flavors. TOAD assumes relatively simple table and index structures upon which to base these estimates. Although both these screens will function on objects containing newer data types and complex features such as index organized tables, bitmap indexes, compressed tables, and the like, the results may nonetheless be far less accurate. In other words these screens work great for simple tables and indexes, but require improvements for these newer feature-based scenarios. Look for these enhancements in TOAD 7.5 or higher because space management is truly a critical DBA function.

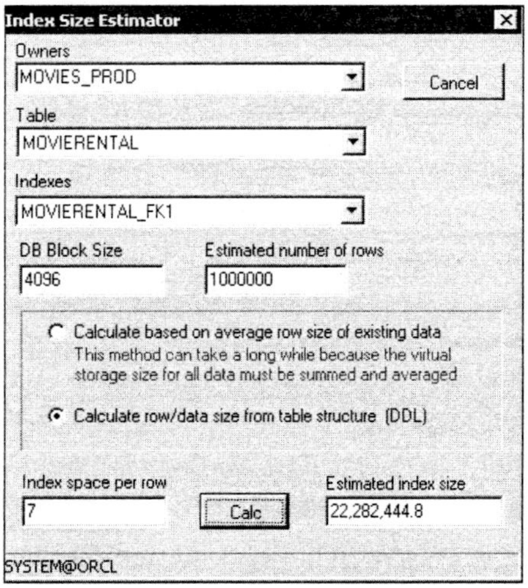

FIGURE 6.14 TOAD Table Size Estimate—calculated.

FIGURE 6.15 TOAD Index Size Estimate—structural.

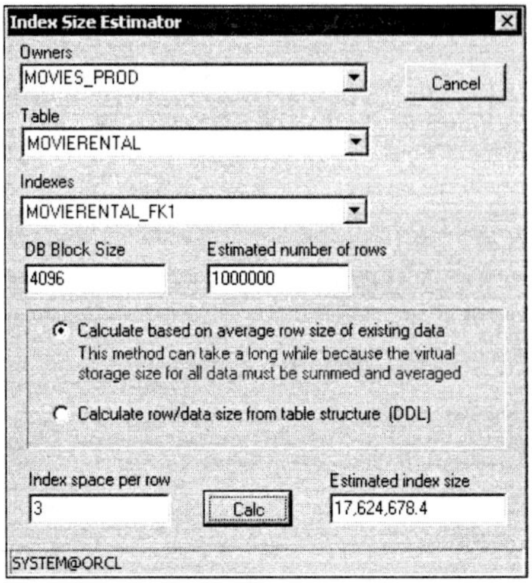

FIGURE 6.16   TOAD Index Size Estimate—calculated.

Analyzing Tables and Indexes

For those DBAs using Oracle's cost-based optimizer, creating and maintaining accurate and timely statistics is both necessary and important. Fortunately, TOAD makes short work of dealing with statistics as it provides two very clean and simple ways to both see and collect them.

For simply examining any table's or index's statistics, you can use TOAD's Schema Browser to pick that object and view its Stats/Size tab as shown in Figure 6.17. Of course, with this approach, you can only see one object's statistics at a time and they're not laid out very aesthetically. The Schema Browser also provides context menu options with multiselect capabilities for invoking the Analyze Tables screen directly as shown in Figure 6.18. With this method, a few mouse clicks and you've analyzed all your tables or indexes. It's quick and easy.

For more involved statistics maintenance from a more global view, TOAD offers the Analyze Tables screen shown in Figure 6.19 and located on the main menu at Tools|Analyze All Tables. This screen presents all the relevant statistics information of concern in a nicely formatted grid, with separate tabs by major statistics type (that is, tables, table partitions, indexes, index partitions, and columns). You merely filter the schema of concern and then multiselect the objects to analyze. Note that this screen also provides the ability to list chained rows and validate object structures. Of course, this requires that you have access to an appropriate CHAINED_ROWS table (such as the one created by Oracle's UTLCHN1.SQL script in the RDBMS admin directory).

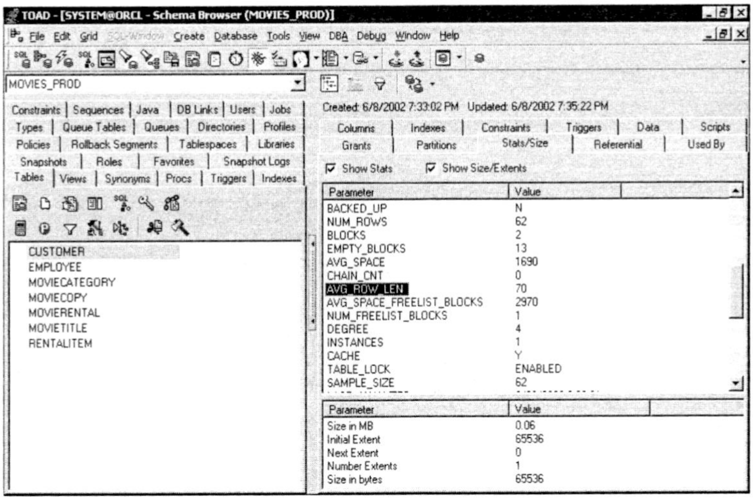

FIGURE 6.17   TOAD Schema Browser—Stats/Size tab.

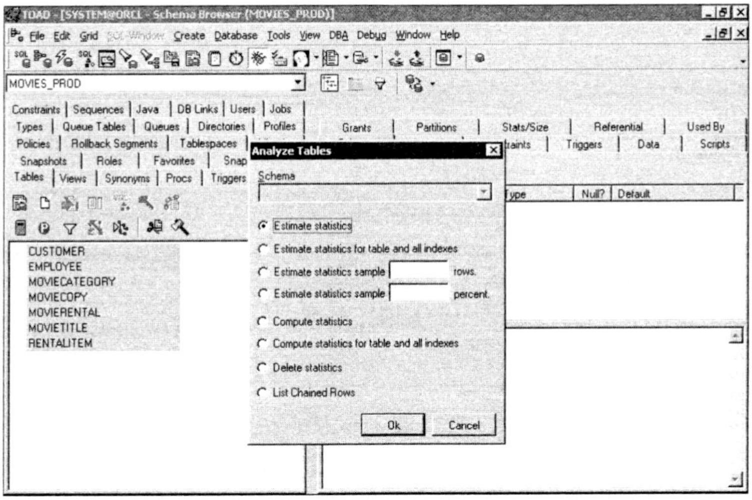

FIGURE 6.18   Analyze via Schema Browser multiselect.

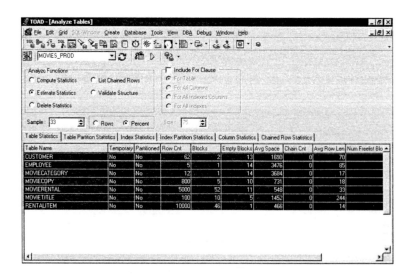

FIGURE 6.19   TOAD Analyze Tables screen.

Rebuilding a Table

Sometimes DBAs may need to rebuild a table. For example, they might simply want
to relocate a table to a different tablespace or rebuild it with different storage parameters. They might need to drop a column or reorder the columns (and their Oracle
version may not support these capabilities natively). Whatever the reasons, the task
of rebuilding a table is very complex. You need to maintain all the same qualities, so
you must preserve definitions for constraints, indexes, views, triggers, grants and
synonyms. Plus you must preserve the data as well. The SQL to accomplish such a
relatively simple task is quite substantial.

TOAD's Rebuild Table screen makes short work of generating the complete script
necessary for rebuilding a table. This screen, which is accessible from the main menu
atTools|Rebuild Table, provides a simple four-tabbed step process as shown in Figure
6.20. First, you visit the Options tab, where you select among a few simple choices. It
is highly recommended that you do check the Unrecoverable/Nologging box to
permit faster index rebuilds. It is also wise to check the box to keep the renamed
original table as a backup of the data. And if your database server has multiple CPUs
or even just exceptional I/O bandwidth, you should also set the parallel optimizer
hint's number of processes.

 There is only one caveat with this screen; you must be connected to the schema owning
the table you want to rebuild.

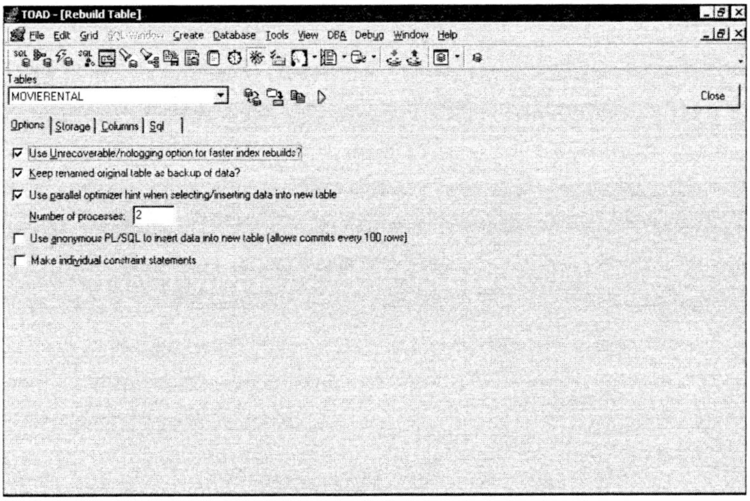

FIGURE 6.20   TOAD Rebuild Table screen—Options.

Second, you visit the Storage tab shown in Figure 6.21, where you select the table's storage options to apply. As was pointed out earlier, you may only need to rebuild the table in order to correct poor storage selections. For example, you may create the table with an initial and next extent size of 64K. Then after the table reaches hundreds or thousands of extents, you may want to rebuild it with 1M extents. This tab provides you with the storage options for using the original parameters or providing new ones. It also permits you to adjust the parallel properties for the table as well.

Third, you visit the Columns tab shown in Figure 6.22, where you select which existing columns to preserve and designate their order within the rebuilt table. On this screen you merely drag and drop the columns into the ordering positions you want. And if you want to drop the column, you just drag and drop it to the bottom panel for columns to exclude. There is also a very useful button to order the columns in the table the same as they are ordered in the primary key. Of course, that may not order all the columns for you, as all the columns may not be in the primary key. But it's useful nonetheless. Do note that if you exclude columns that are used by indexes, TOAD will issue a warning that those indexes will not be re-created.

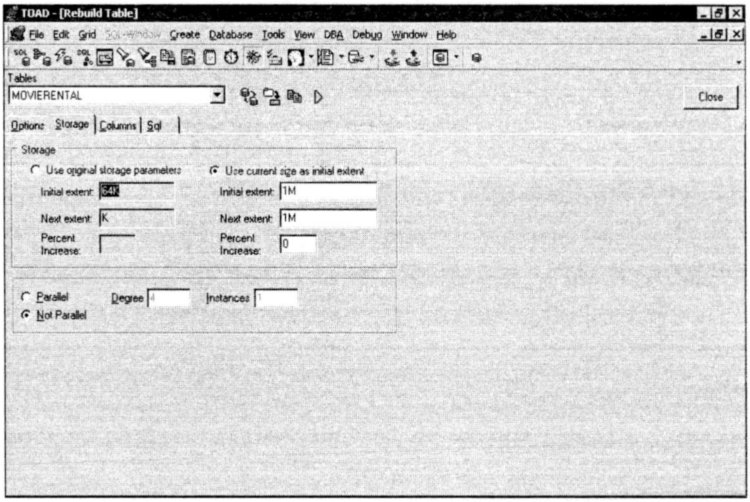

FIGURE 6.21   TOAD Rebuild Table screen—Storage.

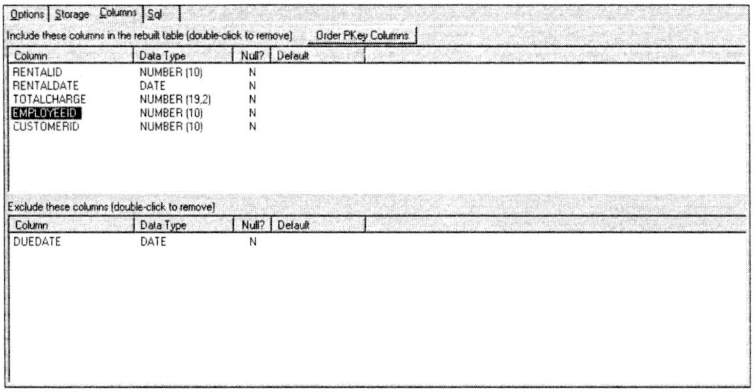

FIGURE 6.22   TOAD Rebuild Table screen—Columns.

Finally you visit the SQL tab shown in Figure 6.23, where you should review the generated script for accuracy. Although you can use the Execute toolbar icon to run the script, it probably makes better sense to either copy it to the clipboard or save it to a file as provided by the remaining toolbar icon options. The main reason is that there is so much to a rebuild table script, that you should review it in detail and possibly consider running it one step at a time. Far too often people choose just to run such complex scripts in their entirety and encounter problems. That's just not the best DBA practice to follow.

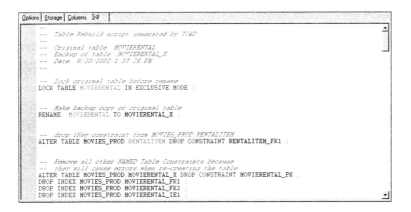

```
Options | Storage | Columns | Sql |
  ---
  --   Table Rebuild script generated by TOAD
  --   Original table MOVIERENTAL
  --   Backup of table MOVIERENTAL_X
  --   Date  8/30/2002 1 07 26 PM

     --   Lock original table before rename
  LOCK TABLE MOVIERENTAL IN EXCLUSIVE MODE ;

     --   Make backup copy of original table
  RENAME  MOVIERENTAL TO MOVIERENTAL_X ;

     --   drop fKey constraint from MOVIES_PROD RENTALITEM
  ALTER TABLE MOVIES_PROD RENTALITEM DROP CONSTRAINT RENTALITEM_FK1 ;

     --   Remove all other NAMED Table Constraints because
     --   they will cause errors when re-creating the table
  ALTER TABLE MOVIES_PROD MOVIERENTAL_X DROP CONSTRAINT MOVIERENTAL_PK ,
  DROP INDEX MOVIES_PROD MOVIERENTAL_FK1 ;
  DROP INDEX MOVIES_PROD MOVIERENTAL_FK2 ;
  DROP INDEX MOVIES_PROD MOVIERENTAL_IE1 ;
```

FIGURE 6.23   TOAD Rebuild Table screen—SQL.

Rebuilding Multiple Indexes

Sometimes DBAs may need to rebuild indexes. For example, they might simply want to relocate an index to a different tablespace or rebuild it with different storage parameters. Other times, DBAs need to locate and then rebuild those indexes that have become unusable (that is, corrupted), whose B-trees have become unbalanced, or whose storage parameters were inappropriately sized for their growth needs. Whatever the reasons, TOAD provides a simple yet potent screen for making index rebuilds of any type a snap. Plus this screen can be run from the command line with e-mail notification capabilities. So TOAD can now fully automate your entire index rebuild candidate detection and code execution process via the Windows scheduler.

The Rebuild Multiple Indexes screen is accessible from the main menu at Tools|Rebuild Multiple Indexes and is shown in Figure 6.24. When you first enter this screen, it will be blank. You must first load into this screen those indexes that you want to work with. You can accomplish this by selecting one of the four identical icons that look like a disk with an arrow pointing to a file folder, which represent Load My Indexes, Load Indexes by User, Load Indexes by Tablespace, and Load Indexes by Table. Figure 6.24 shows the Load Indexes by User window. After you've made an index filtering selection, the screen will be populated with all those indexes, their relevant sizing

Load Indexes By User	
OWNER	Index_and_Partition_Count
DSS	294
MOVIES_DEV	32
MOVIES_IOT	71
MOVIES_LOCAL	29
MOVIES_PART	65
MOVIES_PROD	29
MOVIES_TEST	29
OUTLN	3
STAGING	94
SYS	309
SYSTEM	187
TOAD	10

Make the appropriate selection(s) and click OK

OK   Cancel

FIGURE 6.24   TOAD Rebuild Multiple Indexes—filtering.

information, and check boxes for whether or not to include them for consideration as shown in Figure 6.25.

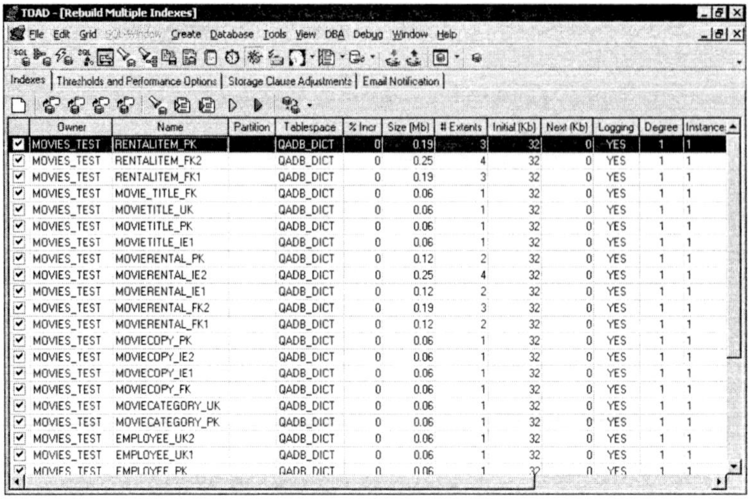

FIGURE 6.25   TOAD Rebuild Multiple Indexes—selection.

After you've filtered and marked those indexes you're interested in, you can have TOAD review them by using the Examine Checked Indexes and Make Recommendations button (the flashlight shining on a disk icon). TOAD will display a dialog to warn you that the checked indexes will be examined, which will require a momentary lock on each index. After that process has completed, the screen will look like Figure 6.26. Note that a grid line has been added directly beneath each index on whether that index needs to be rebuilt or not. It also indicates why for those that are indicated as needing to be rebuilt. Do note that this can take a while if you select a schema or tablespace with lots of indexes. Be patient; TOAD displays its progress at the bottom of the window.

At this point, you could simply rebuild the indexes by using one of the toolbar icons related to execution: Rebuild Recommended Indexes or Rebuild Checked Indexes. Or you could copy the generated rebuild code to the clipboard for your own manual execution using either the Create Script to Rebuild Recommended Indexes or Create Script to Rebuild Checked Indexes icon. However, these index rebuild recommendations and the resulting code generated were made based on some default settings that most DBAs should review and adjust to their own specific needs. This is accomplished by using both the Thresholds and Performance Options tab shown in Figure 6.27 and the Storage Clause Adjustments tab shown in Figures 6.28 and 6.29.

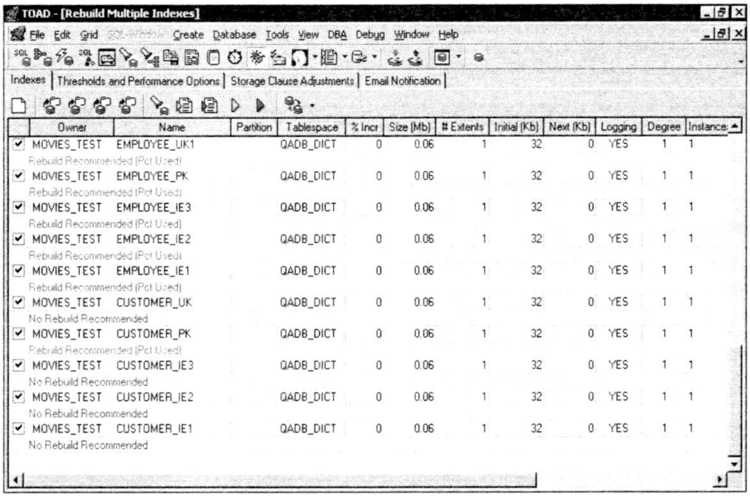

FIGURE 6.26   TOAD Rebuild Multiple Indexes—results.

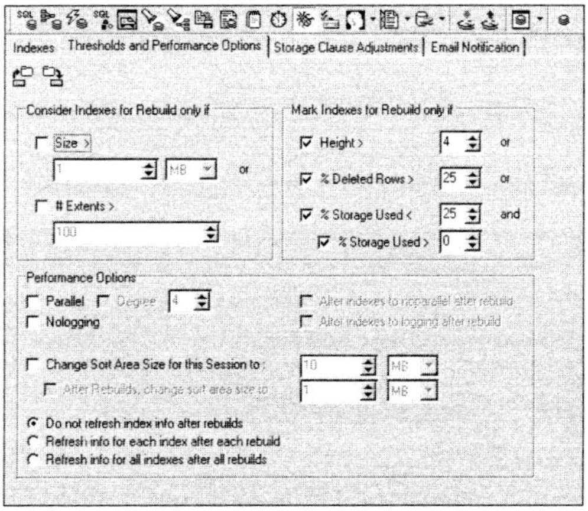

The top half of the Thresholds and Performance Options tab provides for advanced rebuild recommendation filtering based on thresholds. You can indicate to consider indexes only if they are bigger than a certain size or if they contain more than a specified number of extents. This would be useful for filtering out smaller minutia. You also can define when to mark indexes for rebuild based on their height, deleted rows percentage, and storage utilization. An index suffers height growth when there are B-tree splits, at which time it should be rebuilt. An index suffers from deleted row space consumption when lots of rows are deleted that are only marked as unused in the B-tree,

FIGURE 6.27   TOAD Rebuild Multiple Indexes—Thresholds and Performance.

at which time the index should be rebuilt. And finally, you don't want indexes with too much or too little space.

The bottom half of the Thresholds and Performance Options tab provides for advanced rebuild recommendation code generation based on performance options.

You can indicate whether or not to rebuild the indexes in parallel and with nologging. Plus you can indicate whether to or not to set the indexes to nonparallel and logging after the rebuild is complete. You also can adjust your session's sort area size to accommodate the index creation sort space demands, plus reset that sort size after the process is complete.

The Storage Clause Adjustments tab offers numerous and key capabilities related to Extents and Tablespaces, shown in Figures 6.28 and 6.29 respectively. These two tabs provide a horde of capabilities, so review the following very carefully.

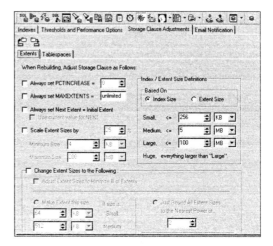

FIGURE 6.28   TOAD Rebuild Multiple Indexes—Extents.

The Extents tab is a bit complicated as it enables you to define three distinct kinds of information. First, the top left portion of the screen offers check boxes for forcing and scaling certain storage parameter values. These options are fairly self-explanatory. The group box on the top right side of the screen permits you to define what is considered small, medium, large and huge based on either index or extent size. These settings are referenced on both the bottom portion of this screen and on the Tablespaces tab shown in Figure 6.29. The group box on the bottom of the screen permits you to force the index extent sizes based on the index's relative size. For example, medium-sized indexes (that is, those less than or equal to 5 megabytes in size) should use 512KB extents. This is a complicated tab. But if you spend the time to set all these options correctly, the rebuild scripts you can generate will be awesome.

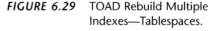

FIGURE 6.29   TOAD Rebuild Multiple Indexes—Tablespaces.

The Tablespaces tab permits you to relocate indexes and index partitions from one tablespace to another. You can move them all or by their size. In Figure 6.29, the settings shown indicate to relocate small indexes to tablespace USER_DICT, medium indexes to tablespace QADB_DICT, large indexes to tablespace QADB_LOCAL, and huge indexes to tablespace DWDB_LOCAL. Moreover, all index partitions are to be rebuilt in tablespace DWDB_LOCAL. Remember, the meaning of small, medium, large, and huge was defined back on the Extents tab in Figure 6.28.

To receive the Rebuild Multiple Index candidate selection and code execution results via e-mail is a simple, two-step process. First you must select the Email Notification tab on this screen and select whether the message should be sent and in what format, as shown in Figure 6.30. The reason for HTML is because TOAD highlights and color-codes the output in a manner conducive to easy reading and focusing on key problems. Second, and only if sending e-mail after completion is enabled, you must visit the TOAD options category for Email Settings and define all the appropriate information as depicted in Figure 6.31.

 Remember that the TOAD Options screen can be opened either by using the Toolbox icon on the main toolbar or from the main menu at View|Options.

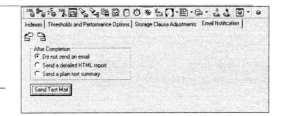

FIGURE 6.30 TOAD Rebuild Multiple Indexes—Email Notification.

You're not quite done yet, though. The ideal scenario would be to have this report waiting for you each morning in your e-mail inbox already prepared and ready for inspection. That way you could start your day by quickly checking the index rebuild report statuses for your databases. To accomplish this, you must schedule this report to run on your Windows machine via the Microsoft Task Scheduler as shown in Figure 6.32. For Windows 2000, this is located at Start|Settings|Control Panel|Scheduled Tasks|Add Scheduled Task.

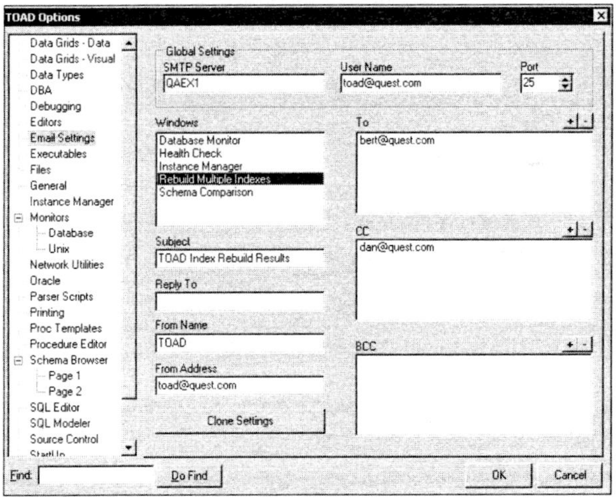

FIGURE 6.31 TOAD e-mail options for rebuilding multiple indexes.

Note that you're simply scheduling Windows on your PC to run TOAD in command-line mode, where you provide the connection information and a rebuild multiple index (RMI) command text file. To produce that file is very simple. You merely need to open the screen, make all your selections, and then choose the Save All Settings to File toolbar icon. The generated file will contain everything necessary to start TOAD, connect to the database, and then run this screen. The generated command file will also contain comments on some commands you can add to tailor its behavior (for example, to close the screen and also shut down when the process is complete).

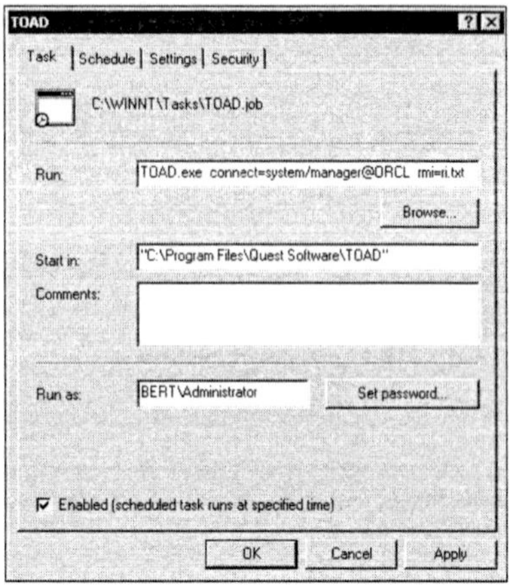

FIGURE 6.32 Windows scheduling of TOAD rebuild multiple indexes.

Repairing Tables with Chained Rows

Sometimes DBAs may need to repair chained rows. Row Fragmentation (RF) or "chaining" occurs when an update increases a row length such that it cannot fit in its current data block and must migrate to a new data block that has sufficient room for the entire row. The only way to correct this problem is to delete those chained rows and re-insert them. This requires creating a temporary table with the same structure as the original to hold those rows between operations. So the actual algorithm is to copy the chained rows to the temporary table, delete them from the original table, and then re-insert them into the original table. TOAD provides the Repair Chained Rows screen, which makes both the detection and correction of chained rows simple and painless. It is located on the main menu at DBA|Repair Chained Rows and is shown in Figure 6.33.

When you initially enter this screen, it will be empty. You must first click the Add button to add the tables from the schemas that you want to analyze for possible chained rows. After you've done that, the screen will look like Figure 6.34. Note that you can then click the Add button again and add additional tables from other schemas. You do not have to look at tables from only one schema at a time. Look again at Figure 6.34; see how there are candidate tables from both the BERT and MOVIES_PROD schemas?

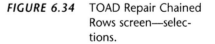

FIGURE 6.33   TOAD Repair Chained Rows screen—Add Tables.

After you've identified the candidate tables for inspection, you click the Analyze button to have TOAD discover which of the tables possess chained rows. Of course, this requires that you have access to an appropriate CHAINED_ROWS table (such as the one created by Oracle's UTLCHN1.SQL script in the RDBMS admin directory). You can specify the name of the chained row table for TOAD to use at the top of the screen. After you click the Analyze button, you will be taken to the Repair tab and shown the tables that contain chained rows and statistics about their situation. As you can see in Figure 6.35, one table was found that has 3934 chained rows.

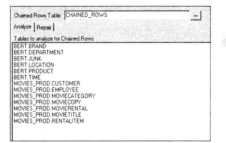

FIGURE 6.34   TOAD Repair Chained Rows screen—selections.

Before clicking the Repair button to fix the chained rows, you have three options to define on this screen. First, there is a check box next to each table indicating whether or not to include it in the repair process. Second, you can optionally specify the name of the temporary table (TOAD will generate unique names for you if this field is left blank). And finally, you can specify the name of the rollback segment to use for the transactions. If you have tables with lots of chained rows, you may need to specify a rollback segment large enough to handle the operations. After you're sure of your settings, simply click the Repair button and TOAD will eliminate all your chained rows. A dialog will be displayed when the operation is complete giving you statistics and information about what just occurred.

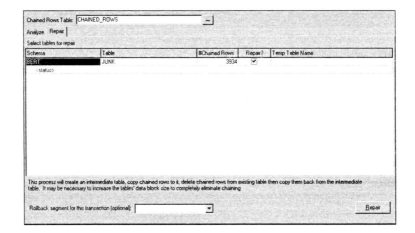

FIGURE 6.35   TOAD Repair Chained Rows screen—results.

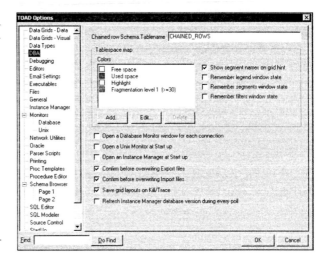

As with any DBA restructuring task, this process could fail for any one of a hundred reasons (i.e. run out of space, rollback segment error, database shutdown, etc.) and leave you with incomplete results. Therefore as a wise precaution, you should always backup the selected tables using either a create table as select or the EXPORT utility.

FIGURE 6.36   TOAD DBA Options for Chained Row Table.

Finally, note that the TOAD Options screen has an option under the DBA category for specifying the default chained row table as depicted in Figure 6.36.

Pinning PL/SQL Code in the SGA

One database tuning technique that isn't used often enough even though it can yield significant improvements is Oracle's ability to pin PL/SQL code within the SGA memory. After the PL/SQL code has been pinned, it cannot be aged out of the SGA memory for any reason. For PL/SQL code that is heavily referenced, this can yield substantial results. The problem is that the method to accomplish this is called to PL/SQL packages provided by Oracle, and not SQL commands. So many DBAs have yet to discover this simple yet powerful tuning technique. TOAD provides a screen that makes this process both simple and quick.

TOAD's Pinned Code screen is shown in Figure 6.37 and is accessible from the main menu at DBA|Pinned Code. Prior to using this screen, you must connect to Oracle as SYS and run the DBMSPOOL.SQL script found in Oracle's RDBMS admin directory. The screen itself is split into two halves. The top half shows any PL/SQL code currently in the SGA and whether or not it's been marked as pinned. The bottom half is a mini-schema browser for navigating schema's PL/SQL code. To pin code that's in the SGA, you merely select it on the grid and click the Pin Selected Code icon (the lock). To pin code not in the SGA, you navigate to it on the mini-schema browser and click the Pin Selected Code button. That's it. It is recommended that you do turn the autorefresh off because this tends to make the screen difficult to use, especially with low refresh intervals.

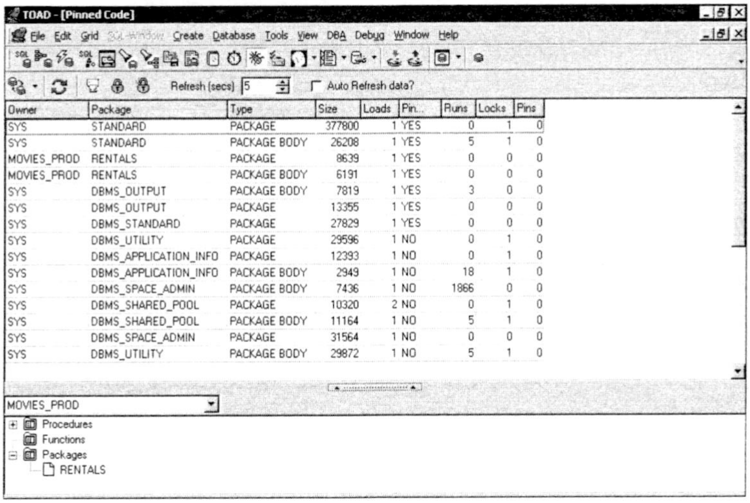

FIGURE 6.37   TOAD Pinned Code screen.

Generating Schema Scripts

Ever needed to reverse-engineer a schema? In the old days when there were just tables, indexes, and views, DBAs simply had a script to reproduce their Data Description Language (DDL) from the online data dictionary. Of course, nowadays there are so many convoluted object types and interdependencies among them that you can't use simple, home-grown scripts any more. So some DBAs will attempt to use data modeling tools like Quest Software's QDesigner or CA's ERwin, but these tools often don't support the more physical aspects of DDL, such as tablespaces and partitions. So what's the poor DBA to do? TOAD comes to the rescue with the perfect solution with the Generate Schema Script screen. Plus this screen can be run from the command line. So TOAD can now fully automate your database reverse-engineering tasks by using the Windows scheduler.

TOAD's Generate Schema Script is accessible from the main menu at DBA|Generate Schema Script. This screen takes you through a simple four-step process to reverse-engineer all your schema's DDL.

The first step is the Source and Destination tab shown in Figure 6.38, which permits you to specify the three major items: source, schema, and file. For source, you indicate whether to reverse-engineer from an online data dictionary or a TOAD schema definition file (a TOAD proprietary format for containing an offline data dictionary and usable by several other TOAD screens). For schema, you select those schemas to reverse-engineer. And for file, you provide the filename to contain either the SQL or TOAD schema definition. Note that if you select multiple schemas and you're generating a DDL file, TOAD has a check box to create a separate DDL file per schema.

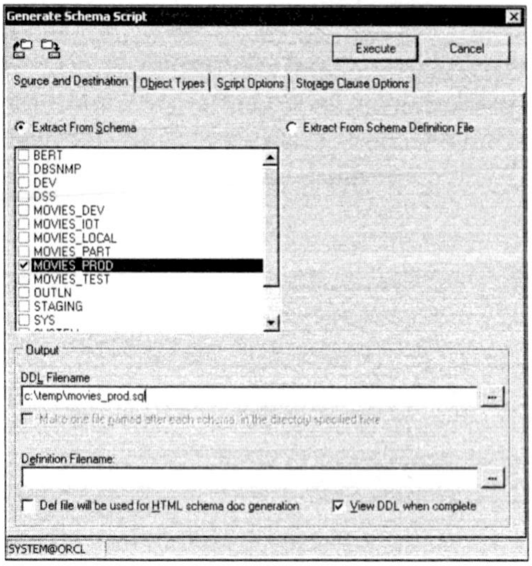

FIGURE 6.38   TOAD Generate Schema Script—Source and Destination.

The second step is the Object Types tab shown in Figure 6.39, which permits you to specify the object types to reverse-engineer. These settings apply to all schemas that are being reverse-engineered. So if you want different settings for different schemas, you'll need to make separate runs for each. Also note that this screen offers context menu options for Select All and Select None. This may not have been readily apparent because this is not really a Windows norm.

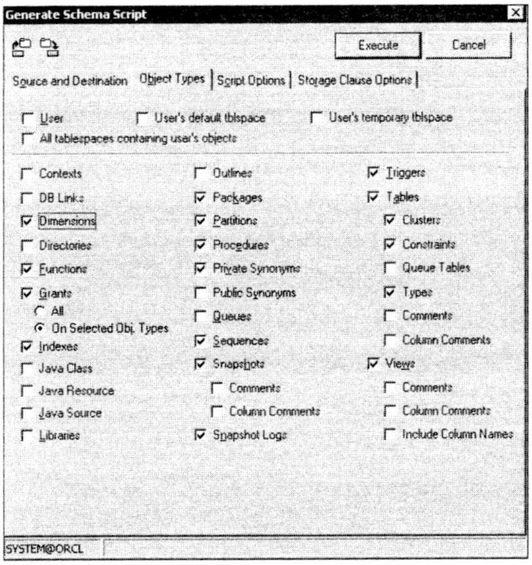

The third step is the Script Options tab shown in Figure 6.40, which enables you to define various SQL code generation options. All but three of these are fairly self-explanatory and require no explanation. The "Exceptions Into" Table field allows you to name the exception table where constraint violation row information is written. The general form of such a table is table name, row id, and error message. So it's just a simple table that contains pointers to other tables whose rows violate constraints. Of course, this requires that you have access to an appropriate EXCEPTION table (such as that created by Oracle's UTLEXCPT.SQL script in the RDBMS admin directory). The Only Extract Object Names Like field lets you filter using simple Oracle pattern matches (for example, LIKE '%X%'). And the Include Schema Name Prefix for Objects field lets you generate statements that look like SCHEMA.OBJECT. This is useful for two reasons. First, you can use a privileged schema like SYSTEM to run the generated script to create the objects in another schema. And second, you can use the Substitute This for Schema Name field to reverse-engineer from one schema into another.

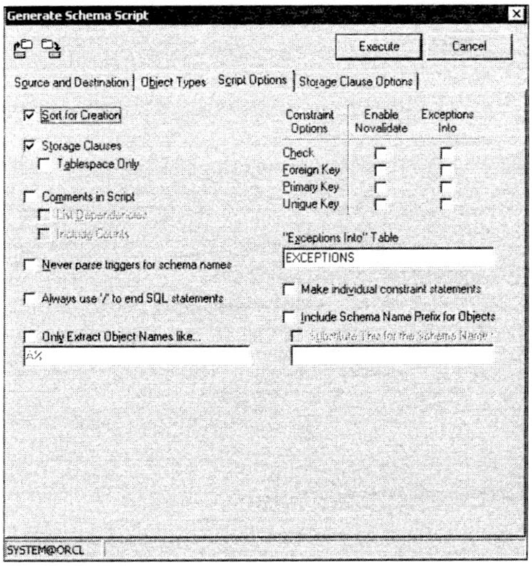

FIGURE 6.39   TOAD Generate Schema Script—Object Types.

FIGURE 6.40   TOAD Generate Schema Script—Script Options.

The fourth step is the Storage Clause Options tab, which offers numerous and key capabilities related to Extents and Tablespaces, shown in Figures 6.41 and 6.42 respectively. These two tabs provide a horde of capabilities, so review the following very carefully.

The Extents tab is a bit complicated as it provides options for you to define three distinct kinds of information. First, the top left portion of the screen offers check boxes for forcing and scaling certain storage parameter values. These options are fairly self-explanatory. The group box on the top right side of the screen permits you to define what is considered small, medium, large, and huge based on either object or extent size. These settings are referenced on both the bottom portion of this screen and on the Tablespaces tab shown in Figure 6.42. The group box on the bottom of the screen permits you to force the object extent sizes based on the object's relative size. For example, medium-sized objects (that is, those less than or equal to 5 megabytes in size) should use 512KB extents. This is a complicated tab. But if you spend the time to set all these options correctly, the reverse-engineered scripts you can generate will be awesome.

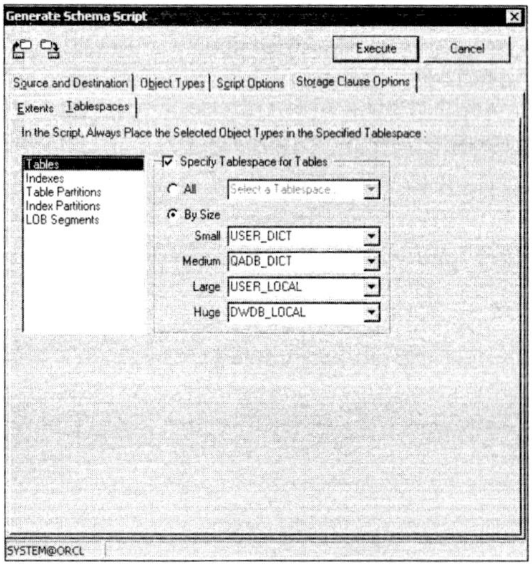

The Tablespaces tab permits you to relocate objects of various types from one tablespace to another. You can move them all or by their size. In Figure 6.42, the settings shown indi-

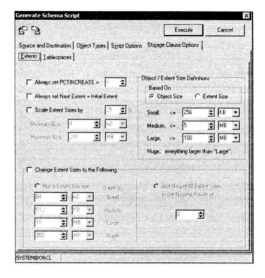

FIGURE 6.41 TOAD Generate Schema Script—Extents.

FIGURE 6.42 TOAD Generate Schema Script—Tablespaces.

cate to relocate small tables to tablespace USER_DICT, medium tables to tablespace QADB_DICT, large tables to tablespace QADB_LOCAL, and huge tables to tablespace DWDB_LOCAL. Note that you need to make these selections for each object type shown on the left side of the screen. Also remember, the meaning of small, medium, large, and huge was defined back on the Extents tab in Figure 6.41.

You're not quite finished yet, though. The ideal scenario would be to have these reverse-engineered DDL scripts waiting for you each morning in your scripts directory, already generated and ready for inspection. That way you could start your day by quickly checking with current scripts to rebuild your schemas if the need arose. You can schedule this report to run on your Windows machine via the Microsoft Task Scheduler as shown in Figure 6.43. For Windows 2000, this is located at Start|Settings|Control Panel|Scheduled Tasks|Add Scheduled Task.

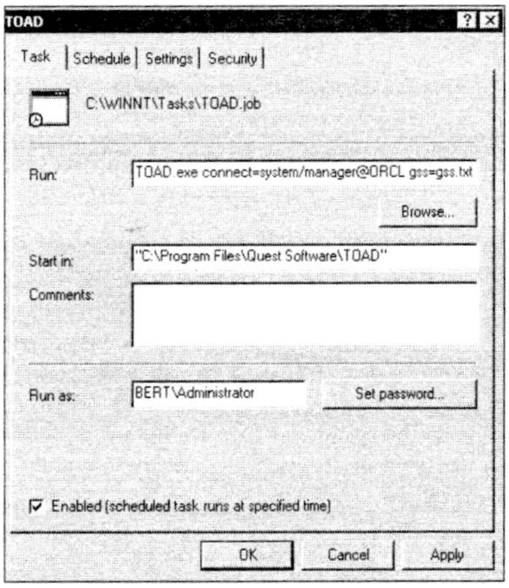

FIGURE 6.43   Windows Scheduling of TOAD Generate Schema Script.

Note that you're simply scheduling Windows on your PC to run TOAD in command-line mode, where you provide the connection information and a generate schema script (GSS) command text file. To produce that file is very simple. You merely need to open the screen, make all your selections, and then choose the Save All Settings to File toolbar icon. The generated file will contain everything necessary to start TOAD, connect to the database, and then run this screen. The generated command file will also contain comments on some commands you can add to tailor its behavior (for example, to close the screen and also shut down when the process is complete).

Comparing Schema Differences

Probably the most challenging DBA task is to maintain database structural integrity and consistency. The DBA must always be able to guarantee that production has not changed, and know how development differs from test and test differs from production. And the devil is in the details (the same as it was with schema generation). In the old days when there were just tables, indexes, and views, DBAs simply had a script to generate the differences via the online data dictionary. Of course nowadays there are so many convoluted object types and interdependencies among them that you can't use simple, home-grown scripts any more. So some DBAs will attempt to use data modeling tools like Quest Software's QDesigner or CA's ERwin, but these tools often don't support the more physical aspects of DDL such as tablespaces and partitions. So what's the poor DBA to do? Again TOAD comes to the rescue with the perfect solution with the Compare Schemas screen. Plus this screen can be run from the command line with e-mail notification capabilities. So TOAD can now fully automate your entire schema comparison process via the Windows scheduler.

The Compare Schemas screen is located on the mainmenu at DBA|Compare Schemas and is shown in Figure 6.44. It's just a simple three-step process to successfully compare even the most complex schemas. First, you visit the Schemas tab and select both your reference and comparison schemas (which are just the source and target, respectively). There is also a handy switch button for reversing the selection, as it's very easy to realize when you view the output that you've chosen them backwards. Also note that you can use TOAD schema definition files as both the source and target. As was previously documented for the Generate Schema Script screen, a TOAD schema definition file is a proprietary format for containing an offline data dictionary and usable by several other TOAD screens.

Next you visit the Options tab, which itself has two tabs under it. In the Options tab's Object Types to Compare tab shown in Figure 6.45, you can select what kinds of database objects you want to compare and the filename for the generated synchronization script. Also note that this screen offers context menu options for Select All and Select None. This may not have been readily apparent because this is not really a Windows norm.

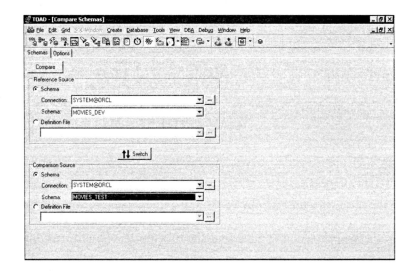

FIGURE 6.44   TOAD Compare Schemas—Source and Target.

Then you visit the Options tab's Options tab shown in Figure 6.46, which enables you to select the comparison process control options. For example, you can choose to ignore storage clauses because the development database is sized differently than production and you know this. All but two of these are fairly self-explanatory and require no explanation. The Only Compare Object Names Like field lets you filter using simple Oracle pattern matches (for example, LIKE '%X%'). And the Stop When # Differences Exceeds check box permits you to define after how many differences the comparison process ends. This is very handy when you have lots of differences and are willing to capitulate (that is, stop) after a certain threshold.

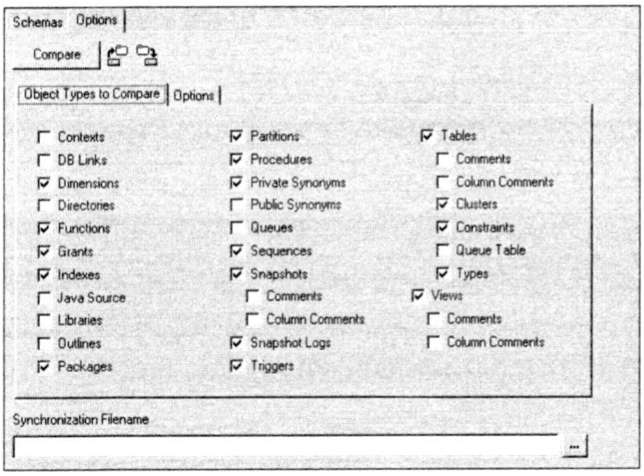

Now you click the Compare button and wait for the results as shown in Figure 6.47. Note that you actually have three results tabs from which to choose. The Results (Interactive) tab permits you to easily view and navigate all the individual difference results, plus it offers the ability to view the SQL required to synchronize just a selected difference as shown in Figure 6.48. Looking again at Figure 6.47, we see that the Results (Interactive) tab presents three major difference categorizations: objects in both schemas that differ, objects in source but not in target, and objects in target but not in source. Opening up the objects in both schemas, but which differ node, as shown in Figure 6.49 exposes the myriad of differences between the development and test databases that were compared. TOAD understands and can compare all major Oracle

FIGURE 6.45   TOAD Compare Schemas—Object Types.

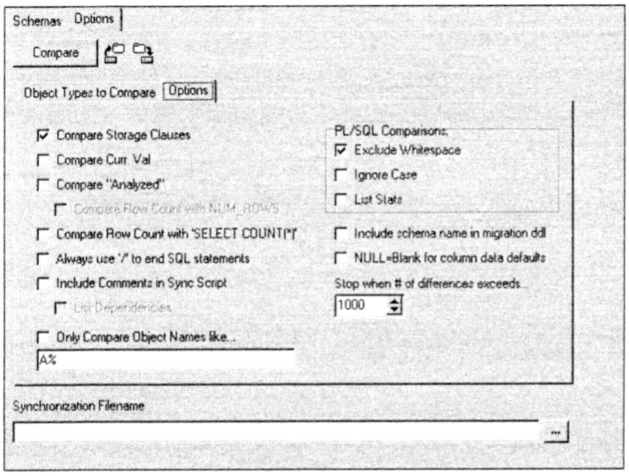

FIGURE 6.46   TOAD Compare Schemas— comparison options.

8i and 9i features, so you can get a boatload of differences. The Results (RTF) tab shows the same information in a rich text format appropriate for printing and the Results (Summary) tab merely displays a high-level synopsis of the differences found. Most TOAD users find the Results (Interactive) tab to be the preferred interface for examining and resolving the database differences.

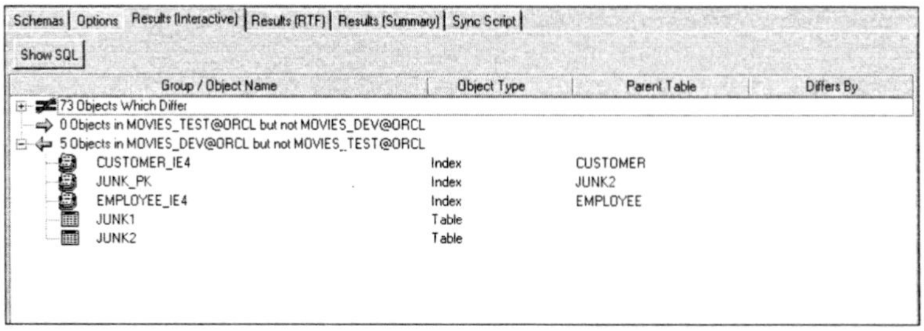

FIGURE 6.47   TOAD Compare Schemas—comparison results.

Finally, you can utilize the Sync Script tab to see all the generated DDL code to synchronize the source and target. You can save the script to a file, print it, load it into the TOAD SQL editor, or just execute it. Note that these scripts can be huge, so the recommendation is to save it to a file and then use TOAD's SQL Editor to run the statements "piecemeal." That way you can control and monitor the entire process. To just blindly execute a huge script that will be altering your database is not very good DBA practice. So take care and proceed with caution. An example synchronization script is shown in Figure 6.50.

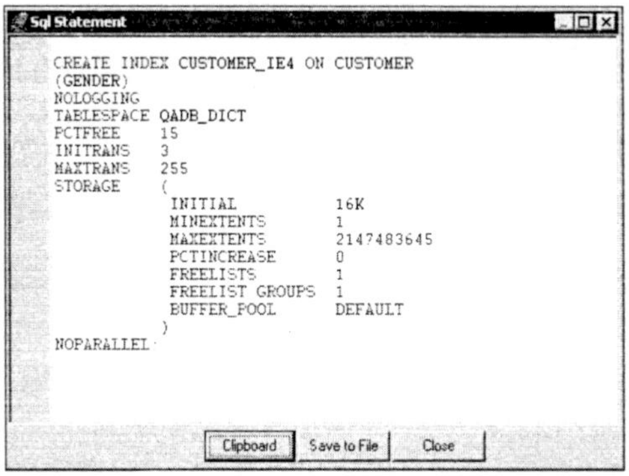

FIGURE 6.48   TOAD Compare Schemas—individual sync code.

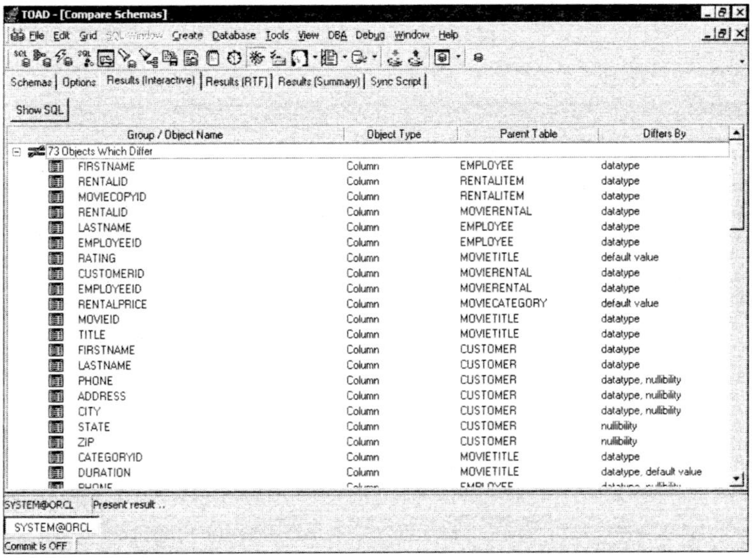

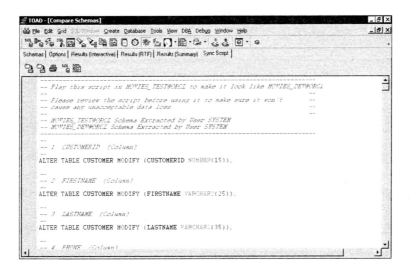

FIGURE 6.49 TOAD Compare Schemas—details of the differences.

FIGURE 6.50 TOAD Compare Schemas—Sync Script.

To receive the Compare Schemas comparison results via e-mail is a simple process. You merely visit the TOAD Options category for Email Settings and define all the appropriate information as depicted in Figure 6.51.

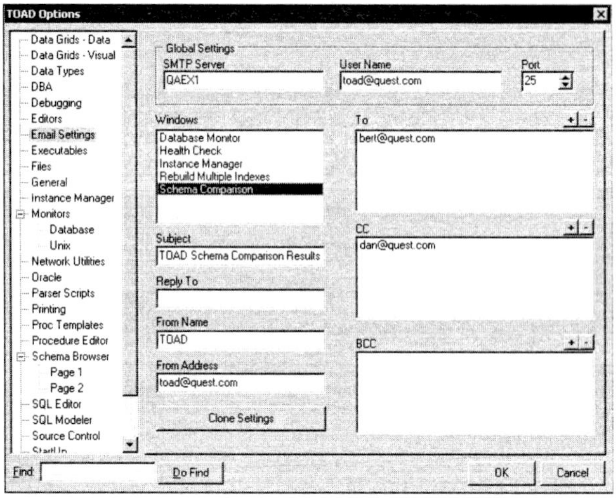

It would be ideal to have this report waiting for you each morning in your e-mail inbox so that you can start your day by checking the schema comparison statuses of all your databases. You can schedule this report to run on your Windows machine via the Microsoft Task Scheduler as shown in Figure 6.52. For Windows 2000, this is located at Start|Settings|Control Panel|Scheduled Tasks|Add Scheduled Task.

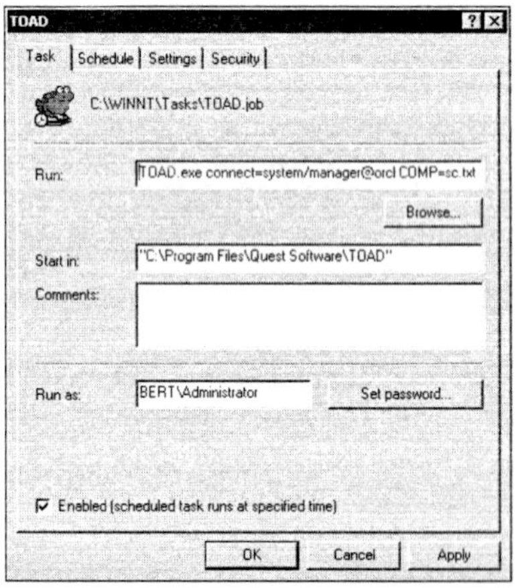

FIGURE 6.51   TOAD E-Mail Options for Compare Schemas.

FIGURE 6.52   Windows scheduling of TOAD Compare Schemas.

Note that you're simply scheduling Windows on your PC to run TOAD in command-line mode, where you provide the connection information and a compare schemas (COMP) command text file. To produce that file is very simple. You merely need to open the screen, make all your selections, and then choose the Save All Settings to File toolbar icon. The generated file will contain everything necessary to start TOAD, connect to the database, and then run this screen. The generated command file will also contain comments on some commands you can add to tailor its behavior (for example, to close the screen and also shut down when the process is complete).

Monitoring a Database Instance

On occasion, database performance becomes an issue and demands a DBA's attention. No matter how hard the DBA tries, the following bad performance scenario always happens. The telephone rings, the pager goes off, or someone walks into your cubicle because all of a sudden and without cause, database performance came to a grinding halt. Moreover, it's always the case that no one has changed anything or has issued a questionable query. They all swear it happened suddenly and for absolutely no reason. No one is ever to blame.

Fortunately TOAD has a screen for high-level monitoring exactly what's going on inside the database, and thus exposes why its performance has tanked—it's the Monitor Database screen, shown in Figures 6.53 and 6.54, and accessible from the main menu at DBA|Monitor Database. This screen graphically represents major database performance functional areas of key concern to the DBA. In essence, this screen presents a fifty-thousand-foot view of what's happening inside the database. Often one or more graphs will reveal some problem area, such as too much physical I/O or too many wait states of a specific nature. The DBA then utilizes this information to modify database conditions or parameters in order to alleviate the problems.

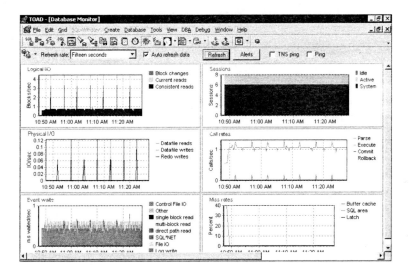

FIGURE 6.53   TOAD Database Monitor—left side.

One really useful feature on this screen that's not readily apparent is the ability to both print and zoom in on a single graph via context menu options. For example, if the database wait states were a problem, you could zoom into that graph as shown in Figure 6.55. Also, did you notice the TOAD tray icon? It animates whenever minimum or maximum thresholds are crossed. You can set these via the TOAD Options screen category for Monitors/Database as shown in Figure 6.56. Besides thresholds, you can specify whether or not to enable alerts, scripts that run for an alert, or to use the tray icon. Plus you can specify a script to run for each threshold.

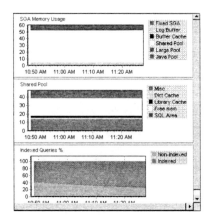

FIGURE 6.54   TOAD Database Monitor—right side.

Setting alerts to signal and scripts to automatically execute upon thresholds permits DBA's to proactively monitor and self diagnosis their databases. For example sending an email that space is running out and automatically running a clean-up script to buy the DBA time until he's received that message may well prevent unnecessary user errors or database downtime.

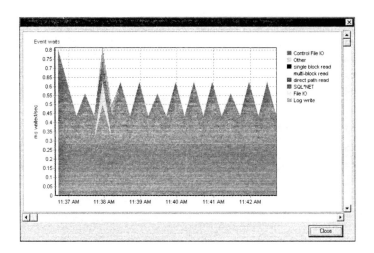

FIGURE 6.55   TOAD Database Monitor—zoom in.

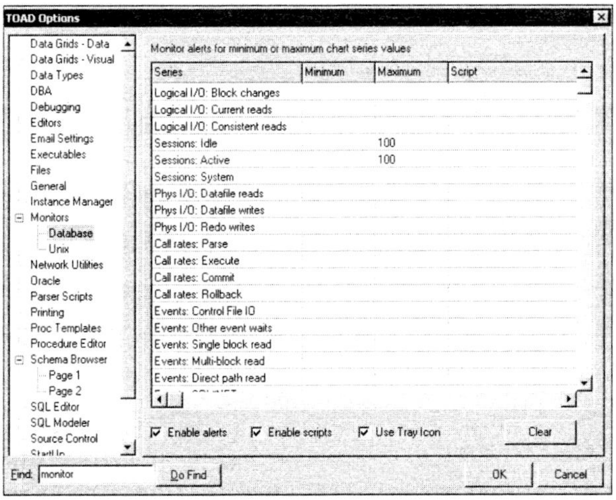

FIGURE 6.56 TOAD Monitor Options for Monitor Database.

Finally, you may find the Monitor Database screen so useful as a DBA that you want it to automatically launch every time you start up TOAD or connect to a database. You can accomplish this by simply checking the box for Open Database Monitor Window for Each Connection field in the TOAD Options screen under the DBA category as shown in Figure 6.57.

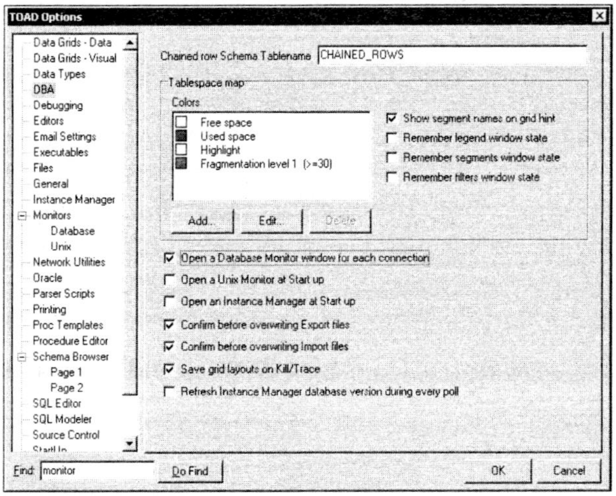

FIGURE 6.57 TOAD DBA Options for Monitor Database.

Examining Server Statistics

Sometimes while troubleshooting database performance issues, you may prefer to see major database performance functional areas of key concern in a tabular or grid format. In other words you want similar information as what's in the Monitor Database screen, but not displayed as graphs. In that case, you could run TOAD's Server Statistics screen shown in Figure 6.58 and located on the main menu at DBA|Server Statistics. This screen breaks up that performance information into five tabs, of which only the first tab supports thresholds and messages based on crossing them. Of course, reasonable default thresholds are supplied.

Note that this is somewhat of an older-style screen with far fewer bells and whistles than the Monitor Database screen. For example, it does not display a tray icon and thus has no possible animation. And the threshold values are not defined by using the TOAD Options screen, but by editing the TOADStats.ini text file in the TOAD TEMPS directory. The supported threshold categories are as follows:

- dg_row for dictionary gets
- dm_row for dictionary misses
- dcr_row for dictionary cache hit rate
- bcr_row for buffer cache hit ratio
- dsr_row for disk sort ratio
- bbw_row for buffer busy wait ratio
- fbw_row for free buffer wait ratio
- lchr_row for library cache get hit ratio
- lcpr_row for redo space wait ratio
- lcpr_row for library cache pin hit ratio
- rswr_row for redo space wait ratio
- cfr_row for chained fetch ratio
- per_row for parse/execute ratio
- cpo_row for CPU parse overhead
- tsr_row for ratio of rows from idx/total rows
- dbwra_row for DBWR avg scan depth
- dbwrs_row for DBWR avg buffers scanned

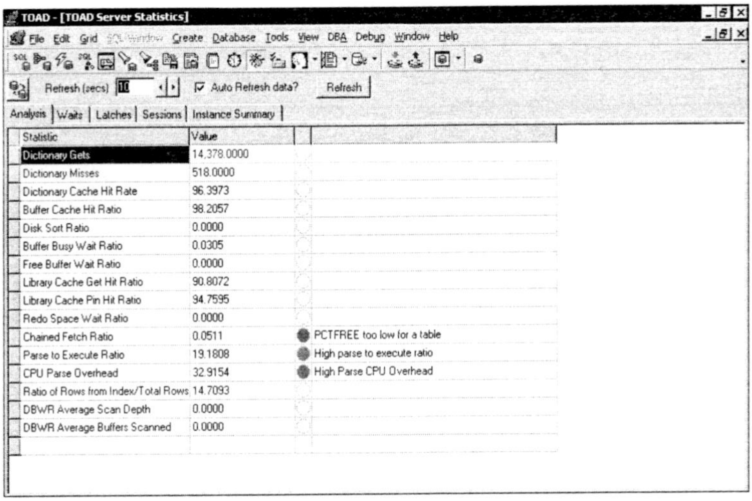

FIGURE 6.58   TOAD Server Statistics screen.

Note that TOAD expects the TOADStats.ini text file to be in the standard Windows INI file format. For each INI file entry, you can define MIN, WARN, MAX, TITLE, and MESSAGE. When a warning threshold is crossed, the circular indicator on the Analysis tab will turn pink. When a maximum threshold is crossed, the circular indicator on the Analysis tab will turn red. A small sample of how to define these INI file settings is shown following:

```
[lcpr_row]
Title=Library Cache Pin Hit Ratio
Min=80
Warn=90
ErrorMsg=Shared Pool area too small

[per_row]
Title=Parse to Execute Ratio
Warn=17
Max=20
ErrorMsg=High parse to execute ratio
```

Examining Control Files

TOAD provides the Control Files screen for viewing information about control files as shown in Figure 6.59 and located on the main menu at DBA|Control Files. This screen merely permits the DBA to view information about both the control files and their detailed record sections. There also is no capability for TOAD to issue an ALTER DATABASE BACKUP CONTROLFILE command. So this screen merely saves the DBA from having to query V$CONTROLFILE and V$CONTROLFILE_RECORD_SECTION tables.

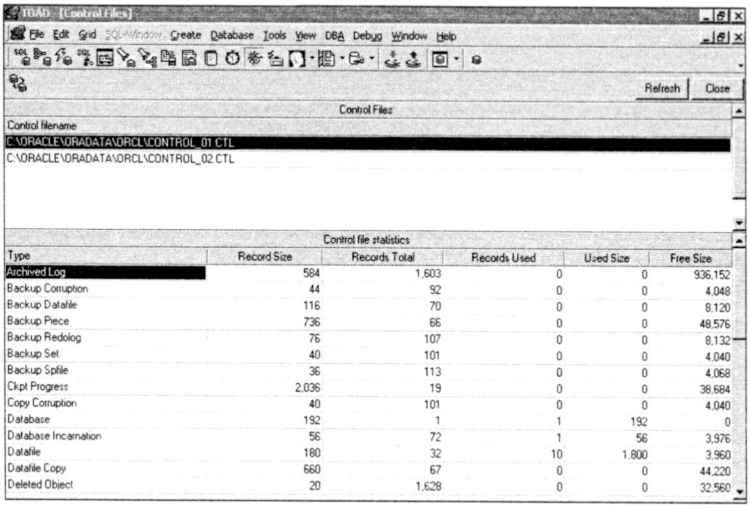

FIGURE 6.59   TOAD Control Files screen.

Managing Redo Log Files

Managing online redo log files is not something that is done very often, but it can have dramatic impact upon a database's performance. Often when a database is initially created, DBAs may specify too few groups or size the members too small. Or if additional volumes are available for database use, the DBA may need to add additional members across different locations for availability purposes. Whatever the reason, there are times when a DBA needs a friendly and efficient interface for managing all aspects of online redo log files. TOAD provides such a screen in the Redo Log Manager screen shown in Figure 6.60 and located on the main menu at DBA|Redo Log Manager.

This screen is very neat and compact, yet it provides a plethora of capabilities. It displays information about the current log file and the last log switch. It supports forcing log switches and adding or dropping of groups and members. It also displays all the members and groups currently allocated. In the case of Figure 6.60, it shows that there are four groups. Two groups have two members each and two groups have but one member each. This reflects an imbalance because ideally you should have equal numbers of members across all groups and those members ought to be the same size. Hence TOAD indicates this imbalance by marking the offending groups in red. Note that the grid permits three different display styles for the member and group information: by icon, file size, and filename. In Figure 6.60, the display is shown using the icon format. The green checks mean OK and the red X's mean not OK (unlike other places in TOAD where these icons mean online and offline). Notice that when sufficient members have been added and the display mode is switched to file size, the screen now appears in all green as shown in Figure 6.61.

The Redo Log Manager screen also displays the status of the archive log mode process, running or not. There is also support for starting and stopping the archive log mode process, as well as manually archiving current, all, next, or group. Plus you can specify the location where the log file

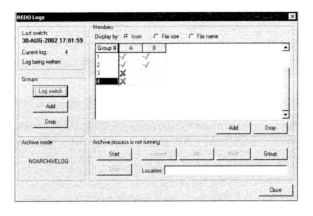

FIGURE 6.60   TOAD Redo Log Manager screen—iconic.

FIGURE 6.61   TOAD Redo Log Manager screen—file size.

should be archived. Remember that you must specify that filename based on the database server environment because the database server process on the database server machine will perform that archive process.

Examining Redo Log File Switches

Sometimes the DBA needs to get an idea of when and how often redo log switches occur. There are two main reasons for this. First, the online redo log member files might be too small and thus too many log switches are occurring. And second, there may be periods of peak database activity that stress or overwhelm the current online redo log files. In either case, the DBA is essentially looking for a very simple historical display of online redo log switching activity. TOAD offers the Log Switch

Frequency Map screen shown in Figure 6.62 and located on the main menu at DBA|
Log Switch Frequency Map. It shows both by day and hour all the online redo log
switching activity for the database.

Date	Day	Total	00	01	02	03	04	05	06	07	08	09	10	11	12	13	14	15	16	17	18	19	20	21	22	23
8/30/2002	Fri	1																		1						
8/29/2002	Thu	1												1												
8/27/2002	Tue	1																	1							
8/25/2002	Sun	1																	1							
8/24/2002	Sat	2									1								1							
8/22/2002	Thu	1																	1							
8/21/2002	Wed	1										1														
8/20/2002	Tue	1										1														
8/18/2002	Sun	1														1										
8/16/2002	Fri	1												1												
8/15/2002	Thu	1										1														
8/14/2002	Wed	2						1											1							
8/12/2002	Mon	4								1		1			2											
8/9/2002	Fri	1									1															
8/8/2002	Thu	4								1	1		1								1					
8/7/2002	Wed	1											1													
8/6/2002	Tue	1									1															
8/5/2002	Mon	1																					1			
8/4/2002	Sun	1								1																
8/2/2002	Fri	5						2	1				2													
7/19/2002	Fri	5						1									1	3								
7/18/2002	Thu	4				1							1				1			1						
7/17/2002	Wed	5															1			3	1					

FIGURE 6.62   TOAD Log Switch Frequency Map screen.

Mining Redo Log Files

Just when you DBAs think things are a bit too quiet and harmonious, someone walks
into your cubicle to announce that they've done a silly thing and need the DBA to
come to their rescue. For example, a developer may have forgotten to place a WHERE
clause on a DELETE command and thus deleted all the rows from a table rather than
just a select few. Beginning with 8i, Oracle provides a set of packages to make such
transaction recoveries possible. But to use the DBMS_LOGMINER packages without a
GUI is a tedious and garish exercise at best. So again TOAD comes to the rescue with
the DBMS_LOGMINER Interface screen shown in Figure 6.63 and accessible from the
main menu at DBA|Log Miner.

The DBMS_LOGMINER Interface screen offers a relatively straightforward, four-step
process whereby DBAs can mine online redo logs to locate and undo transactions.
Prior to invoking this screen, it is advisable to force a log switch via the Redo Log
Manager screen such that you know exactly which redo log files to mine. In the
example shown, the current online redo log was group 4. By forcing the log switch,
the contents of group 4 were now available for mining. After making your log
switch, you open up the DBMS_LOGMINER Interface screen.

Step 1 asks you to define where the log miner packages can query the contents of the data dictionary. With Oracle 9i you have two options: using the online data dictionary (fast and recommended) or using offline dictionaries created by Oracle. In Oracle 8i there is no online data dictionary option; you must create an offline data dictionary file for the packages to reference. When doing an offline data dictionary method, Oracle will need the ability to write to a server directory via the UTL_FILE_DIR INIT.ORA parameter. If this has not been set, you will have to set it and then restart your database. Be patient when creating an offline data dictionary file; this process may take a few minutes.

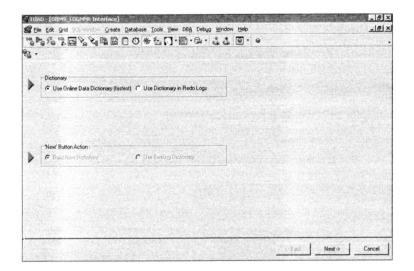

FIGURE 6.63   TOAD DBMS_LOGMINER Interface screen—step 1.

Step 2 permits you to specify which online redo log files to mine as shown in Figure 6.64. In this example, only the fourth redo log file was chosen because the transaction was recent and because online redo log file 4 had been the current group prior to the forced manual log switch. You could of course have chosen more than one online redo log file to mine. Note that the online redo log files are on the database server. So if the example had not been on a local database, you would have had to

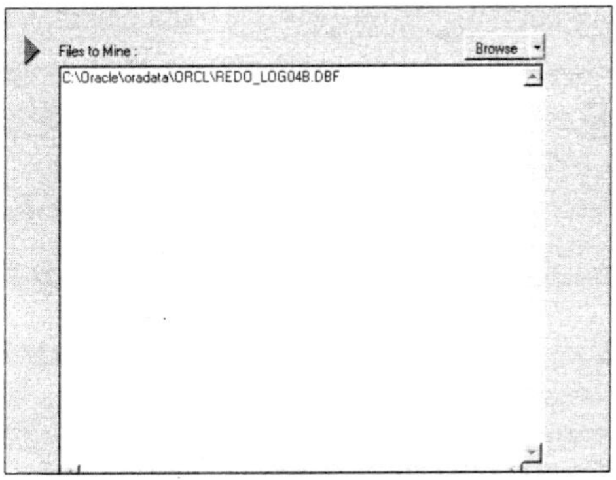

FIGURE 6.64   TOAD DBMS_LOGMINER Interface screen—step 2.

FTP copies of the files onto your PC. Fortunately, TOAD is intelligent enough to recognize that fact and would provide an FTP-style dialog.

Step 3 permits you to filter what will be mined as shown in Figure 6.65. You can limit by the Oracle System Change Number (SCN) or by date and time. Plus there are several useful Oracle 9i options, including one to show committed data only. The goal here is to expedite the log file mining process and also shorten the obtained results displayed. A typical database may have redo log files 100 megabytes or more in size, so any filtering will be advantageous. For the example shown, because the developer just recently issued the DELETE command without the WHERE clause, you could probably restrict based on time with reasonable accuracy.

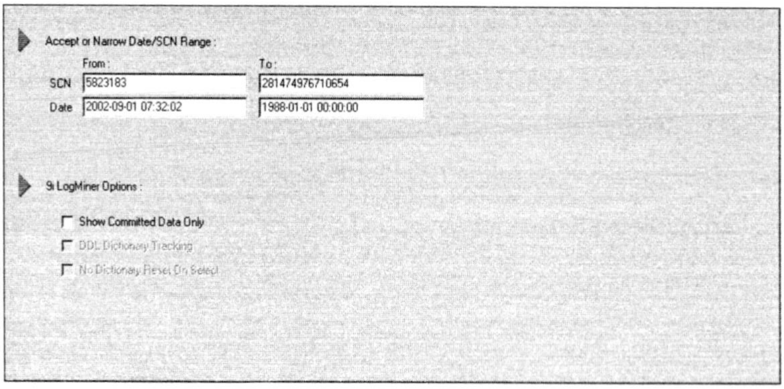

FIGURE 6.65   TOAD DBMS_LOGMINER Interface screen—step 3.

Step 4's screen initially comes up empty. You must select what options you want to see displayed and then click the Execute button. The screen will then show the redo log file mining results as shown in Figure 6.66. Remember this step can take a while, especially for those 100-megabyte redo log files. And even with filtering, the information displayed can still be quite extensive. In the example shown in Figure 6.66, scrolling to the bottom reveals that the last action to occur was delete activity against the MOVIES_DEV.RENTALITEM table followed by a commit. But note that redo log information is recorded at the row level. So in fact, there are 10,000 such entries as the one shown. If the goal is to create a script that perform undo operations for the entire logical transaction, you need to click the Move SQL to SQL Edit Window button and customize the query to your needs as shown in Figure 6.67. Now you have all 10,000 insert commands necessary to re-create the rows mistakenly deleted. You could then execute that query as a script and copy the script output into another SQL Editor window in order to actually run all those commands.

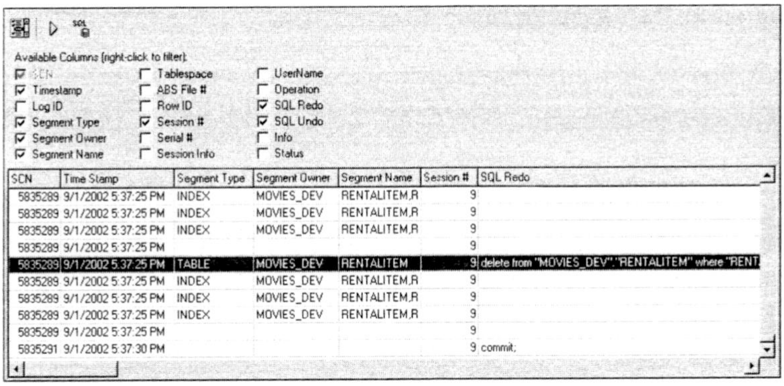

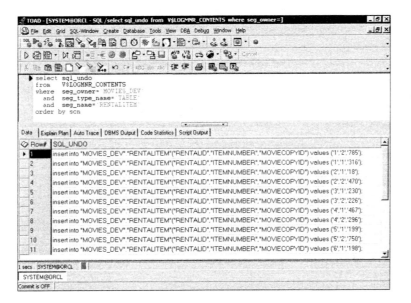

FIGURE 6.66   TOAD DBMS_LOGMINER Interface screen—step 4.

FIGURE 6.67   Building an UNDO script for a transaction.

Monitoring a UNIX Server

DBAs managing Oracle databases on UNIX servers sometimes need the ability to monitor their UNIX boxes. Although some versions of UNIX provide a monitor you that can run on the server itself, this typically requires a graphical UNIX terminal or running an X-Windows server on your PC. However, some DBAs would prefer to monitor their UNIX servers from their PC without the overhead of X-Windows. Thus

TOAD offers its Unix Monitor screen shown in Figure 6.68 and located on the main menu at DBA|OS Utilities|UNIX Monitor. It works for the following UNIX variants: Linux, Solaris, HPUX, AIX, and Tru64. This screen functions by making rexec calls to the database server. So you may need to create a ".rhosts" file on the UNIX server in the account you log in as. Moreover, some UNIX variants require that the init daemon start `rexec` with the "`-c`" option (that is, `rexecd -c`), which eliminates reverse name resolution on the server. Thus getting this screen to work may take a little server-side effort depending on your UNIX variant. So ask your UNIX system administrator for help if you run into problems.

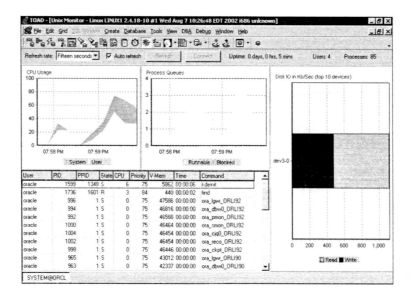

FIGURE 6.68   TOAD UNIX Monitor screen.

Tuning the UNIX Kernel

DBAs managing Oracle databases on UNIX servers must configure the UNIX kernel for their specific database requirements. This is covered in the Oracle Installation Guide for UNIX in Chapter 2 under the section titled "UNIX System Configuration." This is a critical step for both installation success and acceptable database performance. But the installation guide merely provides some suggested values and equations for calculating others. The DBA must therefore manually perform these calculations and then configure the kernel, assuming that the DBA knows the steps for doing so (the Oracle guides do not provide kernel configuration instructions). So TOAD offers the UNIX Kernel Parms screen to somewhat automate these tasks. It is shown in Figure 6.69 and is accessible from the main menu at DBA|OS Utilities|UNIX

Kernel Parms. You merely specify the UNIX variant, how many database instances, average number of users per database and average degree of parallelism, and then when you click the Calculate button, TOAD provides you both the steps to configure your UNIX kernel and the suggested parameter values for your needs.

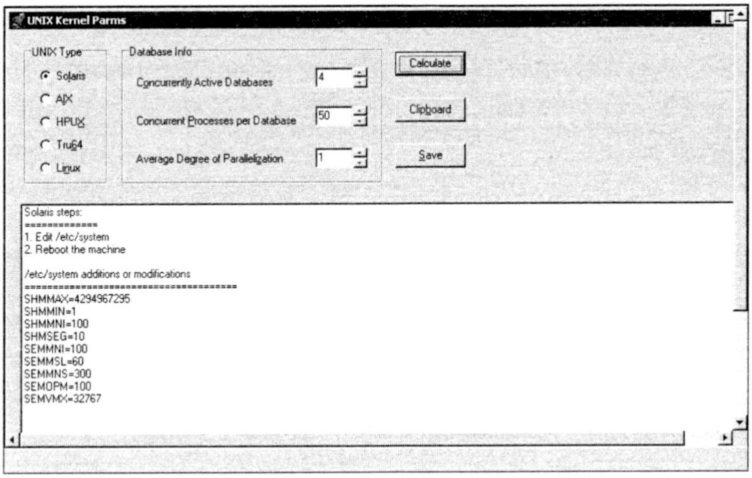

FIGURE 6.69   TOAD UNIX Kernel Parms screen.

Tuning the Windows Registry

DBAs managing Oracle databases on Windows NT/2000/XP servers must configure the Windows registry for their specific database requirements. Unfortunately, this topic is not covered in the Oracle installation guide or documentation. Thus unless the DBA is a Windows guru who already knows the arcane registry tuning techniques available, most if not all of these optimizations never get set. And the performance impact is huge. A typical Windows database server will run anywhere from 50 to 150% faster with just minor registry modifications. The problem is that the DBA must know exactly which Windows registry keys and values to set. TOAD simplifies this entire process via the Windows Registry Parms screen shown in Figure 6.70 and located on the main menu at DBA|OS Utilities|Windows Registry Parms.

This screen lets you specify key registry performance-related settings both quickly and easily. You should check all four of the check boxes (two in Memory Management and two for the NTFS File System) and also select the IO Page Lock Limit that best corresponds to the size of your Windows server. The more memory your server has, the higher you can set the value. You'll have to experiment to be sure, but most servers should benefit from a value of 8K or larger. Note too that you can set both local and remote registries, assuming that you have the proper privileges on the remote Windows server. Finally, this screen can also generate a ".reg" file rather than making the changes live.

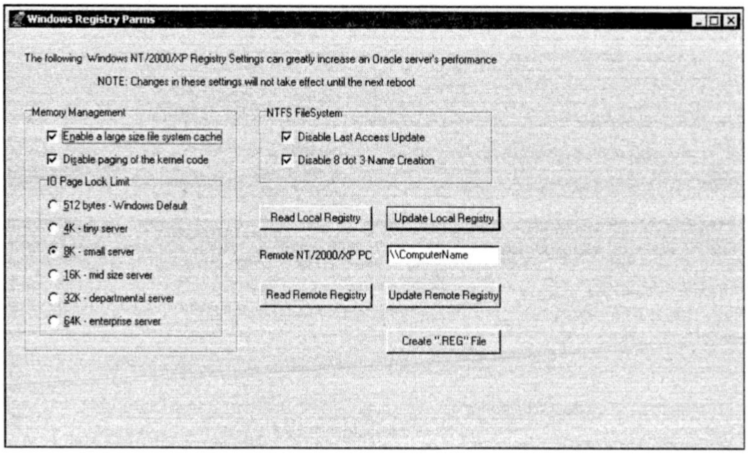

FIGURE 6.70   TOAD Windows Registry Parms screen.

Summary

This chapter covered those database administrative tasks that are considered non-routine. These are the tasks that DBAs need to do weekly, monthly, or infrequently. But all these tasks are nonetheless quite important, such as creating new databases, comparing schemas for differences, or mining redo log files. And without TOAD, these tasks would be very time-consuming for even the most experienced DBA.

The next chapter covers TOAD database reporting capabilities. It covers both TOAD's traditional and new HTML reports.

7

Generating Database Reports via TOAD

Most database application development efforts will at some time require detailed, formatted reports regarding the target database's structure. These reports are for use by a varied cast of players, including project managers, DBAs, application developers, data modelers, and business analysts. Project managers may use the reports for portions of the documentation deliverables. DBAs are often charged with publishing both hardcopy and electronic versions of all the reports. Developers may use the reports as roadmaps while writing complex SQL and PL/SQL code against the reported objects. In addition, for shops doing code reviews, those same roadmap reports will expedite and enhance the code review process. Data modelers may cross-reference the reports with their data models to verify that the database implementation meets their logical design specifications. And finally, business analysts may check the reports against both the data model and their business understandings. These are but a few examples to demonstrate how database application development efforts often require reports.

TOAD offers two key reporting mechanisms to address all such database object reporting needs: Standard Database Reports and the HTML Schema Doc Generator, both of which are covered in this chapter. Moreover, both of these database-reporting options are fully available to both DBAs and developers using TOAD. Although in some shops DBAs produce these database object reports as part of their routine tasks, TOAD does not require DBA privileged access to generate most of these reports. Thus developers and other TOAD users are free to create their own reports whenever needed.

Running Standard Database Reports

Prior to version 7.3, TOAD had only one method of database reporting, the TOAD Reports program for producing standard database reports, shown in Figure 7.1 and located on the main menu at View, Reports. In fact, it's not part of TOAD per se, but rather a separate, standalone executable in the TOAD install directory named TOADReports.exe. You will find the predefined standard reports in the TOAD installation directory under the Reports subdirectory. Note that because these reports run as a separate program and thus an entirely separate process, you can initiate a report and then leave it running—even if you exit the TOAD program entirely.

> Although standard database reports are quite useful and provide parameters for user-specified selection criteria, these reports are nonetheless not creatable or customizable by users. So you have only the predefined standard reports as provided.

As shown in Figure 7.1, the TOAD Reports program first displays a screen for selecting reports and specifying parameters. You then simply choose the report you want in the tree view of available reports. Note that there is a Report Description box in the window's bottom left corner to provide you with a definition of what information that report will provide. Finally, you select the parameters for that report on the right-hand side of the window. But be careful, as the parameters shown will vary depending on the report selected.

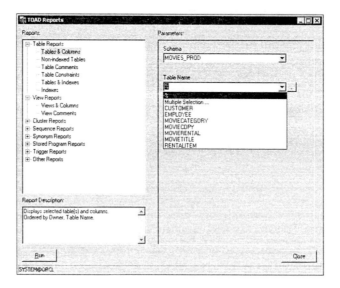

FIGURE 7.1   TOAD Reports—basic selection.

Also note that reports for tables, indexes, and views support a multi-select capability for certain drop-down list selections. In Figure 7.1, in the Table Name drop-down list, there is an entry for Multiple Selection. Selecting that entry will result in the Multiple Selection screen, shown in Figure 7.2. Now you can select multiple entries using standard Windows techniques of Shift-click and Ctrl-click. After you click the OK button in the Multiple Selection screen, you will be returned to the TOAD Reports screen, but the drop-down list will still just show Multiple Selection. You can only see the actual selected entries while the Multiple Selection screen shown in Figure 7.2 is up.

FIGURE 7.2   TOAD Reports—
multiple selection.

After you've selected the report and all its parameters, you click the Run button to execute the report. Be patient as this may take a while if you've selected a schema with many objects. Note that a progress dialog window will display so that you know that TOAD is generating the requested reports. When report generation is complete, a preview window will open where you can examine a report's output as shown in Figure 7.3. This preview window has toolbar buttons to print the report, re-run it (that is, refresh the report output in case of database changes), print the report to a file (that is, save as), and resize the display, plus VCR controls for page navigation.

If you choose to print the report to a file (that is, save as), a report output selection format window will pop up as shown in Figure 7.4. Clicking Next on this screen will open a second screen for specifying the output destination directory and other optional parameters based on the output format selected. For Adobe Acrobat, TOAD generates a single file in PDF version 1.2 (that is, Acrobat version 3.x and higher). For Excel, TOAD generates a single file in Microsoft Excel Worksheets for version 4.0. And for HTML, TOAD generates an HTML file per page of output (with the option to use or not use cascading style sheets). Note that whatever output format is chosen, TOAD does its best to represent the output exactly as shown in the preview.

Print Preview - Tables & Columns

Tables & Columns

SN151
MOVIES_PROD.MOVIECATEGORY

Owner:	MOVIES_PROD
Table Name:	MOVIECATEGORY
Comments:	

Definition:

Valid:	Yes		
Created:	09/22/2002 09:39:49		
Modified:	09/22/2002 10:39:05	Backed Up:	No
Tablespace:	QADB_DICT		
Cluster:	<none>		
Block Min% Free	10	Initial Transactions:	5
Block Min% Use:	80	Maximum Transactions:	255

Storage Parameters:

Initial Extent (B) 65536	Min Extents:	1
Next Extent (B):	Max Extents:	2147483646
Free Lists: 1	Extent Size % Increase	
Free List Groups 1		

Columns:

# Name	Data Type	Nulls?	Default Value
1 CATEGORYID	NUMBER(10)	N	
2 CATEGORYNAME	VARCHAR2(20)	N	
3 RENTALPRICE	NUMBER(19,2)	N	

Page 4 of 4

FIGURE 7.3 TOAD Reports—Preview window.

Finally, note that the category for Other Reports contains several reports that resemble Health Check-type exception reports, as shown in Figure 7.5. All these reports are from a time prior to the TOAD DBA module and its advanced database monitoring screens and health check reports. The categories and reports under the Other Reports node essentially provide an eclectic collection of exception reports that are very much like the DBA module health check reports. However, you must run all these reports individ-

FIGURE 7.4 TOAD Reports—output format.

ually, and thus you do not get one comprehensive report regarding the database's overall health. So if you have the TOAD DBA module, its monitoring screens and database health check reports will be far superior to using the Other Reports for database health checks.

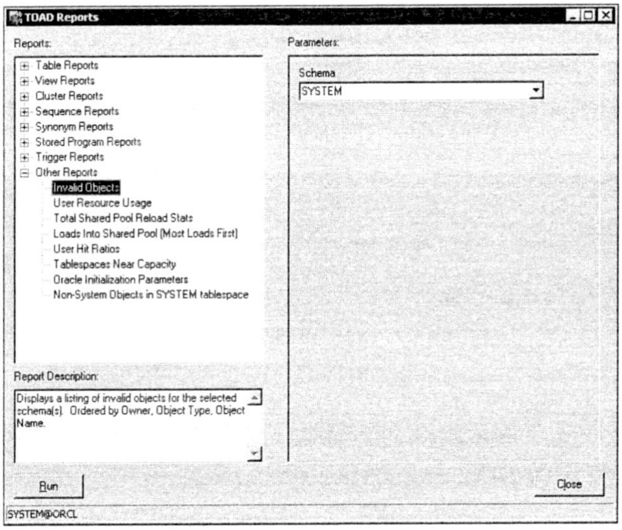

FIGURE 7.5   Other Reports—Health Checks.

Creating HTML Schema Doc Generator Reports

Beginning with TOAD version 7.3, the HTML Schema Doc Generator is the most flexible and featured method for producing database reports. Moreover, TOAD 7.4 adds major performance enhancements for generating HTML reports against schemas with large numbers of database objects. In fact, the QA test scenario was based on an ERP application with many thousands of objects. Plus, the Schema Doc Generator can be run from the command line. Therefore TOAD can now fully automate your entire HTML report generation process via the Windows scheduler.

The HTML Schema Doc Generator screen is accessible from the main menu at Tools, HTML Schema Doc Generator and is shown in Figure 7.6. This screen requires that you visit five tabs in order to specify your entire database reporting needs prior to the report execution. The first tab, Sources, is shown in Figure 7.6. This screen has two sides. The left-hand side permits you to select the schema you want to report on. You may select more than one schema, plus there are context menu options for Check All, Check None, Check My Schema, and Check My Schema only. The right-hand side of the screen is where you can

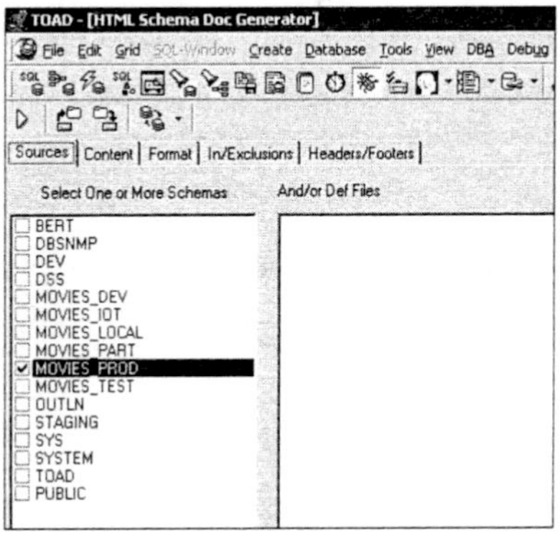

FIGURE 7.6   TOAD HTML Schema Doc Generator—Sources tab.

pick TOAD .def files as the offline data dictionary source for the HTML reports. These .def files are created via the Generate Schema Script utility (documented in Chapter 6). Note that you also must have selected the check box for Def File Will Be Used for HTML Schema Doc Generation (which makes that utility run a bit slower than if merely exporting the basic metadata for script generation).

The second tab, Content, shown in Figure 7.7 permits you to select all the summaries and objects that should be included in the HTML report. For summaries, TOAD merely generates an HTML table with object counts for all those types you request. For descriptions, TOAD simply generates different detailed output based on that object type (for example, describe-like HTML table for tables, a simple HTML text box for PL/SQL procedures, and so on). Also note that this screen offers context menu options for Select All and Select None. This may not be readily apparent because this is not really a Windows norm.

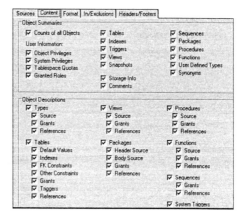

FIGURE 7.7   TOAD HTML Schema Doc Generator—Content tab.

The third tab, Format, shown in Figure 7.8 permits you to specify numerous HTML report generation control parameters. This tab is quite involved and clearly where you should spend most of your customization time and effort. There are numerous options on this tab that are fairly self-explanatory, such as the file options: background, font selections, link colors, and HTML table options. The combinations of these selections provide you with almost limitless HTML formatted output results. However, the Use Existing CSS File check box requires some explanation. When the actual HTML report file

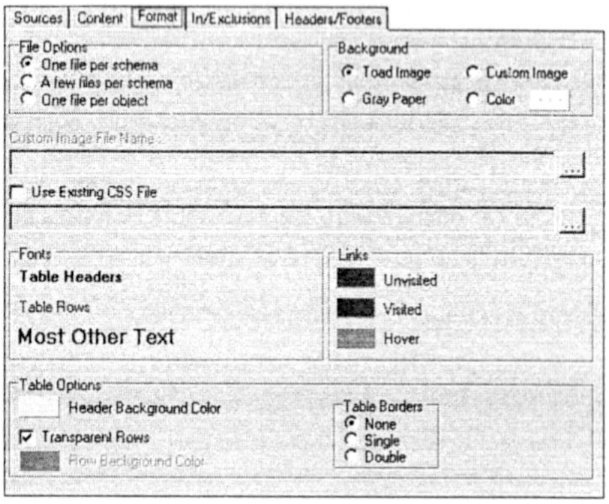

FIGURE 7.8   TOAD HTML Schema Doc Generator—Format tab.

is generated, TOAD also generates a cascading style sheet file (.css) with the same name as the report to contain all your format selections. So if you want to reuse one of your previous report's format selections on another report, you simply check this box and then select that report's .css file. Note that this will disable many of the selections on this screen because you're using the format information from that other cascading style sheet file.

The fourth tab, In/Exclusions, shown in Figure 7.9 permits you to specify complex inclusion and exclusion filter files for tables, views, and procedures. First, you merely select the Create Filter File button to create a base filter file. This is simply a text file that contains the names for the selected schemas. Then you edit that file to either add or remove object names, or better yet to use pattern-matching filtration criteria. For example, you can specify STARTSWITH: string, ENDSWITH: string, or CONTAINS: string. In Figure 7.9, the table exclusion file will eliminate tables with names that start with CUST and end with YEE (which will filter out customer and employee tables). Note that the Procs button will only be displayed after you select to either include or exclude some tables or views via a file. Then you can specify whether or not to include only procedures dependent on the tables that also pass the filters.

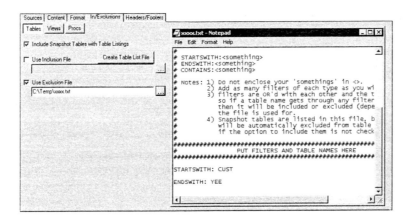

FIGURE 7.9   TOAD HTML Schema Doc Generator—In/Exclusions tab.

The fifth tab, Headers/Footers, shown in Figure 7.10 permits you to specify up to four header and footer lines for each file created by the HTML Schema Doc Generator. You may also modify each line's font selection by merely clicking the label for Font next to each line (which is actually a font button, but does not appear as such until you hover your mouse over it).

After you've visited the various tabs and have made all your selections, you click the Begin HTML Schema Doc Generation button in the upper left of the screen's toolbar to initiate generating the report. If you've selected a large schema or multi-selected numerous schemas, generating the report may require more than a few seconds. After the HTML report has been completely generated TOAD will ask you if you want to view it. If so, TOAD will open the generated HTML report file using your default Web browser and starting with the report's Table of Contents page, as shown in Figure 7.11.

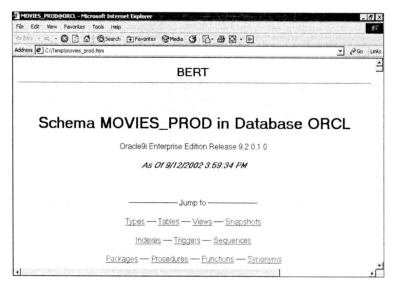

FIGURE 7.10   TOAD HTML Schema Doc Generator—Headers/ Footers tab.

FIGURE 7.11   TOAD HTML Schema Doc Generator—Table of Contents page.

The TOAD HTML report is broken down into various sections, with links to navigate the entire report. The Table of Contents page contains links to each of the database object type sections in the report (which you previously selected for generation via the Contents tab). So for example, selecting Tables takes you to the HTML table listing for the database tables shown in Figure 7.12. What you see here is simply an HTML table listing all the tables found along with some very basic data dictionary information for each. Furthermore, note that each of the table names in that HTML table live links for further drill-down into the generated report.

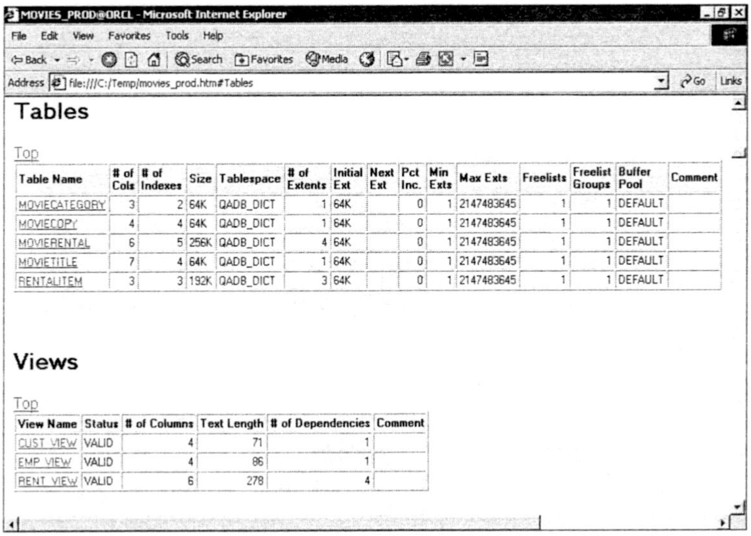

Table Name	# of Cols	# of Indexes	Size	Tablespace	# of Extents	Initial Ext	Next Ext	Pct Inc.	Min Exts	Max Exts	Freelists	Freelist Groups	Buffer Pool	Comment
MOVIECATEGORY	3	2	64K	QADB_DICT	1	64K		0	1	2147483645	1	1	DEFAULT	
MOVIECOPY	4	4	64K	QADB_DICT	1	64K		0	1	2147483645	1	1	DEFAULT	
MOVIERENTAL	6	5	256K	QADB_DICT	4	64K		0	1	2147483645	1	1	DEFAULT	
MOVIETITLE	7	4	64K	QADB_DICT	1	64K		0	1	2147483645	1	1	DEFAULT	
RENTALITEM	3	3	192K	QADB_DICT	3	64K		0	1	2147483645	1	1	DEFAULT	

View Name	Status	# of Columns	Text Length	# of Dependencies	Comment
CUST_VIEW	VALID	4	71	1	
EMP_VIEW	VALID	4	86	1	
RENT_VIEW	VALID	6	278	4	

FIGURE 7.12 TOAD HTML Schema Report—table of tables.

Thus if you're interested in drilling down into one of those tables previously shown, then selecting its link takes you to that table's detailed information section, shown in Figure 7.13. The table is shown in a describe-like fashion, with the corresponding index information in an HTML table that follows. The whole report is interconnected and easy to navigate, as these examples show. As such, many DBA's find that publishing such HTML reports internally on their companies' intranet web sites helps developers and business analysts to better perform their jobs without having to issue numerous and ongoing queries against the production database's data dictionary. In short, these reports become their offline data dictionary published for general use.

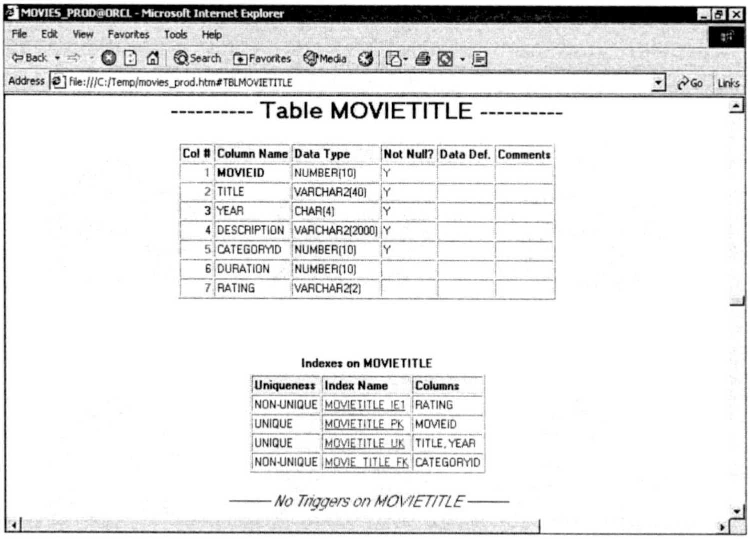

FIGURE 7.13   TOAD HTML Schema Report—specific table.

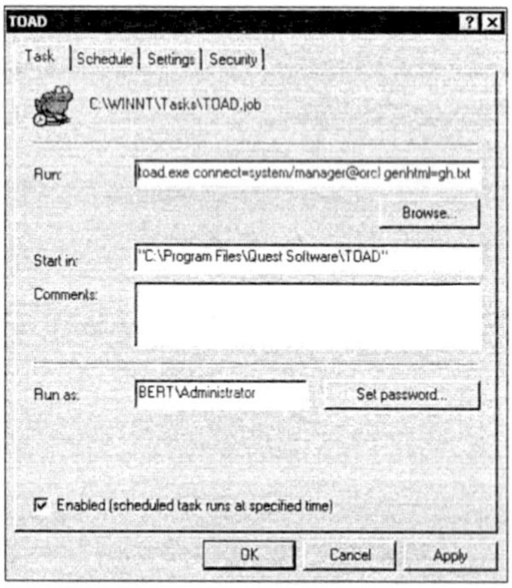

Ideally, you'd like to have this HTML report generated and waiting for you each morning in your HTML report directory. That way you could start your day by quickly checking the HTML Schema Doc report output for your databases. To accomplish this, you must schedule this report to run on your Windows machine via the Microsoft Task Scheduler as shown in Figure 7.14. For Windows 2000, this is located at Start, Settings, Control Panel, Scheduled Tasks, Add Scheduled Task.

Note that you're simply scheduling Windows on your PC to run TOAD in command-line mode, where you provide the connection information and an HTML schema doc generate (that is, GENHTML) command text file. To produce that file is very simple. You merely need to open the HTML Schema Doc Generator screen, make all your selections, and then choose the Save Settings to File toolbar

FIGURE 7.14   Windows Scheduling of TOAD HTML Schema Doc Generator.

icon. The generated file will contain everything necessary to start TOAD, connect to the database, and then run this screen. The generated command file will also contain comments on some commands you can add to tailor its behavior (for example, to close the screen and also shut down when the process is complete).

Running DBA Scripts to Create Reports

There's always that group of hardcore DBAs out there who hate GUIs and software in general. These command-line experts always have a library of scripts they've amassed over the years that they find superior to anything else available. So be it (truth is that I feel that way at times too, so I cannot condemn it). But TOAD can help those DBAs be more productive as well. Chapter 9 introduces TOAD's Script Manager, a cool feature for organizing, executing, and adding menu shortcuts for all your scripts within TOAD. Furthermore, it comes with several useful script category libraries. For example, the DBA and Schema Object categories each contain dozens of useful scripts for reporting on database objects. Figure 7.15 shows that picking the predefined script index_similar.sql from the Script Manager's Quick Pick drop-down list launches that script within a SQL Editor and runs it (see Chapter 9 for more details on how to set up and use the Script Manager). So now power DBAs can easily organize all their report scripts within TOAD.

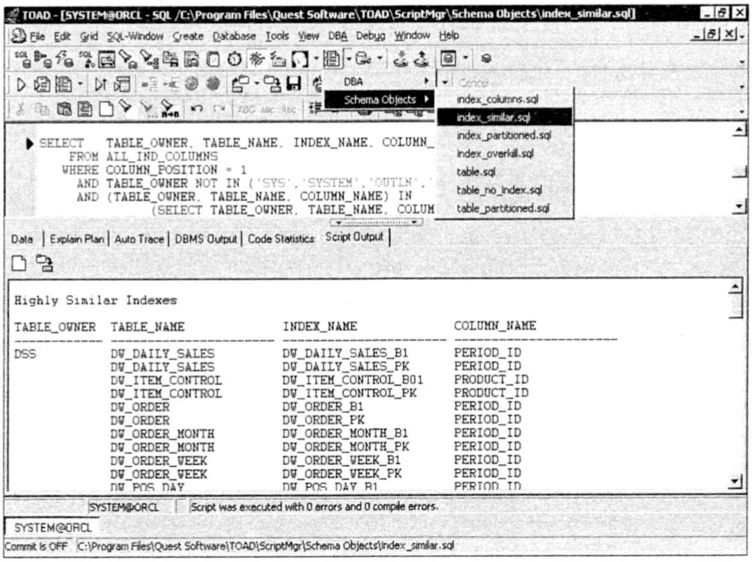

FIGURE 7.15   TOAD Script Manager—running report scripts.

Summary

This brief but important chapter covered TOAD's two primary database object reporting capabilities: Standard Database Reports produced by the TOAD Reports program, and customized reports produced by the HTML Schema Doc Generator. Initially, TOAD attempted to provide predefined reports for every imaginable user need. But users need database object reports at different times and for many different reasons. Therefore as user needs for new reports and customization increased, the new Schema Doc Generator was introduced to meet those needs.

The next chapter covers exporting data out of your database and into files using TOAD's numerous data extraction capabilities. From extracting ASCII delimited text to exporting Oracle dump files, TOAD makes saving data out of the database a snap.

8

Exporting Table Data

This chapter covers the various methods of saving and formatting data from Oracle for use in other applications. For example, it is not an uncommon request at all for DBAs to build a comma-delimited file for use with a spreadsheet application. Conventional methods (that is, SQL*Plus) would take the DBA a half a day or longer. Using TOAD, this task just takes moments.

Overview

You might want to extract data from Oracle for many reasons. You might be prepping data for an end-user's spreadsheet application. This data might have special field delimiter requirements. You might be moving data between versions and instances of Oracle. You might be doing some kind of local backup of special data.

TOAD makes it easy to save data after viewing and export data using both the Oracle utilities and system flat files, with the following methods:

- Save data out of data grid

- Export data via Schema Browser

- Export table data

- Export table data as a flat file

- Use the Export Utility Wizard

Formatting Data for Reporting/Non-Oracle Data Loads

When working with SQL and data in the SQL Editor, you can easily save the data in the Data tab of the output panel. From the menu bar, select Grid, Save As, as illustrated in Figure 8.1.

When you select Save As from this menu, you get the Save Grid Contents screen illustrated in Figure 8.2. This window gives you all kinds of options for creating the output file. The top section (Format) offers choices for the format. Notice that in this section, you can choose to create the data in various Web formats. The second section (Options) allows you to format the data with headings, and quote the character strings (important for some software's import facilities). In the third section (Save To), you can choose whether to copy the data to a file or to the clipboard.

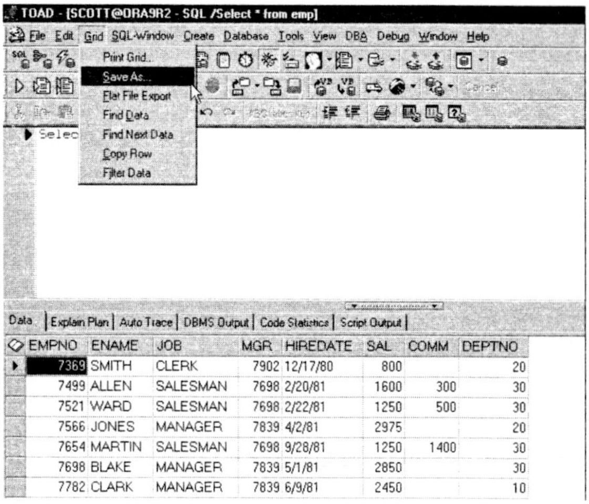

FIGURE 8.1   TOAD SQL Editor options for saving data.

Notice that in the Options section, you can select your delimiter as a field separator. Figure 8.2 shows the delimiter being changed to a colon ':'. Notice the resulting colon-delimited data output in Figure 8.3.

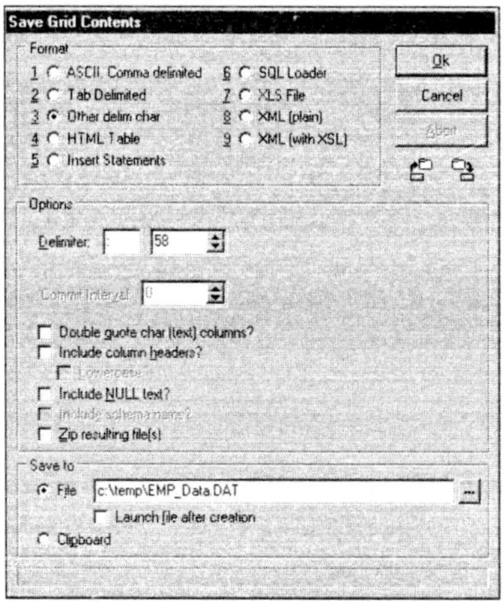

FIGURE 8.2   Options in the Save Grid Contents window.

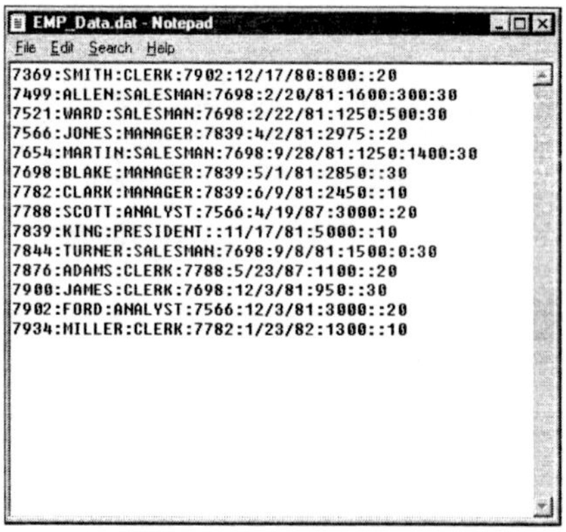

FIGURE 8.3   Colon-delimited data in Notepad.

Formatting Data as INSERT Statements

TOAD allows you to export data from the Schema Browser into INSERT statements. Right-clicking on the table in the Tables tab of the Schema Browser brings up the list of menu items illustrated in Figure 8.4. Select Export Data and you get the Data Export window shown in Figure 8.5. The Columns tab of the Data Export window allows you to select the columns you want.

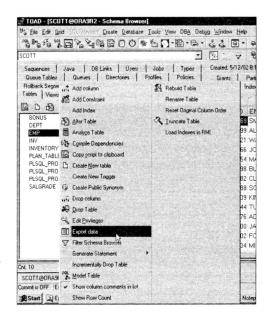

Creating a script with INSERT statements is very useful in moving data between instances of Oracle and even in moving data to other relational databases.

FIGURE 8.4 Exporting data in the Schema Browser.

The Options tab of the Data Export window (see Figure 8.6) allows you to create a file or copy to the clipboard, and add some additional information such as schema owner to the text, add WHERE and ORDER BY clauses, and so on.

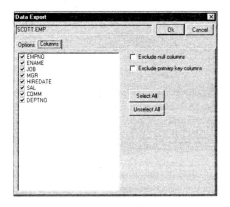

FIGURE 8.5 The Columns tab of the Data Export window.

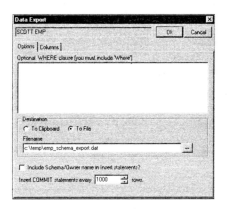

FIGURE 8.6 The Options tab of the Data Export window.

Figure 8.7 shows the output that results from this option. Notice that this option creates a script of INSERT statements.

If you are dealing with a large number of rows, particularly if the rows contain a large amount of data, you might want to do a COMMIT a little bit more frequently than 1000 rows. This really aids Oracle in handling larger transactions and the REDO logs.

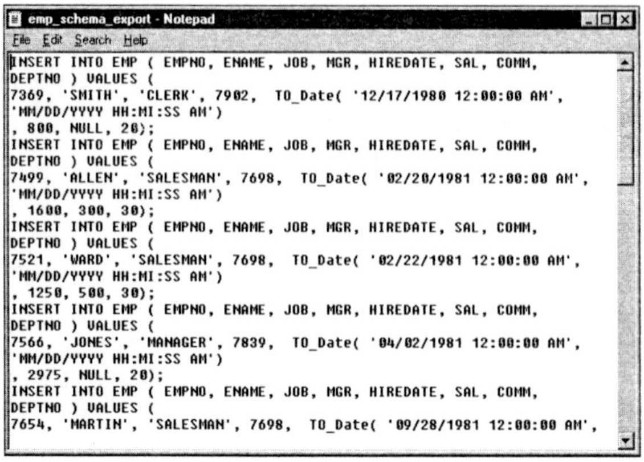

FIGURE 8.7   INSERT-formatted data in Notepad.

Formatting Multiple Table Data as INSERT Statements

TOAD allows you to export many kinds of things from the Database, Export menu, as illustrated in Figure 8.8. When you choose the Table Data submenu, the Data Export window displays. Notice that TOAD can easily create scripts for the various Oracle objects. This section will limit itself to the options that are available from the Data Export window.

FIGURE 8.8   Database Export menu options.

Figures 8.9 and 8.10 show the Tables and Options tabs of the Data Export window, which allow you to make choices for controlling the output. These options are much like those in the Schema Browser except that this window allows you to choose more than one object.

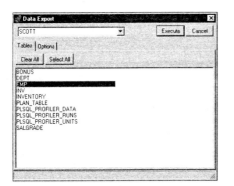

FIGURE 8.9   Export Table selection options.

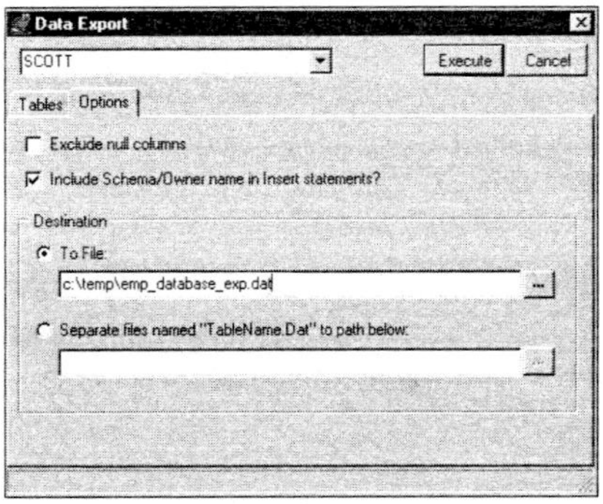

FIGURE 8.10   Export Table Output options.

Figure 8.11 shows what this data looks like formatted in Notepad.

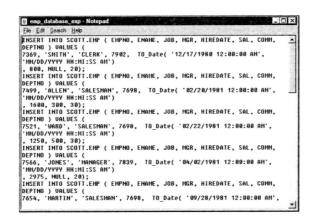

FIGURE 8.11   Multitable INSERT-formatted data in Notepad.

Using the Export Utility Wizard

The Export Utility Wizard gives you a convenient way to use the Oracle Export program. The file that the Oracle Export program produces is in an Oracle proprietary format and can only be used with the Oracle Import facility. TOAD also has an Import Utility Wizard. Export is useful for moving data, performing some kinds of backups (user data and incremental backups), and helping the DBA perform some tasks, such as reorganizations. Figure 8.12 shows how to access this wizard from the DBA, Export Utility Wizard menu.

 It is beyond the scope of this book to discuss all the features and uses of the Oracle Export/Import facility.

FIGURE 8.12   Accessing the Export Utility Wizard.

TOAD sets up the Export facility using most of the features available for export. Notice in Figure 8.13 that Export Tables is selected. As Figure 8.14 shows, you can then select any schema table data.

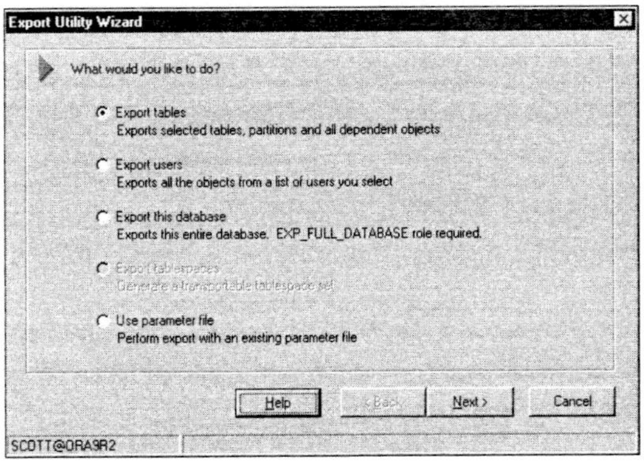

FIGURE 8.13   Export Object type selection.

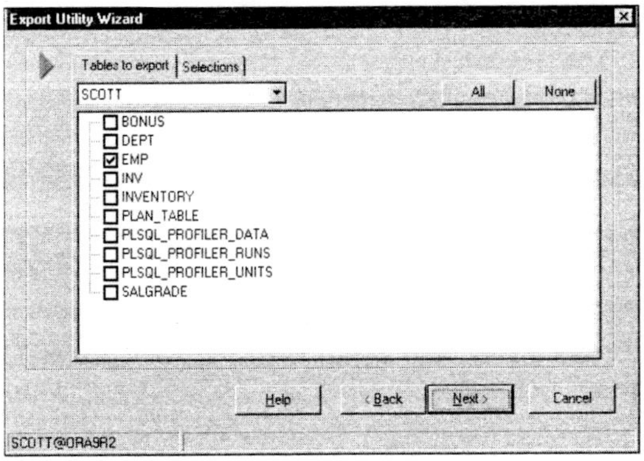

FIGURE 8.14   Export Table selection.

The next screen in the wizard, shown in Figure 8.15, brings up specific Export options. The screen shown in Figure 8.16 allows you to choose the file creation names and locations.

For this example, we will choose just to build the parameter file; see Figure 8.17. Figure 8.18 illustrates the Export Parameter file that we just created.

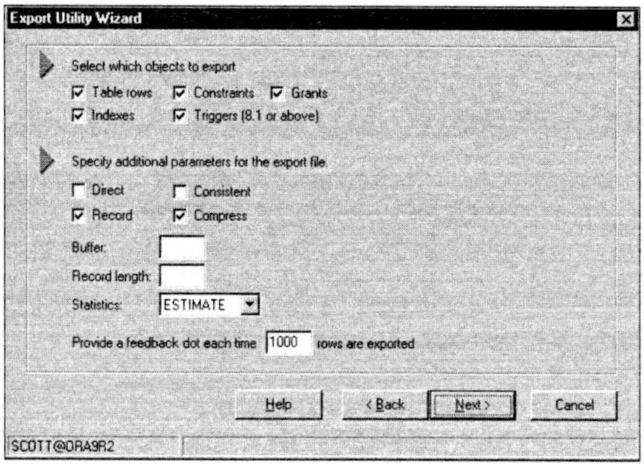

FIGURE 8.15   Oracle Export options.

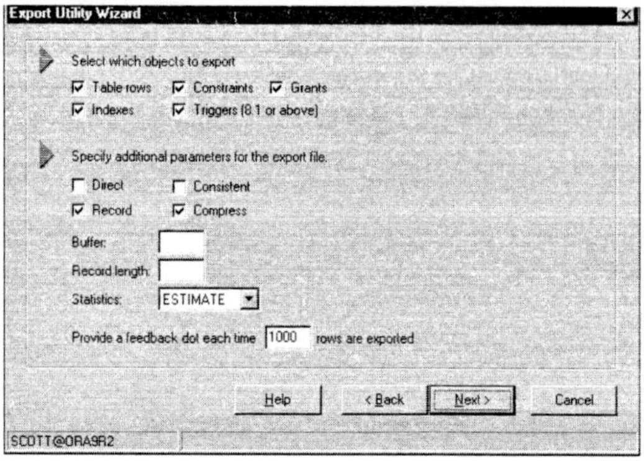

FIGURE 8.16   Export file location and names.

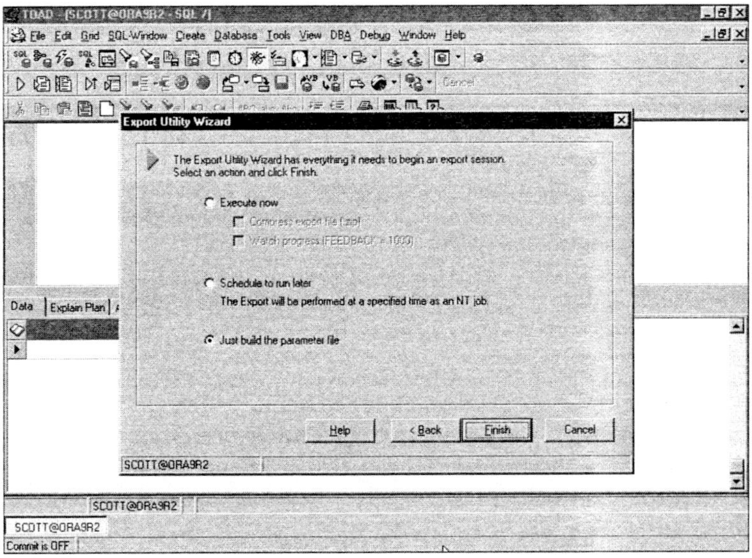

FIGURE 8.17   Export runtime options.

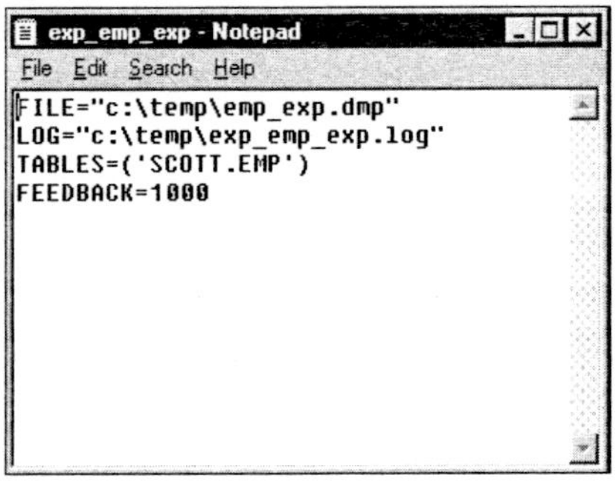

FIGURE 8.18   Export Parameter file in Notepad.

Summary

This chapter covered getting data out of Oracle into various formats. TOAD easily allows you to format data into a variety of output styles, delimited files, and scripts that contain INSERT statements around the data.

The next chapter covers other useful TOAD features that are useful to either the Oracle developer or the Oracle DBA.

9

Using Other Powerful TOAD Tools

TOAD is truly the be-all, Swiss army knife of Oracle tools. It has features for DBAs, developers, business analysts, and just about anyone else who needs to do Oracle-related work. So far, the chapters have been organized for basic operation and by job function. But there are so many features in TOAD that a chapter is needed to cover some functionalities that don't fit so neatly in the other chapters. That's not to say that these TOAD features are less useful, but more likely that they may span job functions. For example, both developers and DBAs need to manage their scripts, perform FTP of files, and possibly telnet to remote servers. So these tasks are not special or relegated to just one type of TOAD user per se, but are generally utilized by many different categories of users. Moreover, some of these features have less to do with the Oracle database than they have to do with TOAD and its operation. So again, these features would apply to just about any type of TOAD user.

So now let's examine in more detail all those features above and beyond SQL or PL/SQL coding and DBA tasks. This chapter outlines all those features that people attending TOAD user groups often don't know about. Their reaction to these features is to say "Wow, since when could TOAD do that? "

Browsing Master-Detail Data

When doing relational database work (regardless of whether you are a DBA, developer, or business analyst), the time comes when you must be able to inspect and sometimes modify data. Of course, you could use TOAD's SQL

Editor window with its data grid, but today's highly normalized databases would make "one table at a time" efforts tedious and error-prone. What's generally necessary is a screen where you can easily see a table, its related tables, and their synchronized data (that is, focus on parent sets and focus on children to the same base record). TOAD has just such a screen in its Master Detail Browser, shown in Figure 9.1 and located on the main menu at Tools, Master Detail Browser.

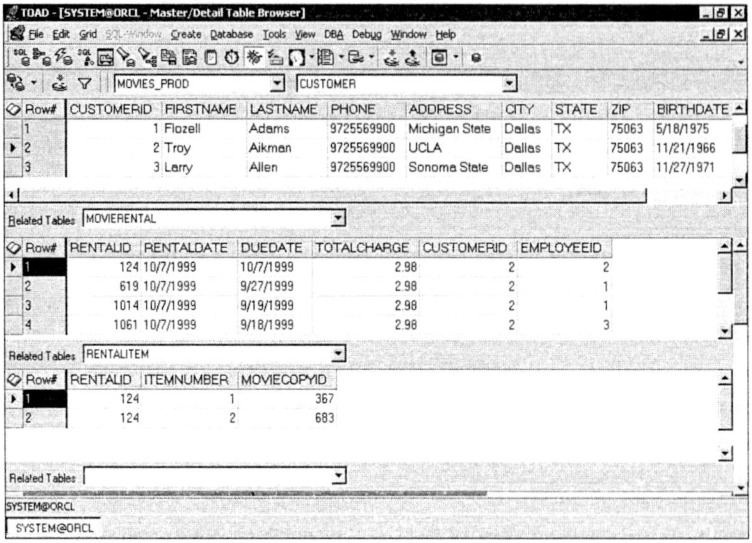

FIGURE 9.1   TOAD Master Detail Browser screen.

When you first enter this screen, the data grids will be blank. You must first select a base schema and table for which you want to see the results. For a database schema possessing referential integrity constraints (that is, foreign keys), selecting a table for the topmost data grid automatically results in TOAD populating the related table selections and querying their data. Plus all these grids are kept synchronized. You navigate the grid results, and the lower grids' data are kept completely synchronized to your selections. So with this one screen, you can now inspect and update all your data within the context of its complete and accurate relational environment.

Even though TOAD only retrieves 25 rows at a time for data grids, selecting a parent table that has numerous detail data grids and many rows per grid can result in this screen taking a very long time to initially locate all the candidate rows and then populate all the data grids even for the limited number of rows being returned. Moreover, the related data grid synchronization as you navigate can also slow things down further. Thus TOAD offers the ability to filter the parent table. You simply click the Filter/Sort main table data button, which will open up the dialog shown in Figures 9.2 and 9.3. This screen offers two tabs: one for sorting and one for filtering.

After you've made your sort and filter selections, click OK. TOAD will now change the color of the filter toolbar icon to red as an indicator that it's active, and then apply both the filter and sort operations to the first data grid. Figure 9.4 shows the results of using filters and sorts (note how the filter icon is now red indicating that it's active).

Of course, after you've inspected the data and found those rows that require modification, it's the exact same process as used in the SQL Editor data grid (refer back to Chapter 3). You can make those modifications directly in the data grid by simply selecting the cell and making the change. For numeric fields, a built-in calculator is available, as shown in Figure 9.5. For Date fields, there is a built-in calendar, as shown in Figure 9.6.

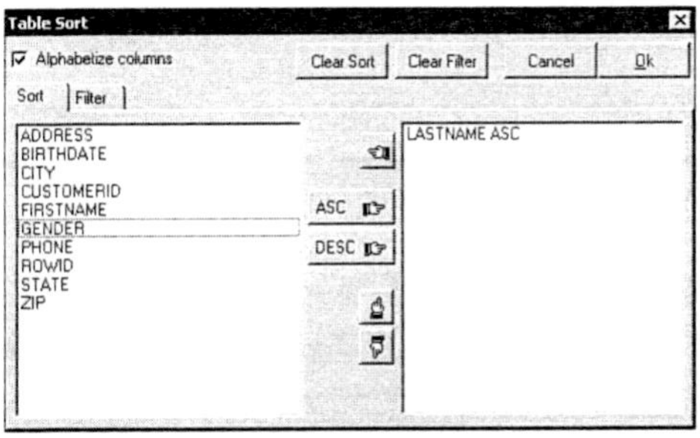

FIGURE 9.2 TOAD Master Detail Browser—Sort tab.

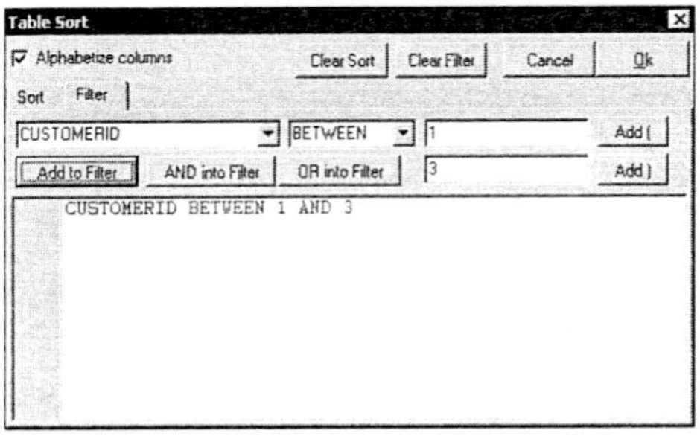

FIGURE 9.3 TOAD Master Detail Browser—Filter tab.

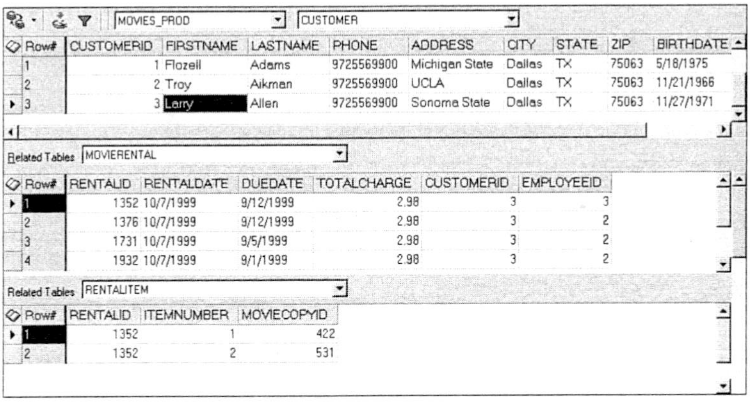

FIGURE 9.4 TOAD Master Detail—filtered results.

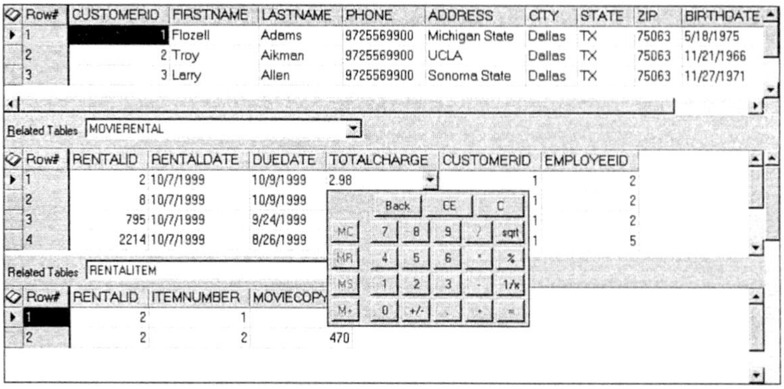

FIGURE 9.5   TOAD Master Detail—Calculator.

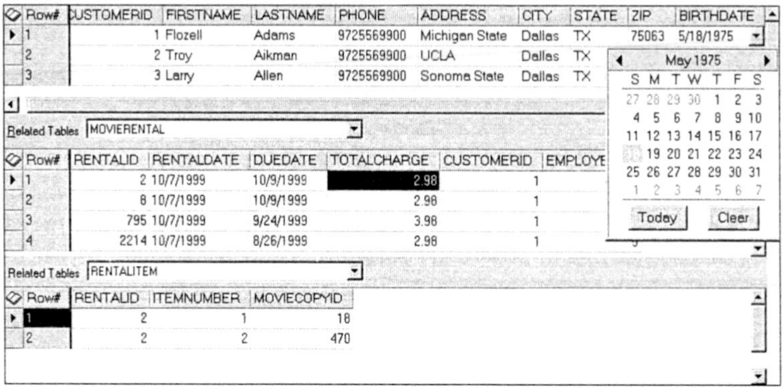

FIGURE 9.6   TOAD Master Detail—Calendar.

Plus, you can switch to single-record view mode for editing as shown in Figure 9.7 by merely clicking on the Single Record View icon in the upper-left corner of the desired data grid. Finally, this screen's data grids also offer context menu options for Print Grid and Save as. Refer back to Chapter 3 for more details.

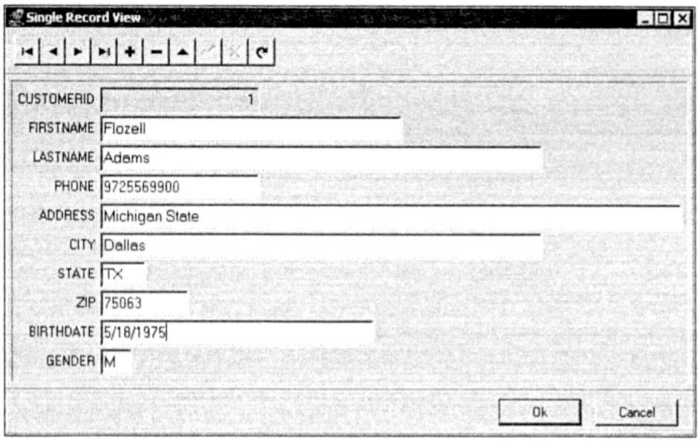

FIGURE 9.7   TOAD Master Detail—single-record view.

Modeling Complex SQL Visually

Not everyone is comfortable with writing SQL, especially complex joins with group operations, HAVING clauses, and sorts. What many people want is a visual query builder that enables them to model what they want and that can then generate the SQL that's required. For this need, TOAD offers the SQL Modeler shown in Figure 9.8 and located on the main menu at Database, SQL Modeler. And though this screen may look very simple, it's one of the most feature-rich and powerful screens within TOAD. There are very few SQL coding techniques that cannot be successfully modeled here and then generated.

When you first enter this screen, both the top left and bottom portions of the screen will be empty. These are the model area and Criteria/Generated Query/Results/Explain Plan tab area, respectively. Only the top right portion of the screen will contain information. This area is known as the table selector. There are splitters between all three of these areas for resizing to best suit your screen resolution and other needs or tastes.

There are just three simple steps to begin using the TOAD SQL Modeler. First, you must select a schema from the drop-down list in the table selector area, which then populates the objects from which you can select. Then you drag and drop tables, views, or synonyms from the table selector area into the model area. And finally, you check those columns in the selected objects of the model area that you want projected. While you're doing these basic steps, the Criteria tab area will begin to fill in as shown in Figure 9.8. That's all there is to it. You're now visually creating your SQL queries (that is, SELECT commands). However, there is a lot more you can do with this screen than these basic steps.

The SQL Modeler has numerous options that warrant discussion before proceeding with describing how this screen works. Unlike many other TOAD screens where the options can be discussed last as they do not radically change screen interaction, the options for the SQL Modeler must be discussed first because they do in fact significantly change the way you work with the screen. If you open a context menu in the model area as shown in Figure 9.9, you will see numerous options. You can specify on the Show submenu what level of information will be displayed in the model area for a selected object. In the example, Join Text, Primary Keys, and Indexes have been selected. Note that if you choose too many display options, the objects in the model area become much bigger and things very quickly become cramped.

Two other options worth noting from this menu are Copy Model Image to Clipboard and Full Screen Mode [F2]. Some people will use the model image with data type, primary keys, and indexes selected as sort of a poor man's ERD (entity relationship diagram). And toggling back and forth between full-screen modes is often necessary when working with more than a few objects.

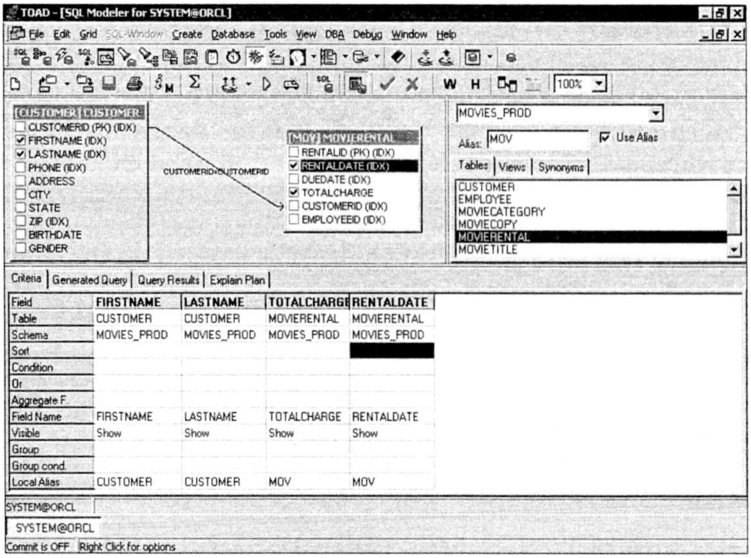

FIGURE 9.8   TOAD SQL Modeler—basic operation.

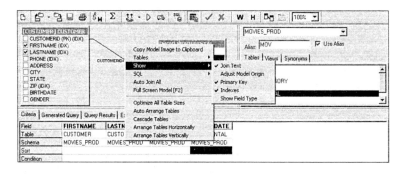

FIGURE 9.9   TOAD SQL Modeler—model area options.

Note that there are many options within TOAD related to using the SQL Modeler screen. The TOAD Options screen can be opened either by using the Toolbox icon on the main toolbar or from the main menu at View, Options. The basic SQL Modeler options shown in Figure 9.10 fall into one of three categories. First, there are options for defining fonts and colors for text and relationship lines. Second, there are options for defining the functions available for WHERE clauses and calculated fields (covered in the following paragraphs). And third, there are options that control the behavior of objects newly selected into the model area:

- Automatic Autojoin is a relationship line automatically drawn between related objects.

- Use Schema Name in Generated SQL is the generated SQL format `schema.object.column` or `object.column`.

- Automatically Select All Columns selects all the columns of the selected objects already checked.

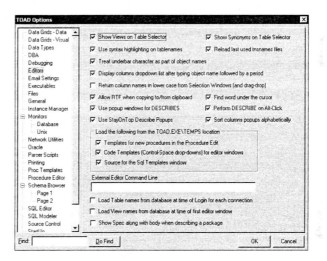

FIGURE 9.10 TOAD basic options for SQL Modeler.

However, it's the less obvious options shown in Figure 9.11 that are most problematic. Probably the most frequently asked technical support question is: How do I get views and synonyms to show up in the table selector for the SQL Modeler? The answer is simply to check both Show Views on Table Selector and Show Synonyms on Table Selector in the TOAD Options for Editors (the default for both is unchecked). So few people find this on their own, that beginning with TOAD 7.4 the defaults have been changed to those options being checked. So this issue will fade as time goes on.

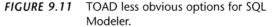

FIGURE 9.11 TOAD less obvious options for SQL Modeler.

With all your SQL Modeler options properly set, you can now effectively work on visually constructing and generating your SQL queries. Look back at the model area in Figure 9.8; the tables CUSTOMER and MOVIERENTAL were selected—the column CUSTOMERID joins them. In addition, the columns FIRSTNAME, LASTNAME, RENTALDATE, and TOTALCHARGE were selected for projection. Thus the field grid in the Criteria tab area has four columns, one for each of the selected table columns. But this in itself would do nothing more than generate a simple SELECT column FROM table command. It's now time to begin filling in the details that will result in more useful and meaningful queries. There are a lot of steps to go through, but that's because the SELECT command has so many options and the SQL Modeler addresses most of them.

The goal is to build a query using the selections in Figure 9.8 that finds all customers who have rentals in the past five years that totaled at least $2.00 and to display their total charges and the average number of days they kept a movie. Sounds pretty easy in English, but the steps to model and the code generated will most likely surprise you. That's OK, because TOAD's SQL Modeler can handle this and much more complex needs.

The first few steps are quite easy and involve merely making some very minor Criteria tab field grid selections. You'll want the resulting data sorted on output, so you'll need to define the sort options. You merely double-click in the column's Sort cell as shown in Figure 9.12 and select either No Sort, Ascending, or Descending. You can even define multiple sort fields as shown in Figure 9.13: ASC(1) and ASC(2). These last two screens have in effect added a multicolumn ORDER BY clause to the generated SQL.

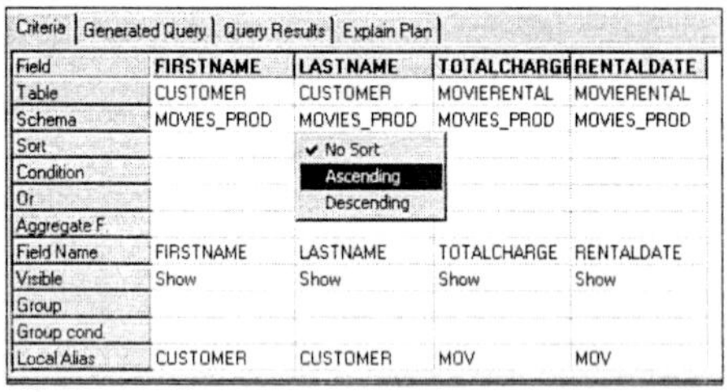

FIGURE 9.12   TOAD SQL Modeler— defining sorts.

Next you need to specify that the TOTALCHARGE column should sum all of the total charges. For this, you merely double-click in the column's Aggregate F. cell as shown in Figure 9.14 and select the appropriate group function—in this case SUM. This will result in a SELECT SUM(TOTALCHARGE) in the generated code.

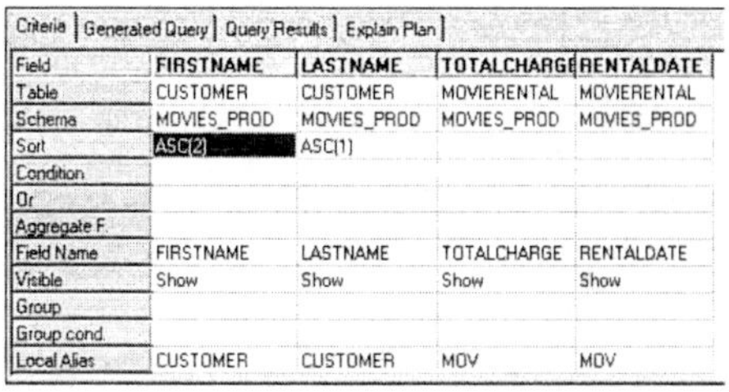

FIGURE 9.13   TOAD SQL Modeler— multiple sorts.

Then you need to define the restriction that only movie rentals for the past five years are included. Note that there are two issues here. First, you don't need to project this column, just restrict on it. So you can mark it as non-displayed by double-clicking in the Visible cell for the column to toggle from Show to Not Shown, as shown in Figure 9.15.

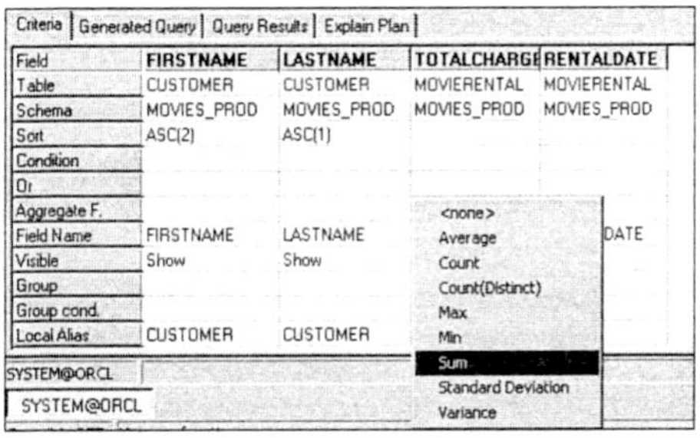

FIGURE 9.14   TOAD SQL Modeler—group function.

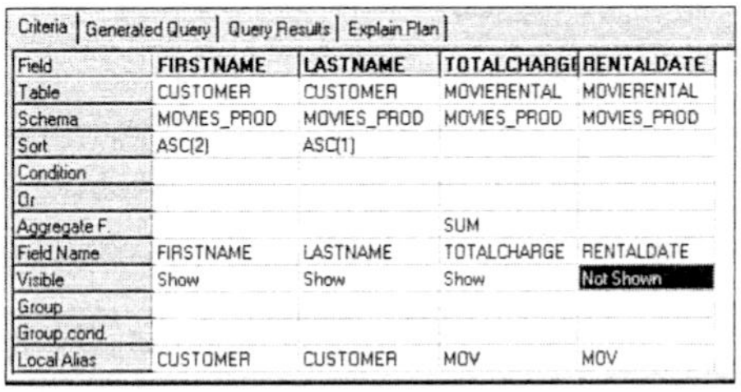

Second, you need to define the restriction (that is, the WHERE clause) by simply double-clicking in the Condition cell for the desired column. This will launch the WHERE Definition screen shown in Figure 9.16. Here you simply define the restriction operator and its value or values. You can also specify a subquery from another SQL Modeler query (that is, a .DML file) or switch to expert mode as shown in Figure 9.17. Note that after you switch to expert mode for a particular field, you cannot switch back.

FIGURE 9.15   TOAD SQL Modeler—not shown.

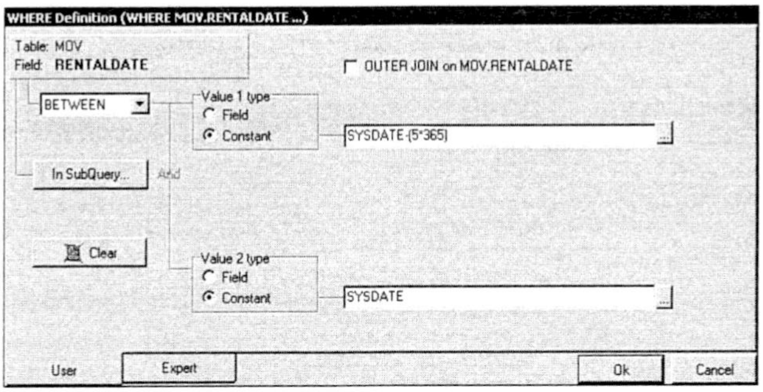

FIGURE 9.16   TOAD SQL Modeler—simple restriction.

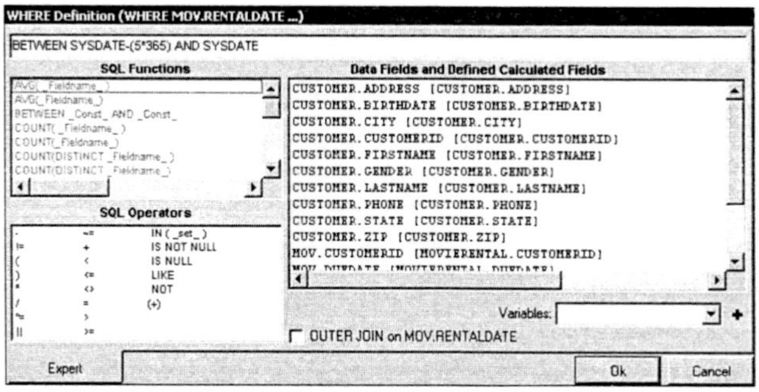

FIGURE 9.17   TOAD SQL Modeler—expert restriction.

Now comes a complex question: How do you display the days rented when there is no such column? Neither CUSTOMER nor MOVIERENTAL has a DAYS_RENTED column. But look again at MOVIERENTAL; it does have columns for RENTALDATE and DUEDATE. If you assume that the DUEDATE minus the RENTALDATE is the number of days rented, you can calculate this value. TOAD's SQL Modeler offers the Calculate Fields toolbar button (the sigma symbol) for just this scenario. You click this button to launch the Calculated Fields screen as shown in Figure 9.18.

You supply a calculated field name and press the + key, which launches the Calculated Field Definition screen as shown in Figure 9.19. Here you define the calculation expression to use. This is essentially the same screen as the WHERE Definition screen back in Figure 9.17 (minus the outer-join option).

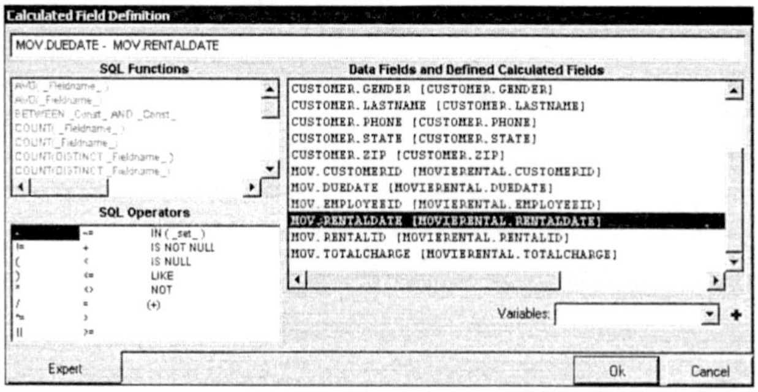

FIGURE 9.18   TOAD SQL Modeler—calculated fields.

FIGURE 9.19   TOAD SQL Modeler—define calculation.

Then after the expression is defined, you must finally associate the calculated field with a table as shown in Figure 9.20. This is where the calculated field will show up back in the model area as shown in Figure 9.21. See how DAYS_RENTED is now part of the MOVIERENTAL table? Finally, note that DAYS_RENTED also has its Aggregate F. value set to AVG because this was part of the original request. This was done manually after defining the calculated field.

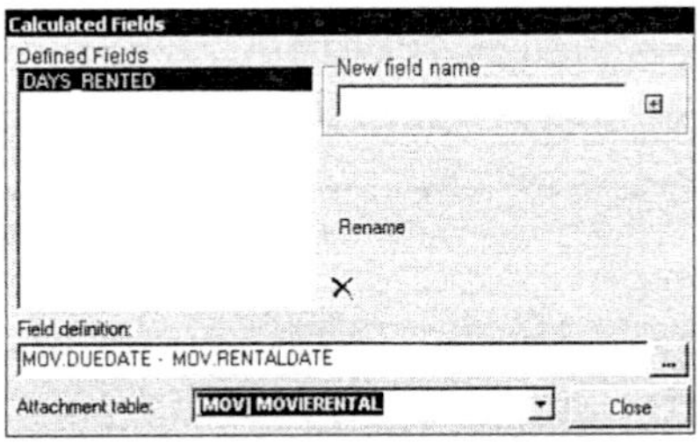

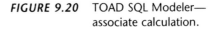

FIGURE 9.20 TOAD SQL Modeler—associate calculation.

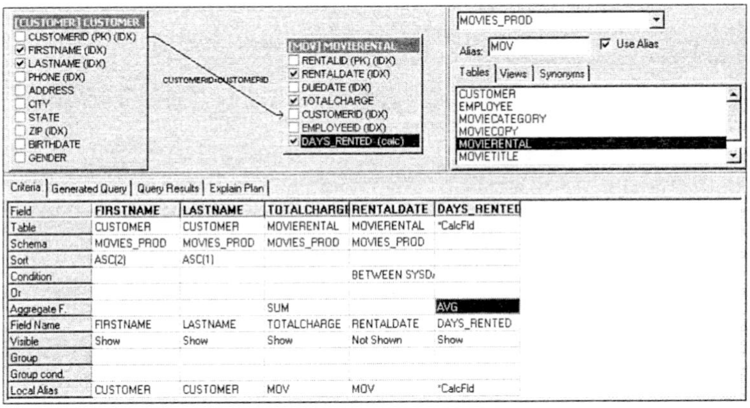

FIGURE 9.21 TOAD SQL Modeler—calculated field's home.

All that's left now is to define the grouping information and you're ready to go. There's just one simple golden rule to remember—all displayed fields that do not have aggregate functions must be grouped. So in Figure 9.22, the fields for FIRSTNAME and LAST-NAME have been indicated as grouped. This was accomplished by merely double-clicking in their Group cells to toggle from ungrouped to grouped.

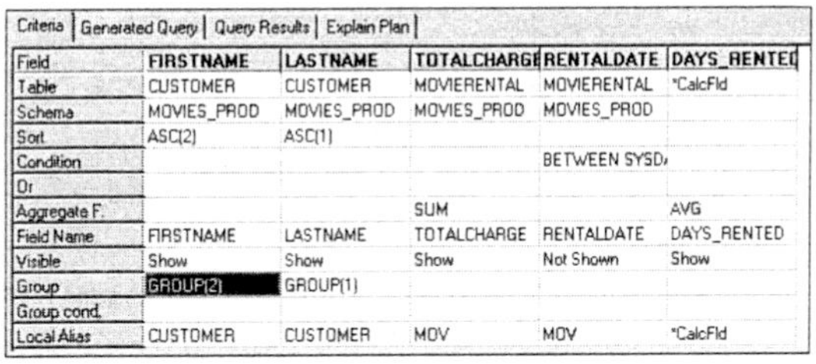

FIGURE 9.22 TOAD SQL Modeler—grouped columns.

But wait, there was one more key requirement—only for total charges whose sum was at least $2.00. The idea is to eliminate people with one-time rentals for less than two bucks. You cannot accomplish this with a WHERE clause because it must be restricted based upon the results of the aggregate or group operation. Therefore you must click the toolbar button for Global Having Condition editor (the H button) and launch the screen shown in Figure 9.23.

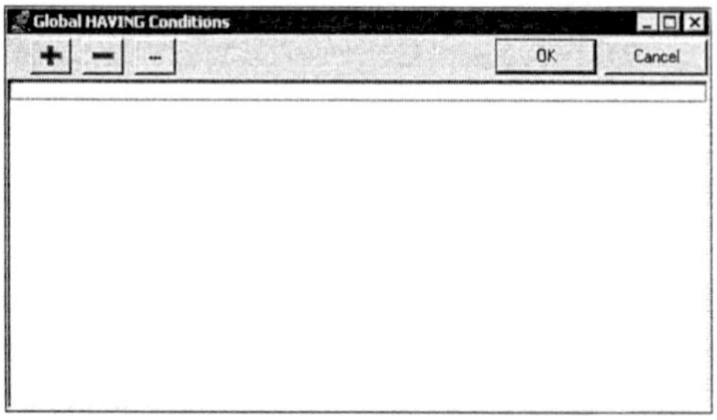

FIGURE 9.23   TOAD SQL Modeler—global HAVING conditions.

Here you simply press the + key to create a new HAVING condition, and it launches you into the Global Having Definition screen shown in Figure 9.24. As with calculated fields, this is essentially the same screen as the WHERE Definition screen back in Figure 9.17 (minus the outer-join option). With that, you've now fully modeled the requested query.

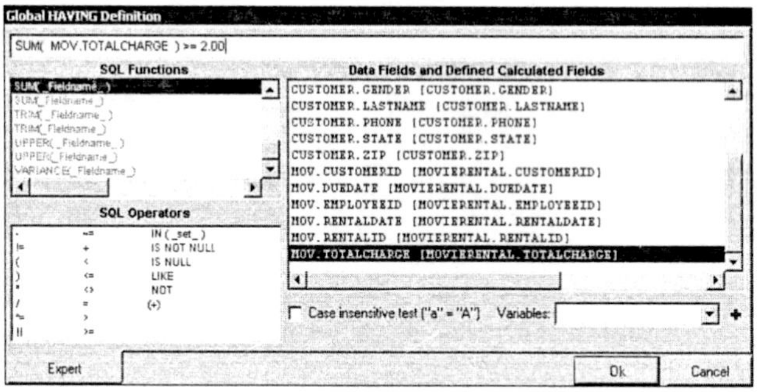

FIGURE 9.24   TOAD SQL Modeler—Global HAVING expression.

The Generated Query tab will now contain the generated SQL as shown in Figure 9.25. For many people, writing a query such as this would have been beyond their skill set. Yet with the aid of a screen like the SQL Modeler, just about anyone can easily write effective and efficient SQL queries against even the most complex database design. And although you can run the queries here directly as shown in Figure 9.26, you can just as easily send the generated SQL to the TOAD SQL Editor by using the View SQL in SQL Window button on the SQL Modeler toolbar. Now you have all of TOAD's SQL editing, tuning, execution, save as and printing options (refer back to Chapter 3). So even very experienced SQL developers could use the SQL Modeler to initiate the construction of their SQL code.

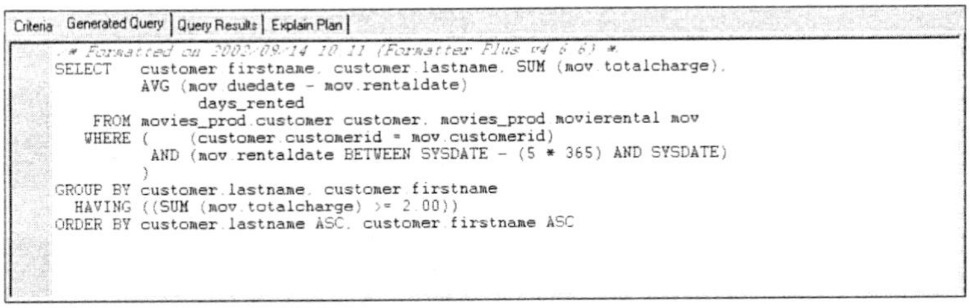

FIGURE 9.25   TOAD SQL Modeler—generated SQL.

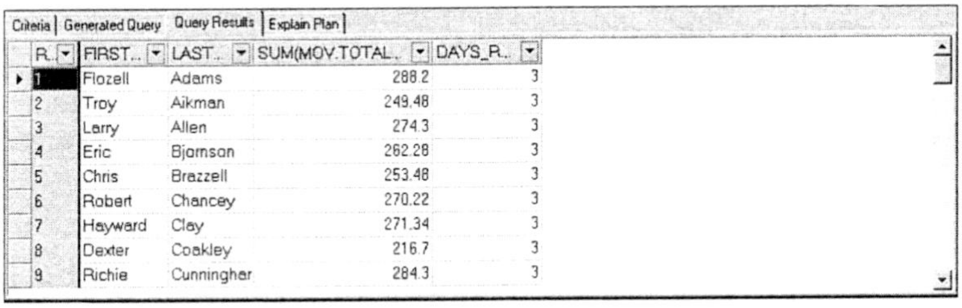

FIGURE 9.26   TOAD SQL Modeler—query results.

Generating Entity Relationship Diagrams

Sometimes a DBA or developer would like a mini-ERD (entity relationship diagram) for just a few tables of interest. For example, the developer might be writing code against a set of tables and would like to have a roadmap of their structure to code against. Having such a diagram can increase productivity while decreasing errors. For those shops that have a data-modeling tool such as Quest Software's QDesigner, this is no problem. But if your shop just has TOAD, you can still create basic, simple ERDs using the SQL Modeler (although indirectly). However, the process is significantly different than modeling SQL code as covered in the preceding section.

First, you merely select a table of interest in the Schema Browser and right-click to get a context menu selection of Model Table as shown in Figure 9.27. TOAD will then prompt you via a pop-up for how many referential levels deep to model, as shown in Figure 9.28. For example, if you want a table, its children, and its grandchildren—you would specify two levels deep. Of course, this all requires foreign keys (that is, referential integrity) in order to work.

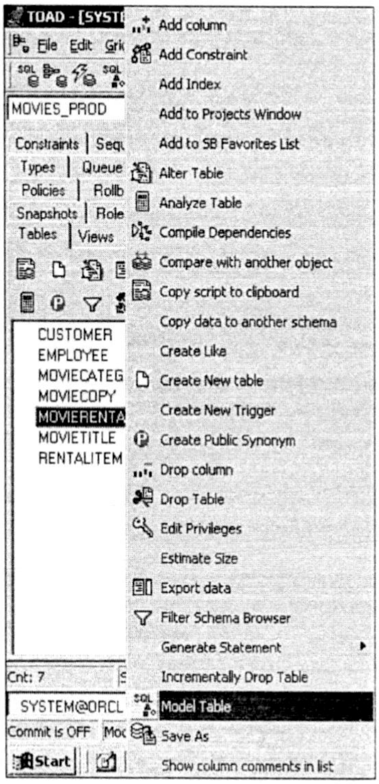

FIGURE 9.27 TOAD SQL Modeler—model table.

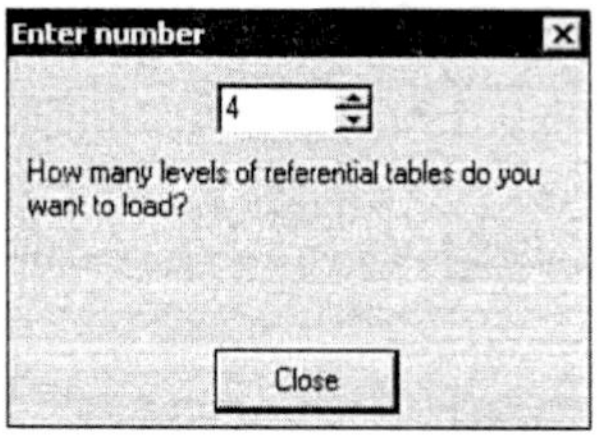

FIGURE 9.28 TOAD SQL Modeler—levels to model.

TOAD then launches you into the SQL Modeler with the tables that meet your selection criteria. You can then toggle to full-screen mode by pressing F2 and clean up the layout as shown in Figure 9.29. There is also an option now in TOAD to launch table models in full-screen mode by default. It's located in the TOAD Options for SQL Modeler, under the General category.

Finally, you can use Copy Model Image to Clipboard to copy the mini-ERD to a program such as Microsoft Paint as shown in Figure 9.30. And voilà, you have a poor man's ERD. Note that this technique only works reasonably well for small to medium object counts. It's not a true replacement for a data-modeling tool.

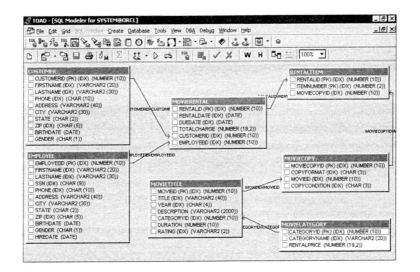

FIGURE 9.29   TOAD SQL Modeler—mini-ERD.

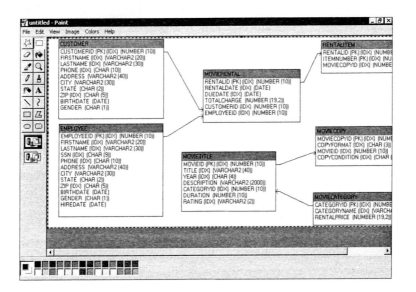

FIGURE 9.30   Poor man's ERD copied to MS Paint.

Registering External Programs

There are times while you're in TOAD when you
need to jump into another program, such as Quest
Software's QDesigner or Oracle's SQL Plus. But you
don't want to go out to the Windows Start menu
because you'd have to repeat information, such as
your database connection user id and password. So
TOAD has an intelligent and customizable program
launcher that makes opening other programs clean
and simple. It's the TOAD Tool Options window,
shown in Figure 9.31 and accessed by using the
Configure/Execute External Tools icon on the main
toolbar. TOAD knows about key Windows and Quest
applications, and can automatically add them to the
external tools list via the Auto Add button; the tools
list is shown in Figure 9.32.

FIGURE 9.31 TOAD External Tools—configuration.

After you've added your external tool definitions, TOAD will show them in the external
tools drop-down list as shown in Figure 9.33.
Note that the icon on the main toolbar has
changed to that of the last run external
tool—in this case, MS Paint.

Finally, you can also manually create external tool definitions. Figure 9.34 shows
adding Oracle's SQL Plus. Note that by using
the macros for $UID, $UPW, and $SID, SQL
Plus will launch with the same connection
information as the current TOAD connection.

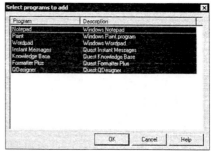

FIGURE 9.32 TOAD External Tools—auto add.

FIGURE 9.33 TOAD External Tools—drop-down list.

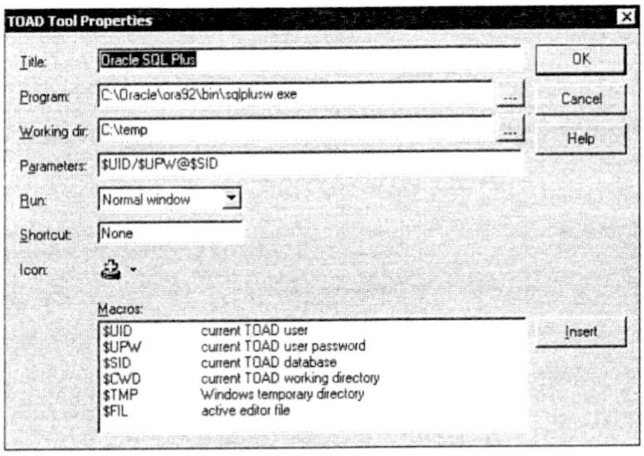

FIGURE 9.34 TOAD External Tools—manual definition.

Comparing Files for Differences

One fundamental task that nearly everyone needs to do is to compare text files for differences. Of course, Windows offers the COMP command, and UNIX has diff. But both of these are command-line utilities without advanced GUIs or reporting capabilities. So TOAD offers the Compare Files utility shown in Figure 9.35 and located on the main menu at File, Compare Files.

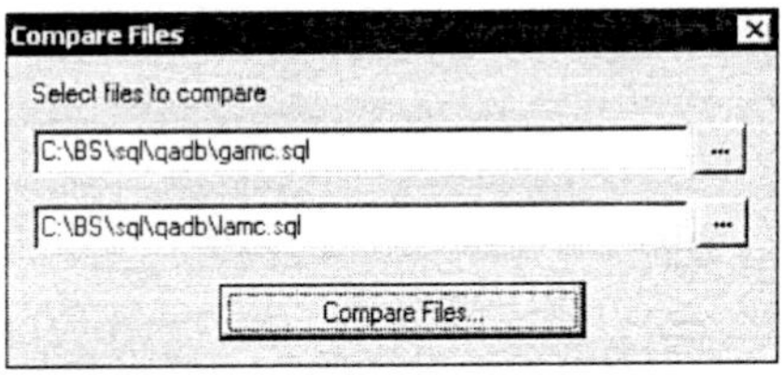

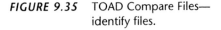

FIGURE 9.35 TOAD Compare Files—identify files.

You merely select the two source files and then click the Compare Files button. TOAD then launches its awesome File Differences Viewer shown in Figure 9.36. Not only does this viewer offer the typical VCR button interface for navigating through the differences, but it also has advanced filtering and searching capabilities.

Numerous additional display options settings are available by clicking the difference viewer's toolbar icon for options, which launches the Viewer Options screen shown in Figure 9.37.

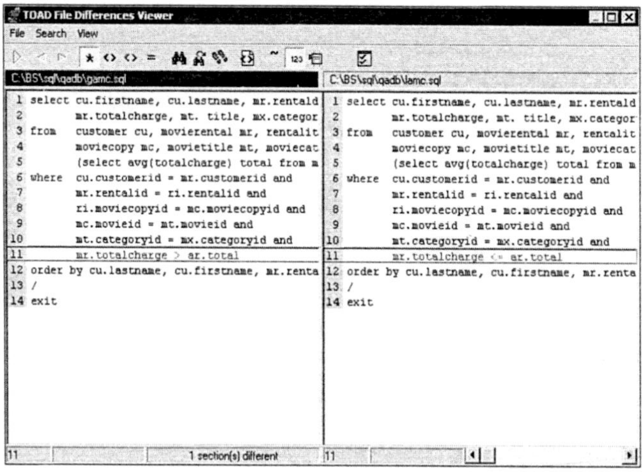

FIGURE 9.36   TOAD Compare Files—File Differences Viewer.

And for really large files with many differences, you can show a thumbnail view of the overall differences in the files as shown in Figure 9.38. This makes navigation much simpler and is the recommended way to work with this screen.

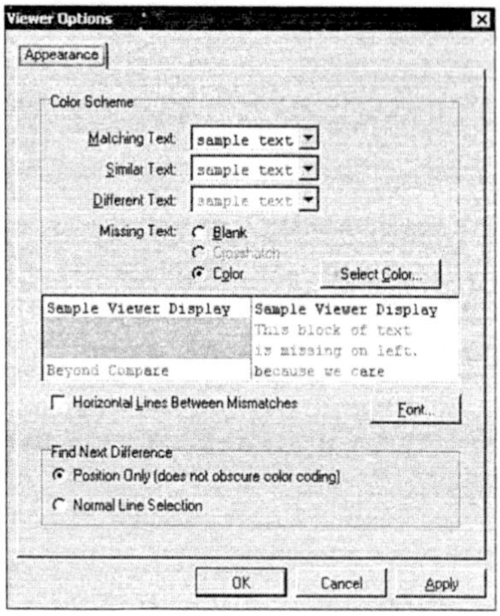

FIGURE 9.37   TOAD Compare Files—Viewer Options.

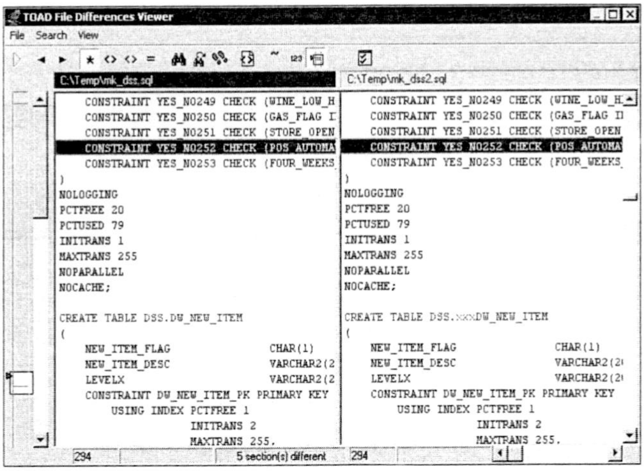

FIGURE 9.38   TOAD Compare Files—thumbnail view.

Using FTP and Network Utilities

On occasion, both developers and DBAs need the ability to work with remote
servers. For example, the PL/SQL source code may be under version control under
SCCS on UNIX. So in order to perform their programming assignments, a developer
may need to log in to the UNIX server to check out PL/SQL code and then FTP the
files down to their PC for development work within TOAD. Then when they're
finished, they would need to FTP the files back up to the server and check them back
in. Rather than requiring use of separate tools, TOAD now supports these functionalities. The idea is that TOAD should support the complete development life cycle,
which quite often includes such steps. Thus TOAD offers the FTP screen and
Network Utilities to meet these needs.

The FTP screen is shown in Figure 9.39 and is located on the main menu at File, FTP.
The first thing you must do is to connect to your FTP server by clicking the Connect
button, which opens the Server Settings window for the connection information.

After you've entered this information, clicking the OK button causes the FTP connection to be established and results in the right side of the screen being filled as shown
in Figure 9.40. To move files, you merely select a file and either click the < and >
buttons or drag and drop the files from one side to the other. Note the buttons to
the right of both the local and remote file listings. These buttons permit typical
directory and file operations such that the FTP interface can be used as sort of a poor
man's explorer—even for a remote UNIX server.

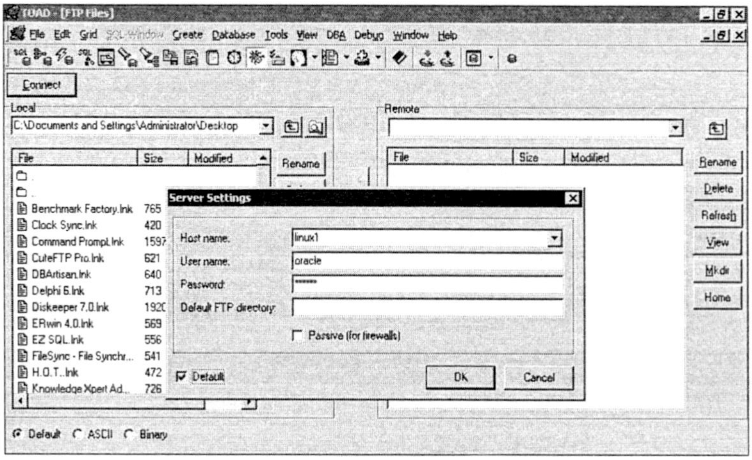

FIGURE 9.39   TOAD FTP—connection information.

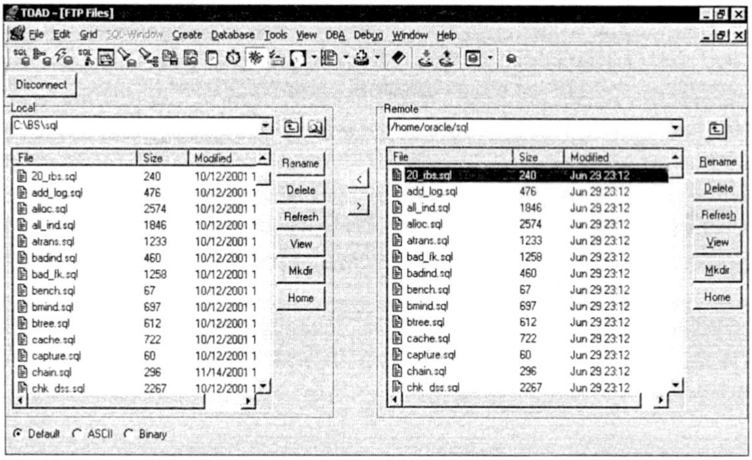

FIGURE 9.40   TOAD FTP—side-by-side display.

The Network Utilities screen is a multi-tabbed interface supporting the five key networking capabilities. The Telnet tab shown in Figure 9.41 provides basic telnet capabilities as a remote server command-line interface. It does not handle special control characters required for full-screen command usage (such as editing a file). You merely provide the host name or IP and click the Connect button to initiate a telnet session.

The Rexec tab shown in Figure 9.42 provides complete rexec (that is, remote execution) capabilities. You provide the host name or IP, user id, password, and a command string, and then click the Execute button. It can handle multiple commands by including command separators. It can also handle command strings much longer than the text field provided. So it's not uncommon to copy very long commands from an editor such as Notepad and paste them into the command text field.

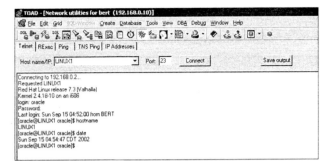

FIGURE 9.41   TOAD Network Utilities—the Telnet tab.

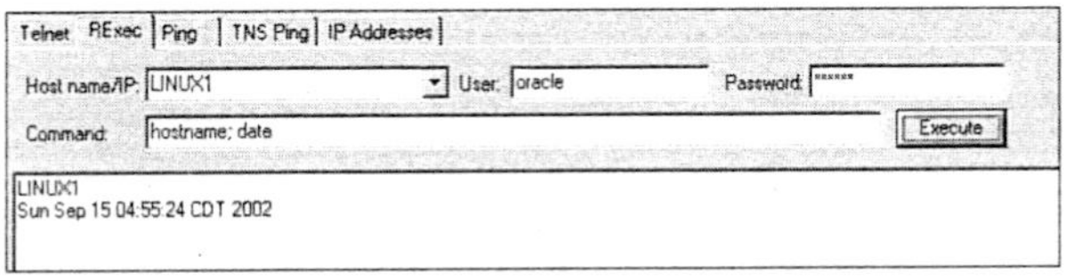

FIGURE 9.42   TOAD Network Utilities—the Rexec tab.

The last three Network Utilities tabs are very simple, yet useful. The Ping tab shown in Figure 9.43 provides a GUI for basic network ping testing. You simply enter the host name or IP and click the Start button. It will repeat the test every interval time period until the Stop button is clicked.

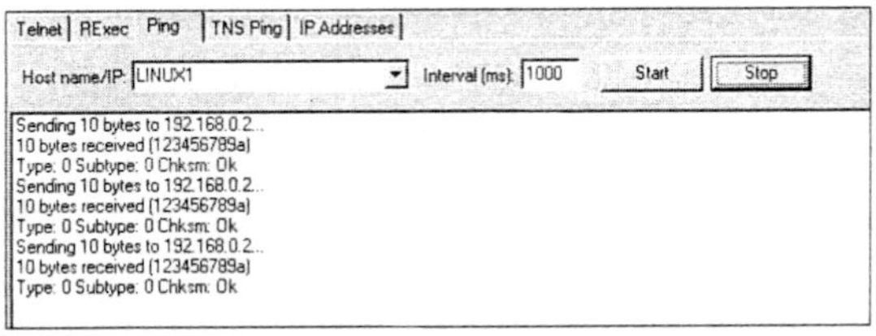

FIGURE 9.43   TOAD Network Utilities—the Ping tab.

The TNS Ping tab shown in Figure 9.44 provides a GUI for basic Oracle TNS ping testing. You merely enter the database SID you want to verify is listening and click the TNS Ping button.

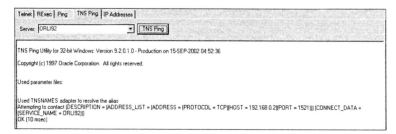

FIGURE 9.44   TOAD Network Utilities—the TNS Ping tab.

Finally, the IP Addresses tab shown in Figure 9.45 provides a simple name and IP search capability. You enter the host name or IP and it finds the complete host information. In the example, entering a host name of Solaris and clicking the Find button identifies that the correct IP address is 192.168.0.6.

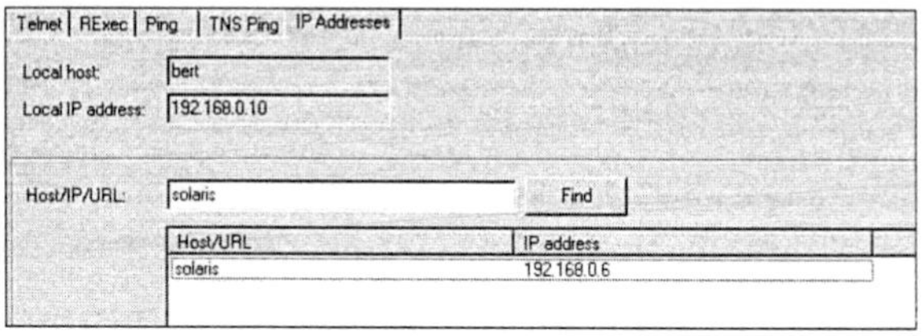

FIGURE 9.45   TOAD Network Utilities—the IP Addresses tab.

Editing Oracle TNS Name Files

Any developer or DBA who works with multiple Oracle databases on many different servers will invariably end up at some point with a need to modify their Oracle TNS Names file. Some people will just open the file in a text editor and have at it. Others will use Oracle's Java utilities: Net Manager and Net Configuration Assistant. But all these approaches require leaving TOAD. And as before, the new and basic idea is that TOAD should support the complete development life cycle—so that you never have to leave TOAD.

Thus TOAD offers the TNSNames Editor screen shown in Figure 9.46 and located on the main menu at Tools, TNSNames Editor. As you can see, this screen permits you to open two files so that you can see differences and copy entries between them using the < and > buttons.

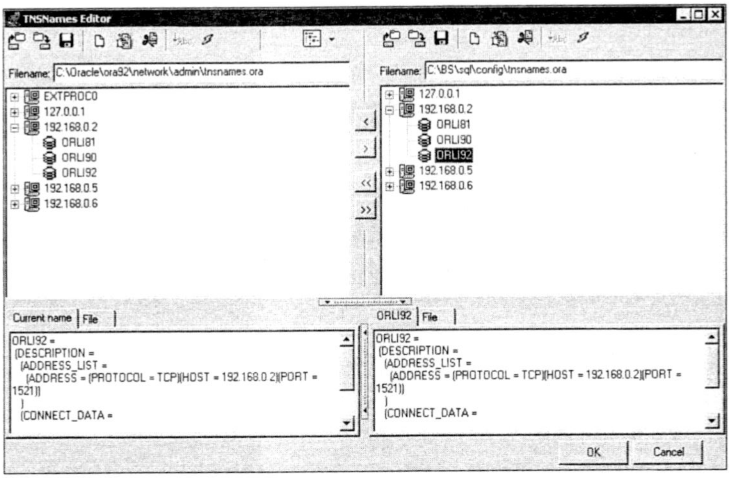

FIGURE 9.46   TOAD TNS Names Editor—side by side.

You also can create or edit services as shown in Figure 9.47. This is much easier than remembering the cryptic and cumbersome syntax involved—no more counting and matching parentheses. Plus it supports the more sophisticated options via the Advanced button as shown in Figure 9.48.

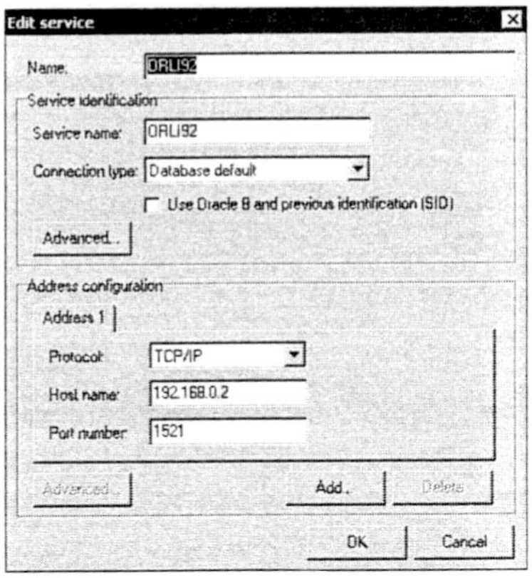

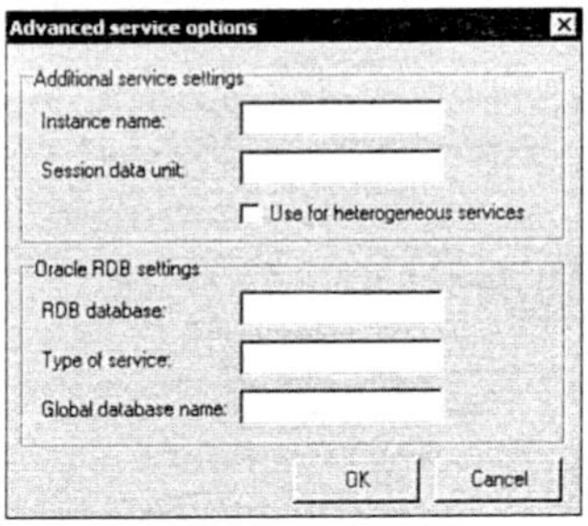

FIGURE 9.48   TOAD TNS Names Editor— Advanced Service Options.

FIGURE 9.47   TOAD TNS Names Editor—Add/Edit Service.

Tracing Execution Using TKPROF

In the old days before Oracle debuggers and profilers became available, the only way to see what was going on inside your program was the TKPROF utility. This was an undocumented tool first available in Oracle version 5. But then Oracle support began having people utilize it to troubleshoot their problems, so Oracle made it an official utility in Oracle version 6. And although today's debugger and profilers are snazzy, TKPROF still offers some value during application development. So TOAD offers the TKProf Interface. However, there are some preparatory steps you must perform in order to effectively utilize this utility.

Capturing Trace Output to Profile

First, you must start the trace for the session you want to monitor. The easiest way to do this is via TOAD's Kill/Trace Session screen shown in Figure 9.49 and located on the main menu at DBA, Kill/Trace Session. You merely need to click the green lantern toolbar button to initiate tracing that session.

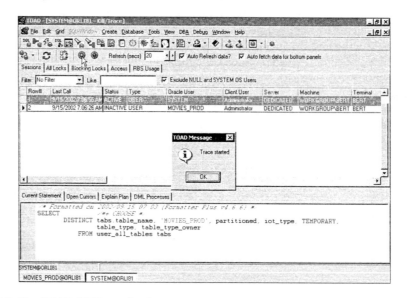

FIGURE 9.49   TOAD Kill/Trace Session—start a trace.

Second, you need to run some application code such as that shown in Figure 9.50, which runs the CHECK_DUPLICATES package. Third, you should return to the Kill/Trace Session window and stop the trace (this time clicking the red lantern toolbar button).

Remember that Oracle's trace files are created on the database server under the UDUMP directory. So if you're working with UNIX instead of a local Windows database, you'll have to FTP down the recently generated trace file as shown in Figure 9.51. With that, you've now completed the preparatory steps for successfully using TOAD's TKProf Interface.

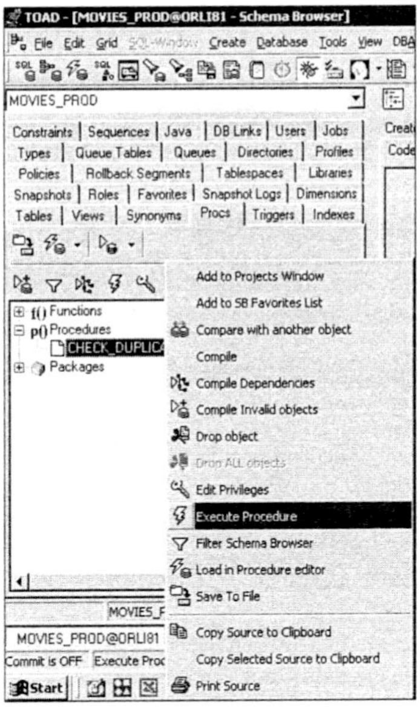

FIGURE 9.50   TOAD Schema Browser— execute some code.

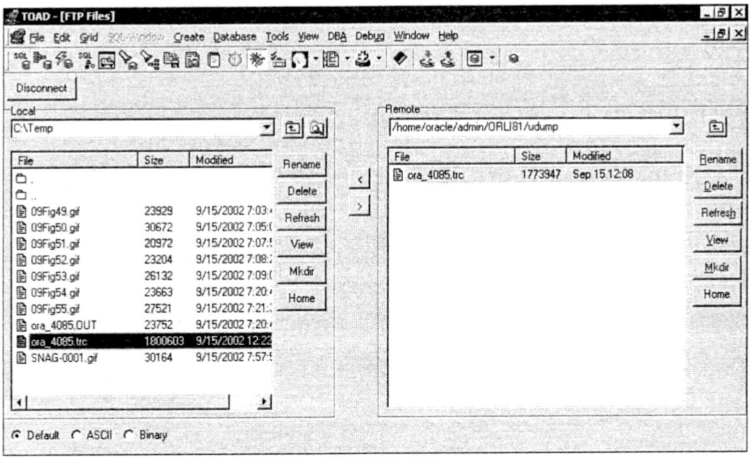

FIGURE 9.51   TOAD FTP—download the trace file.

Profiling the Captured Trace Output

The TKProf Interface screen is shown in Figure 9.52 and is located on the main menu at Tools, TKProf Interface. It's a simple three-step wizard. First you specify the Oracle trace files you want to have decoded, as shown in Figure 9.52. When TKPROF is run, it will produce an output file by the same name but with a .OUT extension, which you can change here.

FIGURE 9.52 TOAD TKPROF Wizard—Step 1.

Second, you check the sort criteria you want used during TKPROF's run as shown in Figure 9.53. Note that you can select multiple items here. The example shown as the selection for # of Physical Reads from Disk During Fetch is often a good place to start. Remember, disk IO is not our friend—so finding high physical disk IO rates is generally the quickest and easiest way to make the most improvement for the least effort.

And third, you can define additional TKPROF parameters such as who to connect as for explain plans and whose explain plan table to use. This is shown in Figure 9.54. After you click the Finish button, TOAD spawns a TKPROF command-line execution using the information you've supplied. And if View Output Files When Finished is checked, TOAD will open the results in Notepad as shown in Figure 9.55.

FIGURE 9.53 TOAD TKPROF Wizard—Step 2.

```
ora_4085.OUT - Notepad
File  Edit  Format  Help

Select /*+ CHOOSE */ object_name, object_type, status from
  user_objects where
  object_type in ( 'FUNCTION','PROCEDURE','PACKAGE','PACKAGE BODY')
order by 1, 2

call     count        cpu    elapsed       disk      query    current
------  -------  ---------  ---------  ---------  ---------  ---------
Parse        1       0.00       0.07          1          0          1
Execute      1       0.01       0.00          0          0          0
Fetch        1       0.00       0.00          0          5          0
------  -------  ---------  ---------  ---------  ---------  ---------
total        3       0.01       0.07          1          5          1

Misses in library cache during parse: 1
Optimizer goal: CHOOSE
Parsing user id: 18

Rows     Row Source Operation
------   ---------------------------------------------------
    3    SORT ORDER BY
    3     VIEW USER_OBJECTS
    3      UNION-ALL
    3       FILTER
    4        TABLE ACCESS BY INDEX ROWID OBJ$
   46         INDEX RANGE SCAN (object id 34)
    0       FILTER
    0        INDEX RANGE SCAN (object id 105)
    0        TABLE ACCESS BY INDEX ROWID IND$
    0         INDEX UNIQUE SCAN (object id 36)
*****************************************************************
select /*+ CHOOSE */ TEXT
from
 ALL_SOURCE where OWNER=:owner and NAME=:name and TYPE=:type order by
```

FIGURE 9.54   TOAD TKPROF Wizard—Step 3.

```
ora_4085.OUT - Notepad
File  Edit  Format  Help

Select /*+ CHOOSE */ object_name, object_type, status from
  user_objects where
  object_type in ( 'FUNCTION','PROCEDURE','PACKAGE','PACKAGE BODY')
order by 1, 2

call     count        cpu    elapsed       disk      query    current
------  -------  ---------  ---------  ---------  ---------  ---------
Parse        1       0.00       0.07          1          0          1
Execute      1       0.01       0.00          0          0          0
Fetch        1       0.00       0.00          0          5          0
------  -------  ---------  ---------  ---------  ---------  ---------
total        3       0.01       0.07          1          5          1

Misses in library cache during parse: 1
Optimizer goal: CHOOSE
Parsing user id: 18

Rows     Row Source Operation
------   ---------------------------------------------------
    3    SORT ORDER BY
    3     VIEW USER_OBJECTS
    3      UNION-ALL
    3       FILTER
    4        TABLE ACCESS BY INDEX ROWID OBJ$
   46         INDEX RANGE SCAN (object id 34)
    0       FILTER
    0        INDEX RANGE SCAN (object id 105)
    0        TABLE ACCESS BY INDEX ROWID IND$
    0         INDEX UNIQUE SCAN (object id 36)
*****************************************************************
select /*+ CHOOSE */ TEXT
from
 ALL_SOURCE where OWNER=:owner and NAME=:name and TYPE=:type order by
```

FIGURE 9.55   TOAD TKPROF—output results.

Subsetting Production Data

Just about every database out there has at least three copies of itself: production, test, and development. Some shops take this even further with separate test and stress-test instances. It's pretty obvious that production is the real deal and hence the source of data for the copies. But how do you make relationally correct, subset copies of production data for both test and development? Oracle provides no tools for simply taking 10% of the production data and copying it to another database. The DBA or developer must either write extensive scripts themselves or utilize TOAD's new Data Subset Wizard (debuted in TOAD 7.3).

TOAD's Data Subset Wizard is a simple four-step utility for automatically generating relationally correct and efficient SQL scripts to copy a user-defined percentage of data from target to source database. This utility works for both the scenario where the target tables already exist and all you need is the data, as well as the scenario where the target objects have not yet been created so that you need both the database objects and their data. The instructions for using the Data Subset Wizard are different for each of these scenarios, so they are covered separately.

The first step in the Data Subset Wizard, shown in Figure 9.56, is simply to define your source and target databases, plus the name of the generated SQL file and whether to open it in Notepad or TOAD's SQL Editor. You can launch this screen from the main menu at Tools, Data Subset Wizard. Regardless of which scenario you are addressing, this first step is the same. Also note that there are Load and Save buttons on this screen. Thus you can save your selections to a named file such that you can run the same choices at a later time. Thus you could create one master set of choices for a subset of production to test, and then reuse those same choices by merely loading that file and just changing the target from test to development.

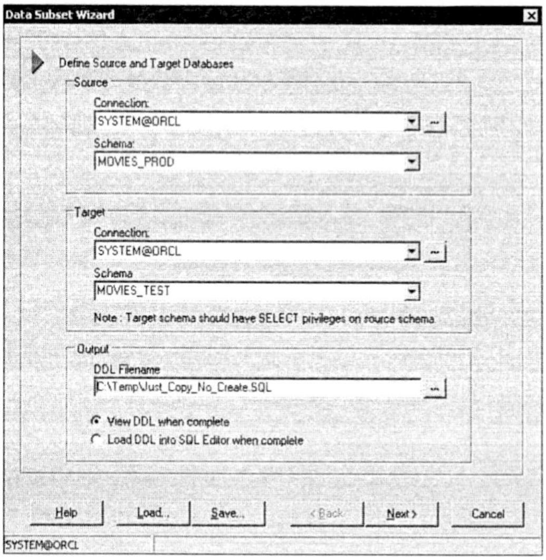

FIGURE 9.56   TOAD Data Subset Wizard—Step 1.

The second step in the Data Subset Wizard, shown in Figure 9.57, is to decide whether you're working with just a subset of data copied to pre-existing target objects or whether the target objects need to be created as well. In this first example, the choice is Do Not Create Any Objects, Just Truncate Tables and Copy Data. This will modify both steps 3 and 4 in the wizard. Note also that the rest of the screen in step 2 is disabled for this option.

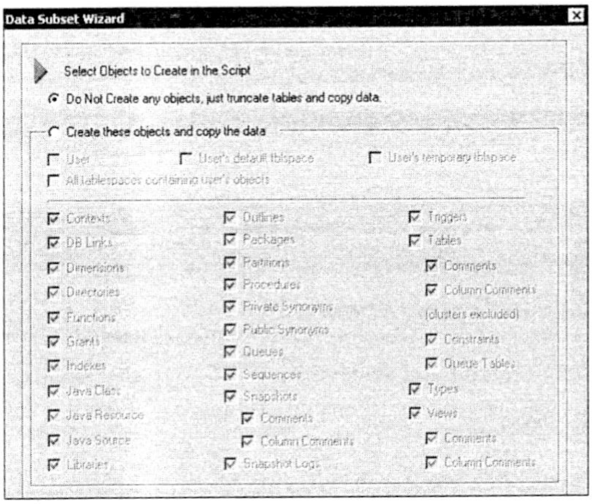

In the third step, shown in Figure 9.58, you specify the percentage of data to copy, whether it's OK to use nologging and parallel DML, and some basic script generation options. Note well the Min # Rows in Lookup Tables value with a default of 10. This specifies the minimum number of rows to copy from source tables if their row count is low. For example, on a table with just 10 rows, you would get all 10 rows (the minimum) rather than just one row (10% of 10).

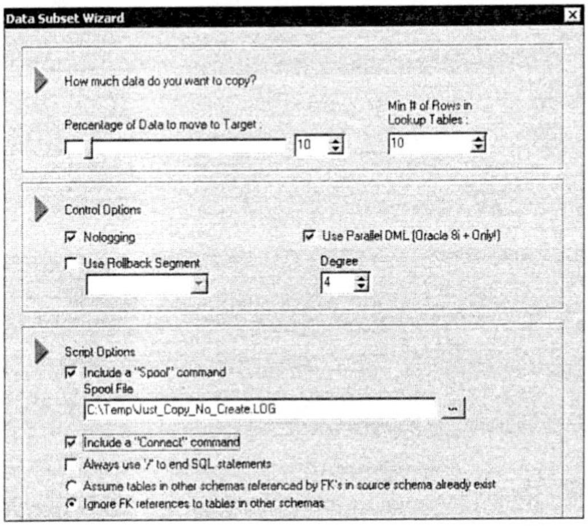

In the fourth step, shown in Figure 9.59, both the Extents and Tablespaces tabs are disabled because you are just truncating pre-existing objects and loading them. So you merely click the Build Script button and get the script shown in Figure 9.60.

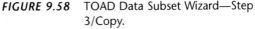

FIGURE 9.57   TOAD Data Subset Wizard—Step 2/Copy.

FIGURE 9.58   TOAD Data Subset Wizard—Step 3/Copy.

When you need to create the database objects as well as populate them with a subset of the source data, you would instead on step 2 check the box for Create These Objects and Copy the Data, as shown in Figure 9.61. Note how this choice enables the rest of this screen's check boxes. You merely check all those objects that you want created and copied into the target database. You can use the context menu for options to Select All and Unselect All.

The third step remains exactly the same and is shown in Figure 9.62. Note that the parallel is for the INSERT SELECT hints and not the CREATE commands. It's step 4 that radically changes when you're both creating and populating rather than just copying the data. So review the following very carefully.

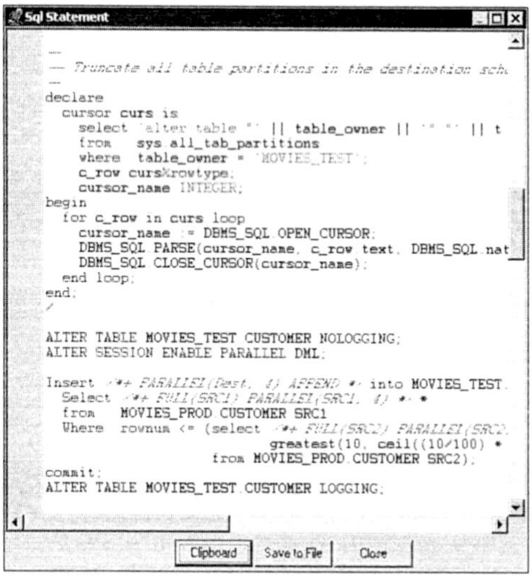

The Extents tab, shown in Figure 9.63, is a bit complicated as it permits you to define three distinct kinds of complex information. First, the top left portion of the screen offers check boxes for forcing and scaling certain storage parameter values. These options are fairly self-explanatory. The group box on the top right side of the screen permits you to define what is considered small, medium, large, and huge based upon either object or extent size. These settings are referenced on both the bottom portion of this screen and on the Tablespaces tab. The group box

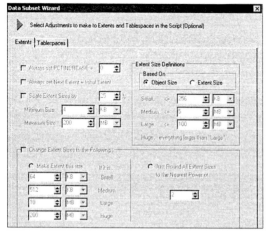

FIGURE 9.59   TOAD Data Subset Wizard—Step 4/Copy.

FIGURE 9.60   TOAD Data Subset Wizard—SQL Script/Copy.

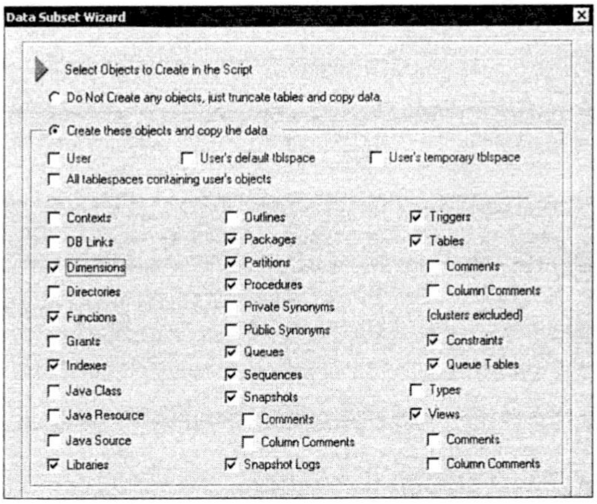

FIGURE 9.61   TOAD Data Subset Wizard—Step 2/Create.

on the bottom of the screen permits you to force the object extent sizes based upon the object's relative size. For example, medium-sized objects (that is, those less than or equal to 5 megabytes in size) should use 512KB extents. This is a complicated tab. But if you spend the time to set all these options correctly, the data subset scripts you can generate will be awesome.

The Tablespaces tab, shown in Figure 9.64, permits you to relocate objects and object partitions from one tablespace to another. You can move them all or by their size. In this example, the settings indicate to relocate small objects to tablespace USER_DICT, medium objects to tablespace USER_DICT, large objects to tablespace QADB_LOCAL, and huge objects to tablespace DWDB_LOCAL. Remember, you already defined the meaning of small, medium, large, and huge back on the Extents tab.

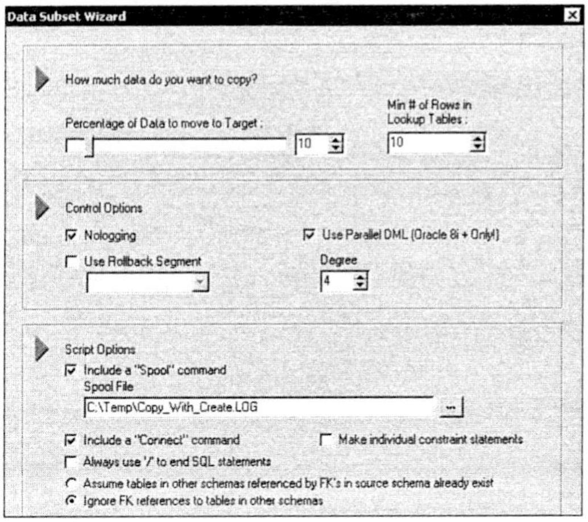

FIGURE 9.62   TOAD Data Subset Wizard—Step 3/Create.

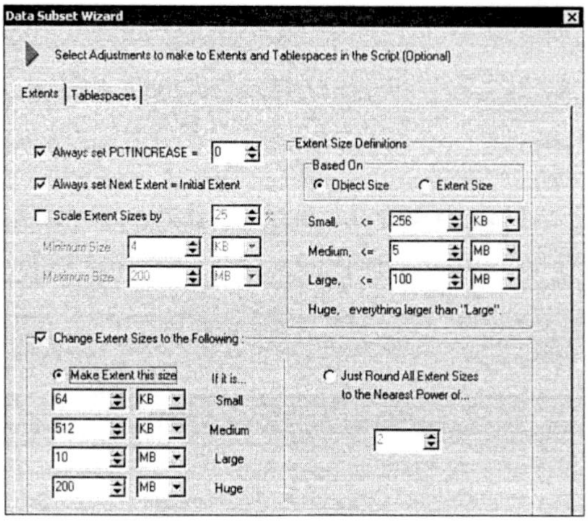

FIGURE 9.63   TOAD Data Subset Wizard—Step 4/Extents.

Now you click the Build Script button and get the script shown in Figure 9.65. Note how the CREATE commands first create the database objects, and then the script is the same as before and copies a subset of the data.

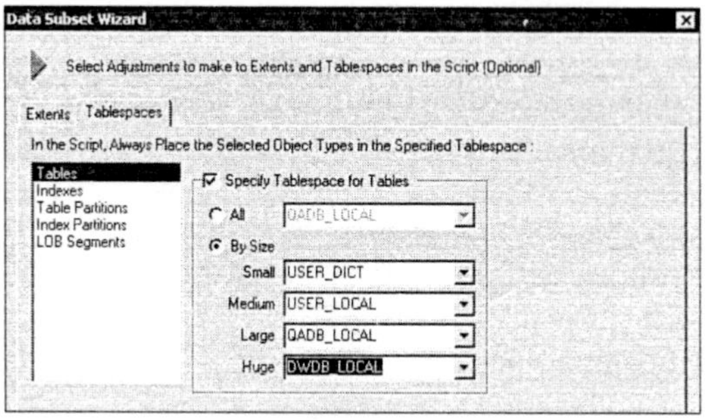

FIGURE 9.64   TOAD Data Subset Wizard—Step 4/Tablespaces.

FIGURE 9.65   TOAD Data Subset Wizard—SQL Script/Create.

Managing SQL Scripts Made Easy

Over time, everybody doing Oracle work, DBAs and developers alike, collects tons of SQL scripts. Wouldn't it be nice if TOAD could help you organize and execute your collections of SQL scripts? TOAD can with the Script Manager screen shown in Figure 9.66. TOAD ships with two useful categories of scripts predefined for you: DBA and Oracle 8i data dictionary. Of course, you can create additional categories. Likewise, you can add scripts to categories (even the predefined ones).

But the real power of the Script Manager lies in three key capabilities. First, you can indicate which scripts should be checked as Quick Scripts as shown in Figure 9.66. This results in the main menu toolbar for the Script Manager having drop-down lists for all those categories containing quick scripts and their scripts as shown in Figure 9.67. Choosing a Quick Script from the main menu toolbar results in that script being loaded into the TOAD SQL Editor and executed as a script.

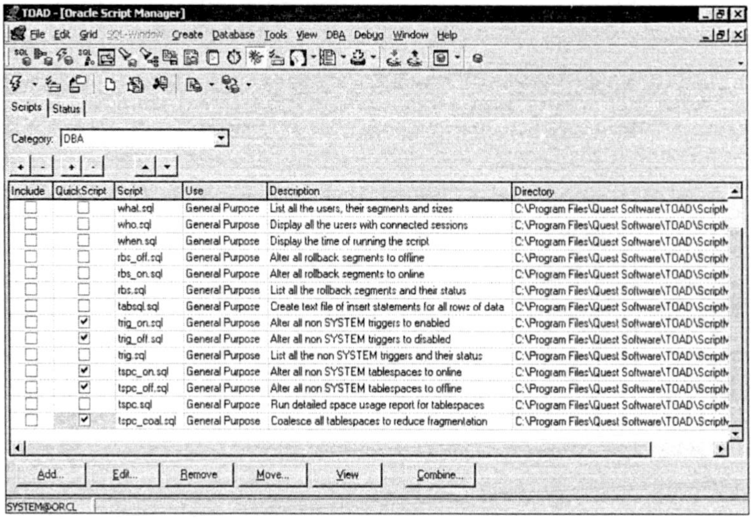

FIGURE 9.66   TOAD Script Manager.

Second, you can include one or more scripts from the Script Manager window and execute them as one concatenated script as shown in Figures 9.68 and 9.69. If you check the Include box for scripts USERS.SQL and WHO.SQL and then click the Execute toolbar icon, these two scripts are run as one in the TOAD SQL Editor.

FIGURE 9.67   TOAD Script Manager—Quick Scripts.

And third, you can create new SQL scripts from the combinations of existing SQL scripts as shown in Figure 9.70 by clicking the Combine button. Thus you can incrementally build upon all your collections of scripts.

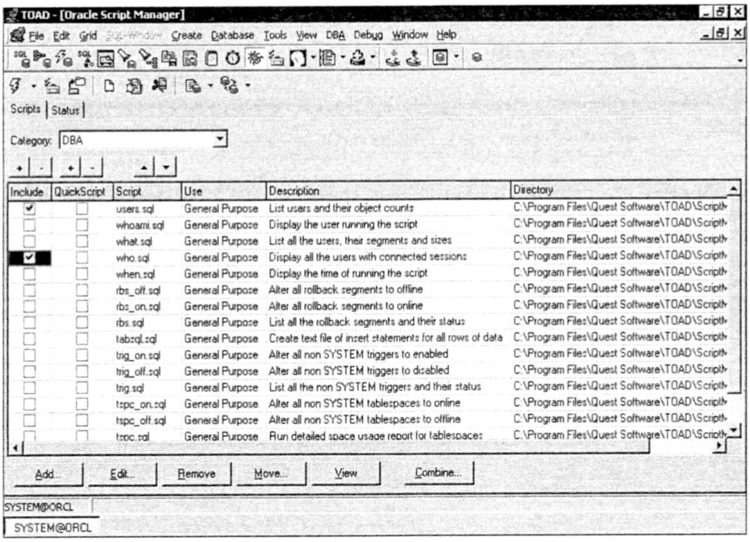

FIGURE 9.68   TOAD Script Manager—Include Scripts.

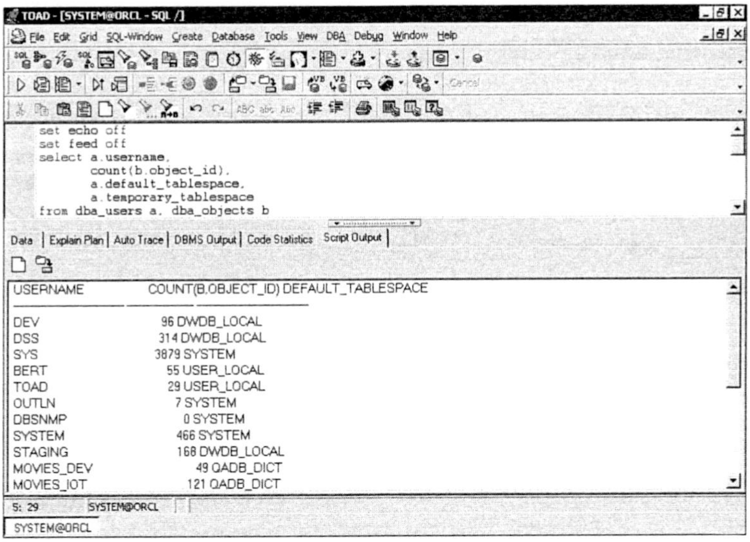

FIGURE 9.69   TOAD Script Manager—Execute Includes.

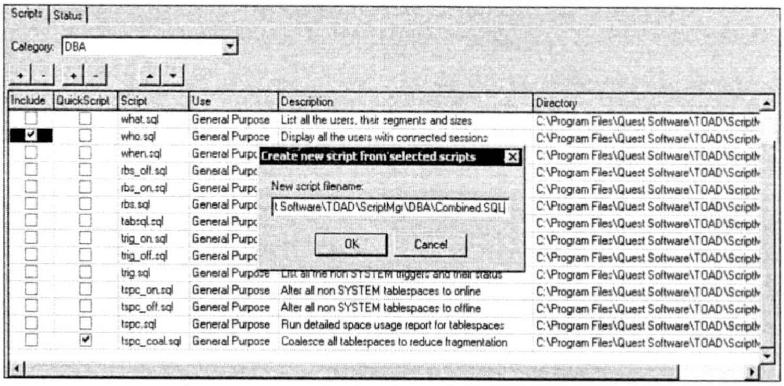

FIGURE 9.70   TOAD Script Manager—Combine Scripts.

Summary

This chapter covered numerous useful and yet often overlooked TOAD features for just about anyone who needs to do Oracle-related work. Often the Swiss army knife has the perfect blade if you just know to look for it. For example, many people need to make subsets of production data for development and test purposes, but few realize that TOAD has a utility that makes the process both simple and fun.

The next chapter covers the complex world of TOAD configurations (that is, marketing bundles) and optional software product add-ons. TOAD is now much more than just a simple tool—it's become a complete tool set.

10

Knowing the TOAD World and Its Add-ons

When you look at all TOAD's features and functionalities covered in this book, it's easy to see why TOAD has become such a huge success. No other single Oracle tool provides so much for so little. People genuinely love the product, often taking it with them from one job to the next. The TOAD phenomenon is truly amazing, because people rarely get so excited about work-related software products! But like the Titanic striking an iceberg, TOAD's impact is immediate and decisive. And as with icebergs, what people see in the product is often just the 10% clearly visible above the water. TOAD has more features lurking below the surface, so many that few people may find them without a little help. Thus this chapter surveys the features of the predefined packages and optional add-ons for TOAD.

Knowing the World According to TOAD

The TOAD world has expanded significantly since its humble freeware beginnings. And at times it can be a bit confusing as to what's available. Essentially, TOAD has configurations and optional add-ons. That's it. TOAD configurations are simply the predefined marketing bundles for various levels of product functionality, whereas add-ons are features or products that can be bundled with a TOAD configuration for an additional cost.

But people interpret the terms "add-ons" and "configurations" as being synonymous, so confusion can result. It's sort of like buying a new automobile. TOAD configurations are much like factory special packages, whereas TOAD add-ons are more like the individual options that can be chosen separate from or along with the factory special packages.

Quest Software currently offers TOAD in the following predefined configurations (note that these have been known to change/evolve over time or for special marketing promotions):

- TOAD Freeware—Free, limited-functionality version of TOAD for use by up to five users within an organization. It expires (times out) every 60 days and can be downloaded for no charge at www.toadsoft.com/lic_agree.html. Note that Quest Software offers no support or documentation for the freeware product.

- TOAD Standard Edition—The premier PL/SQL development and database management tool. It includes Formatter Plus for PL/SQL, which provides expert code formatting, syntax checking, reviews, code profiling, and best practice recommendations.

- TOAD Professional Edition—Includes all the features of TOAD Standard Edition, plus a seamlessly integrated PL/SQL debugger. The debugger provides developers with state-of-the-art features, including simple breakpoints, conditional breakpoints, variable watching, variable setting, call stacks, and much more.

- TOAD Xpert Edition—Includes all the features of TOAD Professional Edition, plus integration with SQLab Xpert tuning functionality. SQLab Xpert provides a world-class SQL tuning workbench with automatic tuning and database structural advice, elevating any DBA or developer to the status of SQL tuning guru.

- TOAD Suite—Includes all the features of TOAD Xpert Edition, plus the additional Quest Software products of Data Factory, Benchmark Factory for Oracle, and QDesigner Physical Architect. Essentially this configuration is just TOAD Xpert Edition with some external add-on products bundled in as well.

Quest Software currently offers the following TOAD add-ons (note that these also have been known to change as new modules emerge or additional products become formally integrated with TOAD):

- Formatter Plus for PL/SQL—Provides expert code formatting, syntax checking, reviews, profiling, and best practice recommendations.

- PL/SQL Debugger—Provides developers with state-of-the-art features, including simple breakpoints, conditional breakpoints, variable watching, variable setting, call stacks, and much more.

- Knowledge Xpert for PL/SQL—Provides a treasure chest of world-class PL/SQL knowledge, expertise, and best practices at your fingertips. Includes online documentation, sample scripts, and the PL/Vision code library with over a thousand useful functions and procedures.

- Knowledge Xpert for Oracle Administration—Provides a treasure chest of world-class DBA knowledge, expertise, and best practices. Includes online documentation, sample scripts, and utilities for database analysis and reverse-engineering.

- Quest DBA Module for TOAD—Adds numerous additional menus, windows, and utilities to TOAD for performing DBA related and privileged tasks. Elevates TOAD from primarily a developer's tool to a complete DBA's management console, on a par with Oracle Enterprise Manager (OEM).

- Benchmark Factory—Provides customizable, industry-standard benchmark test construction and execution for load-testing your databases. Helps you to find your bottlenecks and design flaws before deployment and going live.

- Data Factory—Provides intelligent, synthetic data generation for easily populating test and development databases. Allows developers and QA personnel to focus on the application's functional correctness and adherence to business requirements.

- SQLab Xpert Tuning—Provides a world-class SQL tuning workbench with automatic tuning and database structural advice, elevating any DBA or developer to the status of SQL tuning guru.

- QDesigner—Provides world-class ERD-based, physical data modeling. QDesigner can completely forward- and reverse-engineer database designs, with support for over 30 popular database platforms.

In this chapter, we briefly show some of the many add-ons for TOAD, but we do not cover all of the capabilities of these programs. If you find something of interest in this chapter, go to the Quest Web site or call a Quest sales rep for more information.

Using Formatter Plus for PL/SQL

Formatter Plus for PL/SQL, now included with TOAD Standard Edition, provides expert code formatting, syntax checking, reviews, code profiling, and best practice recommendations. However, many TOAD users barely scratch the surface of this tool's functionality. TOAD users generally locate and utilize the code formatting capabilities offered within TOAD's PL/SQL Editor as shown in Figure 10.1. With a simple context menu selection, the selected code is consistently and expertly formatted.

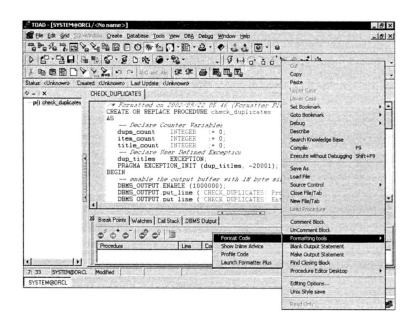

FIGURE 10.1   TOAD PL/SQL Editor—Format Code.

But by merely choosing the last menu option to launch Formatter Plus for PL/SQL instead, a whole plethora of features becomes available. You can do any of the following:

- Define detailed, customized Formatter options, as shown in Figure 10.2. Now Formatter Plus for PL/SQL works the way you want. Define a set of shared corporate standards, and all your PL/SQL code can be formatted to that standard.

- Perform an expert PL/SQL review for code correctness, maintainability, efficiency, readability,

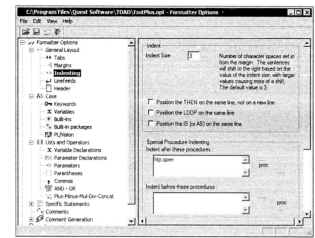

FIGURE 10.2   Formatter Plus—Formatter Options.

and program structure as shown in Figure 10.3. With just the click of a button, you now have the same benefits as if you had performed a code walk-through with a room full of PL/SQL experts.

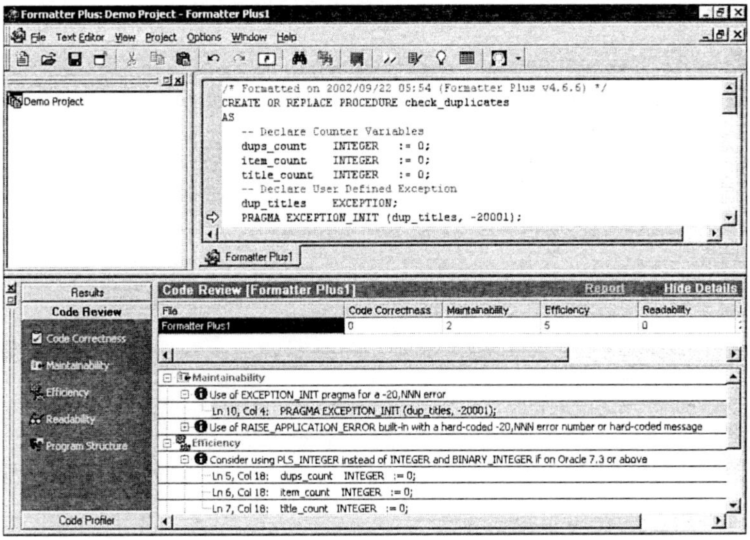

FIGURE 10.3   Formatter Plus—PL/SQL Code Review.

• Perform an expert PL/SQL analysis for each and every programmatic construct, with expert commentary regarding Oracle version dependencies, as shown in Figure 10.4. With just the click of a button, you now have a detailed summarization of the PL/SQL coding techniques used.

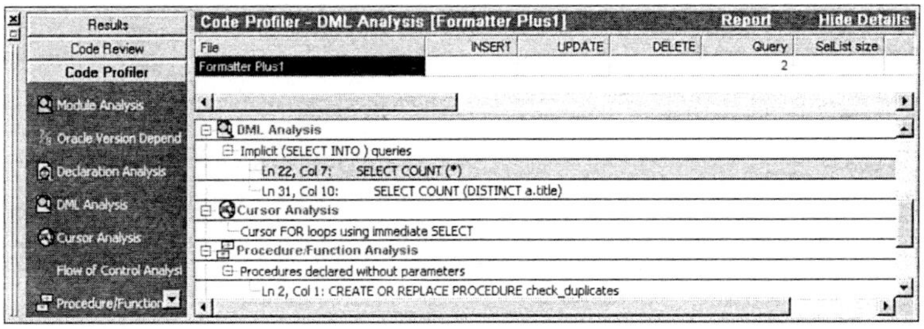

FIGURE 10.4   Formatter Plus—PL/SQL code analysis.

Using the Knowledge Xpert Products

The Knowledge Xpert products present the cumulative knowledge, experience, and wisdom of an army of Oracle experts to you in an easy-to-use format. And although both Knowledge Xpert products can be easily accessed from within TOAD, it's when they're run standalone that they offer the greatest capabilities, as shown in Figures 10.5 and 10.6. Just look at the wealth of topics available. They range from PL/SQL coding best practices to Oracle DBA certification. Even people with 10 or more years of Oracle experience find the Knowledge Xpert products indispensable.

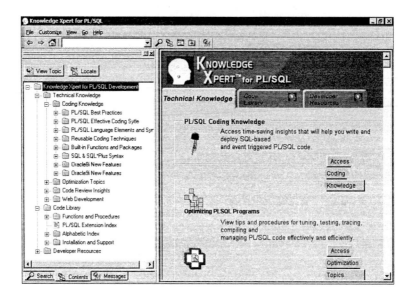

FIGURE 10.5 Knowledge Xpert for PL/SQL.

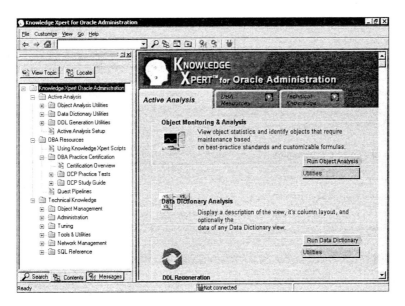

FIGURE 10.6   Knowledge Xpert for Oracle Administration.

Using SQLab Xpert Tuning

Ever wished you could push a button and make all your SQL tuning performance issues go away? Well, you can with TOAD's SQLab Xpert Tuning add-on. SQLab Xpert is by far the world's greatest SQL Tuning tool ever made. SQLab Xpert truly provides a world-class SQL tuning workbench with both automatic tuning and database structural advice, elevating any DBA or SQL developer to the status of SQL tuning guru. Moreover, the steps are both straightforward and simple:

1. In TOAD, you identify SQL code that either runs too slowly or has a suspect explain plan (for example, too many nested loops) as shown in Figure 10.7. Then you merely click the SQLab Xpert Tuning icon on the toolbar to tune the SQL.

2. SQL Xpert displays an effective and efficient SQL tuning workbench with your problematic TOAD SQL copied over as shown in Figure 10.8. You can review the SQL execution plan either via the explain plan tree (which includes the SQL from the WHERE clause attached to each plan step) or the English textual version displayed beneath the tree. You can also review very detailed describe information displayed on the right-hand side for tables, columns, indexes, and statistics.

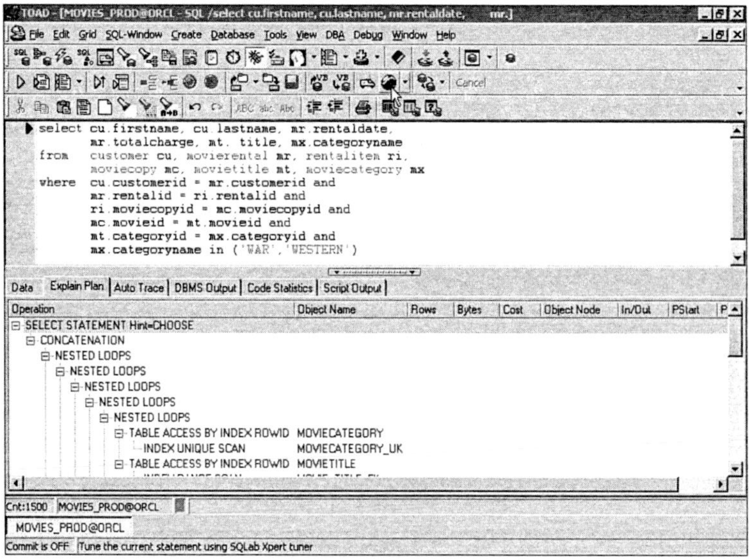

FIGURE 10.7   TOAD SQL Editor—inefficient SQL.

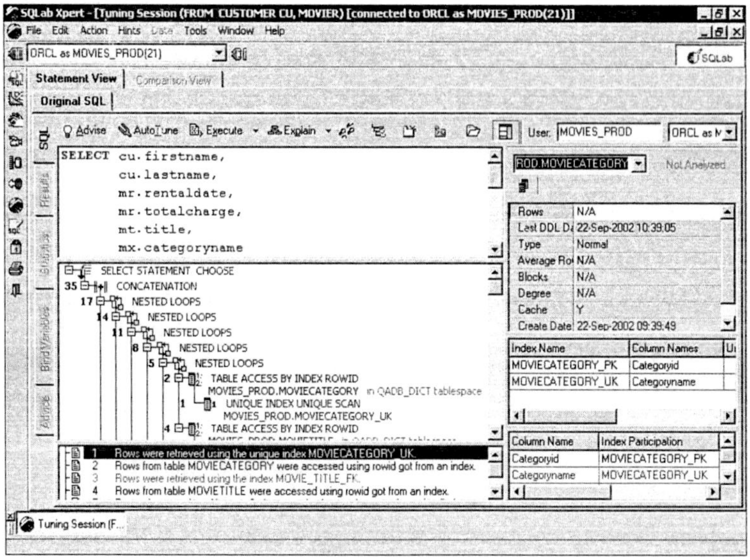

FIGURE 10.8   SQLab Xpert—Tuning Workbench.

3. You can click the Advise button to obtain SQLab Xpert advice as shown in Figure 10.8. Recommendations can include use of hints, creating indexes, dropping indexes, collecting statistics, dropping statistics, and numerous other schema changes as shown in Figure 10.9. Highlighting any recommended advice topic also displays detailed documentation regarding it. Although all the advice is generally educational and useful, you may want to skip directly to the next step if all you want is to tune the SQL.

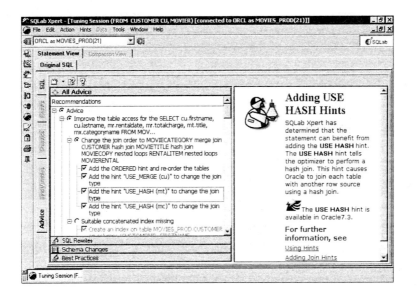

FIGURE 10.9   SQLab Xpert—Tuning Advice.

4. You can click the AutoTune button to have SQL Xpert generate all possible SQL rewrites as shown in Figure 10.10. Note how SQL Xpert knows to generate only rewrites that produce unique explain plans. You may then manually select the ones to keep by using the Select button, although generally it's advisable to use all

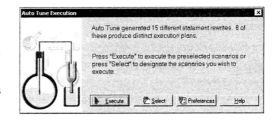

FIGURE 10.10   SQLab Xpert—AutoTune SQL generation.

proposed solutions. You also can specify control parameters for benchmarking the proposed solutions via the Preferences button. You then click the Execute button and wait for SQLab Xpert to benchmark each proposed rewrite (note that this can take a while if the tables are large or many rewrites are proposed).

5. Now review the benchmark results and pick your winner as shown in Figure 10.11. In the sample scenario, rewrite #4 is better than the original SQL. Although both ran in about the same time, rewrite #4 performed approximately 30% fewer logical I/Os. Moreover, it's not at all uncommon for SQLab Xpert to find multiple rewrites that beat the original. And remember that finding a superior SQL rewrite such as in the example takes only three mouse clicks (launch SQLab Xpert, start AutoTune, and Execute the rewrites). SQL tuning has never been so easy.

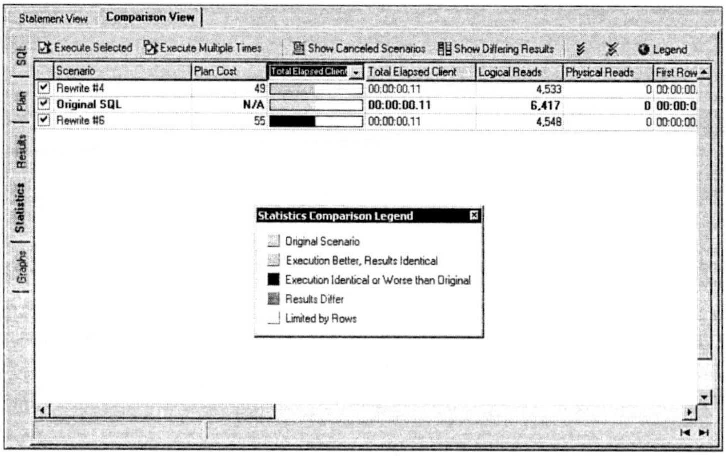

FIGURE 10.11   SQLab Xpert—AutoTune test results.

6. You can review the winning SQL rewrite by merely clicking its tab as shown in Figure 10.12. If you like what you see, just select, copy, and paste it back into TOAD. Your inefficient SQL has now been tuned.

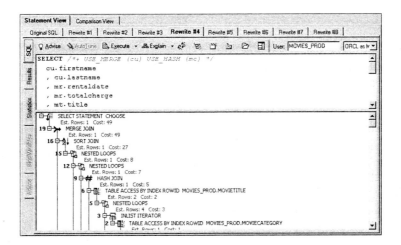

FIGURE 10.12   SQLab Xpert—the best SQL rewrite.

Using Benchmark Factory

Ever needed to benchmark your database platform? Maybe you've installed some new software and/or hardware upgrades and are wondering if they'll make a measurable difference. But who has the time to write extensive benchmark tests? Moreover, who has the knowledge? For example, industry-standard tests such as the TPC-C are controlled as intellectual property and it costs money to buy even just its specification. So what's the poor DBA to do? Use Quest Software's Benchmark Factory, the best and only tool out there for making the construction and execution of industry standard benchmarks a snap. Any DBA can set up and execute any of these tests with just a few mouse clicks. For example, here are the extremely simple steps for running an industry-standard TPC-C benchmark against an Oracle database:

1. Launch Benchmark Factory's New Project Wizard as shown in Figure 10.13 and choose to create a standard benchmark. Click Next to continue.

FIGURE 10.13   Benchmark Factory—New Benchmark Wizard.

2. Restrict the available test type to benchmarks for databases and then select the TPC-C benchmark as shown in Figure 10.14. Although there are numerous database benchmark tests to choose from, the TPC-C is one of the best known and most often quoted.

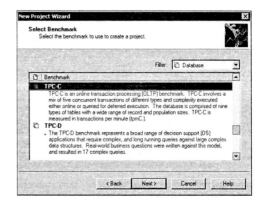

FIGURE 10.14   Benchmark Factory—choose benchmark type.

3. Select the benchmark scale (that is, its size in relative numeric terms, which translates to predefined sizes) as shown in Figure 10.15. The larger the selected scale, the longer initial object creation and population will take. But you need to select a size that makes sense for the number of simulated concurrent users that will access this database during the benchmark's execution.

4. The New Project Wizard will have created a test for you, but only the steps necessary to create and populate the necessary database. You must now select a transaction load scenario and specify the desired properties as shown in Figure 10.16. In this example, the User Load is specified to be 10

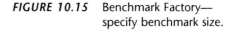

FIGURE 10.15   Benchmark Factory—specify benchmark size.

concurrent database users. This small load makes sense given the prior step's selection of a very small scale for database sizing. Of course, you can easily benchmark terabyte-sized databases with thousands of concurrent users if you want by merely selecting such parameters for the preceding two steps.

5. Go ahead and execute the benchmark steps as shown in Figure 10.17. While the transaction mix is running, you can visually inspect the concurrent session activity using the Agent Station as shown in Figure 10.18. What's really neat is that Benchmark Factory can simulate concurrent user activity either on your PC or a pool of PCs it locates on the network.

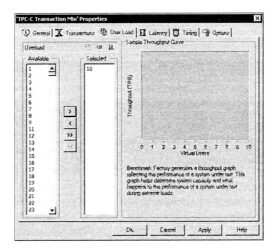

FIGURE 10.16   Benchmark Factory—transaction mix properties.

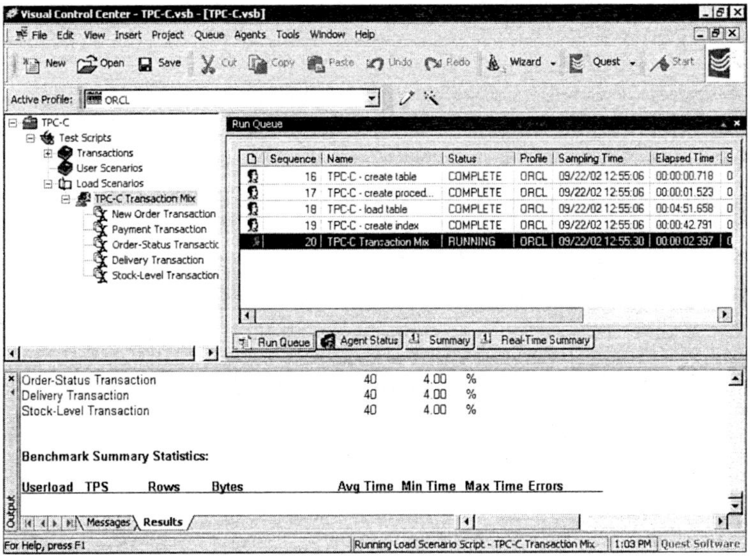

FIGURE 10.17   Benchmark Factory—execute the benchmark.

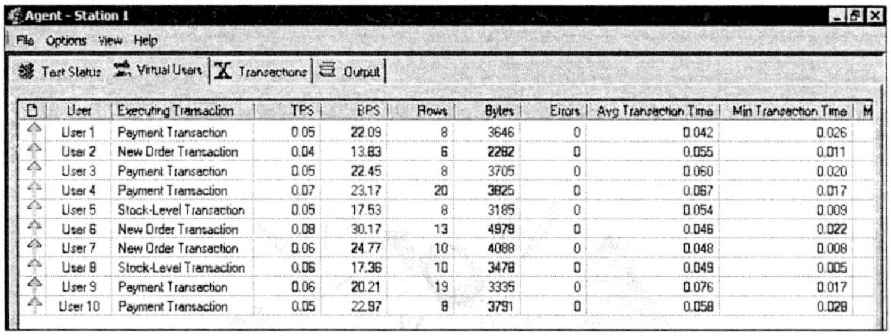

FIGURE 10.18   Benchmark Factory—monitor current sessions.

6. When the benchmark run completes, you simply review the results as shown in Figure 10.19. That's all there is to it. Now anyone can run industry-standard database benchmarks.

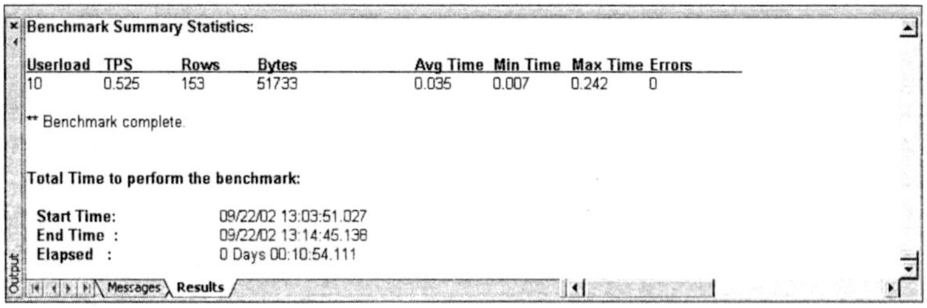

FIGURE 10.19   Benchmark Factory—review the results.

Using QDesigner

Everybody should be doing data modeling. Entity relationship diagrams (ERD) serve as the blueprints for your logical and physical database designs. Can you really imagine a contractor building your house without blueprints? How would you feel if the contractors just started nailing things together based upon their experience and intuition? Well, that's how many databases are put together. It's no wonder that their performance and ability to meet business requirements often fall far short of the desired goal.

QDesigner provides world-class ERD-based, physical data modeling. QDesigner can completely forward- and reverse-engineer database designs, with support for over 30 popular database platforms. QDesigner offers far more features and advanced capabilities than can be described in a few short paragraphs. But for TOAD users, a brief intro on how to reverse-engineer a database into a data model and then forward-engineer that model to generate DDL scripts should suffice to demonstrate QDesigner's usefulness.

To reverse-engineer an existing Oracle database into a QDesigner data model, you perform the following steps:

1. Initiate QDesigner's Reverse Engineering Wizard and specify the source database platform as shown in Figure 10.20. Remember, QDesigner supports over 30 different databases and their numerous versions.

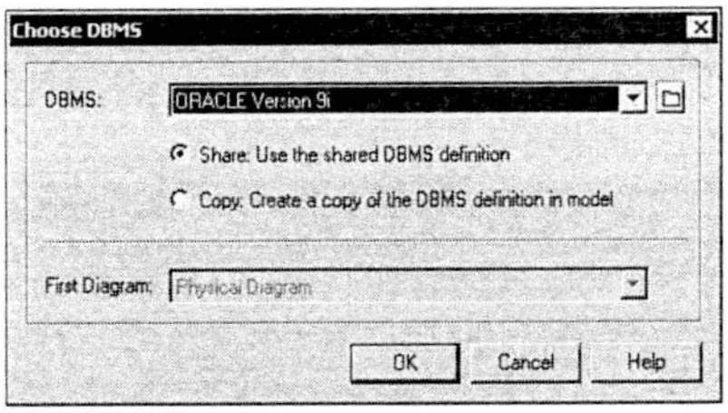

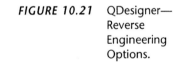

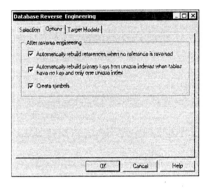

FIGURE 10.20   QDesigner—Reverse Engineering Wizard.

2. Identify the desired database connection information and reverse-engineering options as shown in Figure 10.21. QDesigner can generally infer foreign key relationships in the data model even for databases where referential integrity is not being utilized. Plus QDesigner can also infer primary key constraints for databases just using indexes. This is useful when working with databases built for older versions of Oracle.

3. Select the schema, object types, specific objects, and other options to reverse-engineer as shown in Figure 10.22. Note the total objects selected counter in the bottom right-hand corner of this screen. The more items you pick, the longer it will take to reverse-engineer and more complicated your data model will be.

FIGURE 10.21   QDesigner—Reverse Engineering Options.

4. You now can work with the data model of your database as shown in Figure 10.23. QDesigner offers far too many features to elaborate any further.

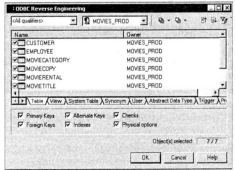

FIGURE 10.22   QDesigner—Reverse Engineering selection.

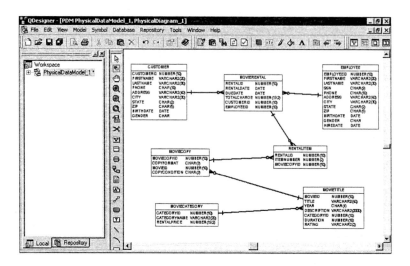

FIGURE 10.23   QDesigner—physical data model.

To forward-engineer a QDesigner model into a DDL script for the modeled objects, you perform the following steps.

1. Initiate QDesigner's Forward Engineering Wizard (that is, Generate Database) and specify the target database generation options as shown in Figure 10.24.

2. Review, modify (if needed) and then execute the generated DDL script as shown in Figure 10.25. Of course, that script can be loaded into TOAD's SQL Editor for review and execution.

FIGURE 10.24   QDesigner—Forward Engineering Wizard.

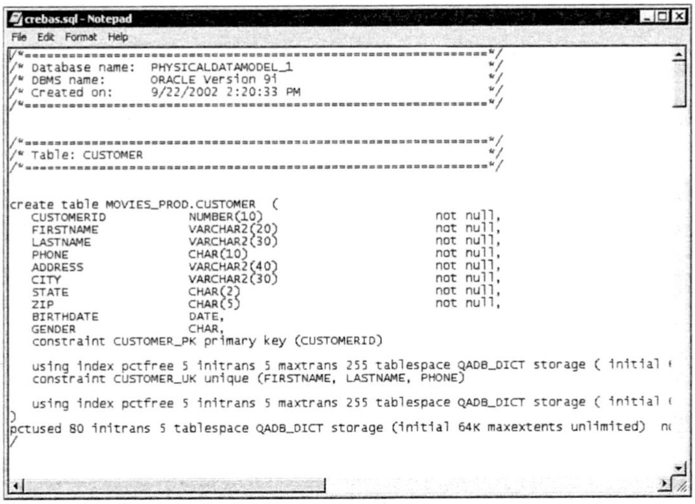

FIGURE 10.25   QDesigner—generated DDL script.

Summary

This chapter attempts to illuminate TOAD's many different predefined packages and their optional add-ons. TOAD has become much more than the simple freeware tool of the past. TOAD now covers the complete development life cycle, from design through deployment—with many options for improved productivity far beyond those offered simply by the graphical IDE. Probably the most important idea to walk away with is that TOAD has now become a platform rather than a product. And as such, TOAD has much more to offer than most people realize.

Index

autosubstitution. *See* automatic replacement

AutoTune button (SQLab Xpert Tuning), 263

B

Back button (New Database wizard), 150

BACKGROUND_DUMP_DEST parameter, 123

backups, 188

Benchmark Factory

Agent Station, 268

benchmark execution, 267

benchmark size, selecting, 266

benchmark type, selecting, 266

New Project Wizard, 265

overview, 257, 265

results, reviewing, 268

transaction mix properties, 266

bind variables, 53, 88

block fetch request, 72

block gets request, 72

breakpoints

options, debugging, 111-112

Set Breakpoint command, 107

Build Init.Ora button, 121

Build Script button (Data Subset Wizard), 250

buttons

Add (Repair Chained Rows option), 170

Add New Folder to Favorites, 35

Add New Sequence, 52, 87

Advanced (TNS Names Editor), 241

Advice (SQLab Xpert Tuning), 263

Alter (Instance Manager), 154

Analyze (Repair Chained Rows option), 171

Auto Add (External Tools), 234

AutoTune (SQLab Xpert Tuning), 263

Back (New Database wizard), 150

Build Init.Ora, 121

Build Script (Data Subset Wizard), 247, 250

Calculate Fields (SQL Modeler), 228-229

Check File Out of Source Control, 82

Combine (Script Manager), 252

Commit, 67

Compile, 99

Compile Dependencies with Debug, 108

Connect (FTP screen), 237

Create Filter File, 203

Create New PL/SQL Object (Procedure Editor), 82, 98

Edit Sequence, 52, 87

Evaluate/Modify, 110

Examine Checked Indexes and Make Recommendations (Rebuild Multiple Indexes), 166

Execute, 65

Execute (SQLab Xpert Tuning), 263

Extent Mgmnt (New Database wizard), 151

Flush the SGA, 138

Halt, 110

Load (Data Subset Wizard), 246

Load File, 82

Load Source from Existing Object, 82

Next (New Database wizard), 150

Print Extents, 131

Refresh Log List, 147

Repair (Repair Chained Rows option), 171

Run (Standard Database Reports), 199

Save (Data Subset Wizard), 246

Save As, 101

Scan SQL, 53

Show Column Select Window, 54-56, 88

Show SQL Template Window, 62, 95

Show Table Select Window, 54, 88